Penguin Education

Family Law
Margaret Puxon

Foundations of Law

Family Law

Margaret Puxon

Penguin Books

Penguin Books Ltd, Harmondsworth,
Middlesex, England
Penguin Books Inc, 7110 Ambassador Road,
Baltimore, Md 21207, USA
Penguin Books Australia Ltd,
Ringwood, Victoria, Australia

First published in Pelican Books 1963
Second edition 1971

Made and printed in Great Britain by
Cox & Wyman Ltd,
London, Reading and Fakenham
Set in Intertype Times

Contents

Introduction

We are all members of a family, and within that family we accept certain rights and obligations without much question. Up to a point the family is a law to itself: it can make its own rules of conduct, impose its own sanctions, and settle disputes which arise between its members. But since each family is also a unit of the state, and the state has an interest in the health and order of its constituent parts, some limit must be set on the freedom of the individual family. In most Western communities the state has been loath to interfere in the family – in England perhaps more than anywhere – but as life becomes more complex and people more crowded together, families impinge more on each other and in the public interest it becomes essential to have a universal code of rules for the family. It is this boundary between private and public life which is the field of family law.

The rules which govern both the community and the conflict of interests between the state and the family are a matter of vital importance to us all. But it is extraordinary how much ignorance there is about this section of the law, even among otherwise well-informed people. Most of us have a fair idea of the general criminal law – that is, the limits which the state imposes on our conduct for the protection of the persons and property of our fellow-citizens – but it is unusual to find anyone except a lawyer who pretends to understand the rules the law applies when called on to intervene in the family, or what legal rights each member has against the other. Perhaps, after all, this ignorance is not so surprising: seen in isolation, family law seems an incomprehensible jumble of rules and remedies; only when it is looked at as part of our history and social evolution does it emerge as the logical framework for our present way of life.

Recent reforms in divorce law, intended to simplify and rationalize, have brought their own difficulties of interpretation and an understanding of family law still depends on appreciation of the way in which that law has evolved.

The fascination of the study of family law lies in the complexity of its origins and the pressures upon it. The family is a fact of nature: the law is neither factual nor natural, but a sophisticated compromise between man's needs and his aspirations. There is a vast difference between the family in a primitive tribe, held together mainly by the need for survival, and that in a modern industrial state, which is regulated and underpinned by the law. But the changes have been brought about by many forces, among which custom and religion were the chief, and the law was a very late arrival.

Custom gradually hardens into law. For many centuries in England the law of the family (apart from the rule of the Church) remained almost entirely the common law – the customary law of the people, unified by the judges of the Royal Courts, and softened by the operation of Equity. But such law grows slowly, and since the industrial revolution social change has been so rapid that the law has had to follow – and on occasions lead – at a speed which is inconsistent with the gentle evolution of custom: statutes, those violent weapons of social growth, have sprouted in profusion to support and regulate the modern family.

Such changes in the law were inevitable. The family could not have survived in its old form, so many forces have there been at work to undermine its structure. First among these is the growth of scientific doubt: how can children be expected to accept without question the authority of parents who do not themselves know with any certainty what is true or false, right or wrong? Then there has been widespread rejection of the authority of religion, weakening the support given to the family by the Church. At the same time there has been a great increase in materialism and the belief that every human being has a 'right' to comfort and happiness, which is to some extent inconsistent with the demands made by family life. This materialism now expresses itself almost universally in the commercialization of sex: the message implied in much advertising and sales talk is that we all have a positive duty to remain attractive to, and be attracted by, the other sex. Since active life is now so much prolonged, these needs are unlikely to be satisfied throughout by the same spouse, so the temptation to change is great. And the increase in the mobility of society makes such change very much easier.

Even more destructive to the permanence of family life has been the liberation of women from their position of inferiority in the home. A woman who owns her own property, builds up her own career, votes in elections and is perpetually wooed and flattered by the advertisers is unlikely to put up with ill-treatment and neglect from her husband: if another man comes along to offer her what she has been taught is her inalienable right – freedom and happiness – she will not be slow to make the change, helped, as we shall see, by the rapid development of the law in her favour. The idealization of romantic love by commercial writers, combined with great freedom of expression in all the arts, has done nothing to help this situation. But though the patriarchal system has broken down, it has not been replaced by a matriarchy – at least, not in this country – and the ideal of a marriage of equal partners is almost impossible to attain, because men and women obstinately refuse to be equal.

It is against this background of change that we shall look at the law of the family. Since the common law of England interfered so little in the family, we shall find that most family law is statutory: but where there is no Act of Parliament to the contrary, the common law still prevails; for example, under the common law a father's rights to the custody of his children are absolute, therefore even today the father, not the mother, has those rights until some Court order, made under statutory powers, has deprived him of them. This common law is to be found in the decisions of the

Courts down the centuries. Certainty is achieved by the rule that Courts are governed by precedent – that is, they must decide every case on the same principles as have been followed by previous cases of a similar nature, the decision of a higher Court always prevailing over that of a lower one, the House of Lords over the Court of Appeal, a decision in the High Court over that of a County Court. But the highest authority is the Supreme Court of Parliament, and statutes which are passed by both Houses and receive the Royal Assent override the common law.

It might be thought that the law would always be clearer if put into the words of an Act of Parliament, but this is by no means so, particularly in the law of divorce. The statutes which lay down the grounds for dissolution of marriage were purposely put into wide terms which gave plenty of scope for judicial interpretation, and it is this which, in spite of recent reforms, makes divorce law so complex. The Judges have for long been forced to find words in which to define matrimonial offences and, words being tricky things, it has proved a difficult task. Parliament and the Courts have been called on to provide a workable system for every type of matrimonial situation, which is not really possible. It is worth remembering this when judicial decisions seem to turn on legal quibbles, and the lives of men and women to depend on semantics. Rules must be drafted, and they must be strictly applied, or there would be no certainty in the law; but no set of rules devised by man can be suited to every situation, and of those who come to the law some will inevitably suffer in the cause of a wider justice.

Some readers may be surprised at the emphasis on the law of property in this book. This is indeed ironical. However materialist our civilization may be today, we tend to a more romantic view of the family than those who made our law. From feudal times through the eighteenth-century squirearchy to the wealthy traders of the Victorian age, the family has been regarded primarily as an instrument for the preservation and transmission of property. This is a concept that the legal mind finds easy to grasp, and so we find that wives and children are even now to some extent regarded by the law as possessions, and even matrimonial misconduct sometimes seems to be looked at more as an offence against property than a personal injury. It is all the more remarkable that family law has, in recent years, found ways to deal with such problems – previously left to the whim of the family – as the welfare of children and the removal of matrimonial misery.

The revised edition of this book comes at a time of great change in family law. For the first time, divorce by consent is recognized by the law, and there will soon be a Family Division which will be the forum for all – or nearly all – disputes relating to marriage and children. Three new Acts of Parliament, which vitally affect children, divorce and matrimonial property, have very recently come into force. This book incorporates the changes in the law brought into force before or in January 1971, and the more important decisions on the new law up to 1 July 1971. But as in many cases old law will have to be applied to new statutory enactments, under new rules of procedure, these reforms do not in general invalidate the propositions of domestic law which are the backbone of the book. It is, for example, clear that the element of 'reform' in the Divorce Reform Act is more apparent than real: while breakdown is to be the only ground for dissolution of marriage, proof of such breakdown is to be found in the old matrimonial offences, sometimes described in different language. Even the old bars to dissolution – connivance, adultery by the petitioner, and condonation – may raise their heads again when 'intolerability and unreasonableness' are considered. (See pp. 132, 133.) Thus we shall be looking back to the old principles, as embodied in the cases, for a long time to come.

I am deeply grateful to Miss Margaret Higgins of the Middle Temple for her reading of the text and her valuable and discerning criticism. I also extend my thanks to Miss Carmel Green of the Inner Temple who has discharged the burden of preparing the index and the tables of statutes and cases with her usual expedition and skill.

Part One **The Marriage**

Introduction

The idea of marriage is so familiar that we seldom pause to analyse it. What sort of legal relationship is it? Who can make a marriage, and how? What does the law recognize as a marriage, and what does the law require of the parties to a marriage before giving such recognition? In what circumstances do our courts recognize foreign marriages? Such questions lead on to an examination of the essentials of marriage: the unity of husband and wife, the rights and duties imposed on each by the law, the effect of marriage on their financial position – including tax and the ownership of property – and the restrictions imposed by the law on disposition of property after death.

After the making and the sharing of the marriage, we approach the broken marriage. While Part Two deals with the mechanics of dissolution, it is necessary first to look at the breakdown as part of the marriage, to see how society has changed in its approach to separation and dissolution, and to investigate the possibilities open to the couple whose marriage has foundered. The progress from the rigidity of the Canon Law to the humane provisions of the Divorce Reform Act, 1969 takes in the growth of legislation relating to legal separation in the magistrates' courts, which even today deal with the great majority of marital breakdowns.

1 Making a Marriage

What is marriage?

In the greater part of the world and for many centuries, marriage has been the basis of the family. But we can only make that statement if we accept a very wide definition of marriage: we must include polygamy as well as monogamy, and the spontaneous unions of the Polynesians as well as the quasi-Christian contracts of the West. Marriage means many different things in different parts of the world – and even within the same community. Even in the Christian countries of the West it is regarded by some as a sacrament, by others as a civil contract, and by most as a mixture of the two. We are concerned with an institution which is an amalgam of tradition, religion, superstition, instinct and reason, and before examining the ways in which the law governs marriage it will be as well to examine the elements which make it up.

Marriage has always had an important economic content, and that has persisted into the Christian era. But Christianity changed marriage perhaps more than any other human institution. The early Church based its attitude to sexual union on the doctrines of St Paul:[1]

1. Now concerning the things whereof ye wrote unto me: It is good for a man not to touch a woman.
2. Nevertheless, to avoid fornication, let every man have his own wife, and let every woman have her own husband.
3. Let the husband render unto the wife due benevolence: and likewise also the wife unto the husband.
4. The wife hath not power of her own body, but the husband: and likewise also the husband hath not power of his own body, but the wife.

1. 1 Corinthians 7, verses 1–7.

5. Defraud ye not one the other, except it be with consent for a time, that ye may give yourselves to fasting and prayer; and come together again, that Satan tempt you not for your incontinency.

6. But I speak this by permission, and not of commandment.

7. For I would that all men were even as I myself. But every man hath his proper gift of God, one after this manner, and another after that.

Elsewhere he said 'I say therefore to the unmarried and widows, it is good for them if they abide even as I [that is, celibate] but if they cannot contain, let them marry; for it is better to marry than burn.'

The harsh doctrine of the early Church that all fornication was to be condemned was something quite new in the civilized world. The Jews had since Abraham condemned adultery, but fornication was acceptable, and it was not until St Paul urged on the early Church that the whole sexual act was deplorable that fornication, as such, was regarded as a sin. (Of course, fornication was always frowned on in young girls, since it meant the deflowering of virgins and therefore deprived husbands of that right.)

St Paul apparently did not even recognize the value of marriage as a basis of family life, since he makes no mention of children in relation to sexual union; his whole attitude to marriage is negative. Happily, the Church, once past the early years of persecution, took a more liberal view: Catholic doctrine, while acknowledging the ascetic ideal of St Paul, recognizes that marriage has other purposes, chief among them the transmission of life and the mutual comfort of the spouses. The Anglican marriage service makes clear the priority of the chief purpose in marriage:

First, it was ordained for the procreation of children. . . . Secondly, it was ordained for a remedy against sin, and to avoid fornication; that such persons as have not the gift of continency might marry. . . . Thirdly, it was ordained for the mutual society, help, and comfort that the one ought to have of the other, both in prosperity and adversity.

The teaching of the Churches, strict or watered-down by centuries of schism and reform, is part of the marriage-bond which the state protects with its laws, the other part being the rights of support and ownership of property, as we shall see later (chapters 12 and 13). Since the Churches are themselves so little agreed about the purposes of marriage, it is small wonder that the law relating to the formation and preservation of marriage in this country is a hotch-potch of contradictory provisions.

In English law the basic definition of marriage has always been, and still is, that which Lord Penzance put into words in *Hyde* v. *Hyde*,[2] 'I conceive that marriage, as understood by Christendom may . . . be defined as the voluntary union for life of one man and one woman to the exclusion of all others.' This definition sets out the three main conditions for a valid English marriage: it must be *voluntary*, it must be *for life*, and it must be *monogamous*. The second condition may seem, indeed it is, something of an anomaly, since English law had already recognized judicial divorce for twenty-nine years when Lord Penzance gave his judgment, and has been making the dissolution of marriage progressively easier ever since. Nevertheless, the condition that marriage must be for life remains true, in the limited sense expressed by the Court of Appeal in *Machinson* v. *Machinson*:[3] at the initiation of the marriage the intention of the parties must be union for life, unless the marriage be previously determined by judicial decree. In other words, the marriage must be, in terms of real property, no more than a life interest determinable on a condition subsequent.

Our law is curious in that there are very few regulations about starting a marriage, while the law relating to the duties of the parties in marriage, and to the dissolution of marriage, is strict and complex. Marriage is one of the easiest contracts to enter into, yet it has very far-reaching consequences, not only for the parties themselves, but for their children and for the whole of society. We will see just how

2. (1886) L.R. 1 P. and D. 130, 133.
3. [1930] P. 217.

easy it is to form this solemn contract, which, in spite of the extension of the law of divorce, is still regarded by the law as binding for life.

Who can marry?[4]

Youth and consanguinity are the two chief bars to marriage. Until very recently, the age of majority was twenty-one and it is not until majority that a person has an unfettered right to marry. The Family Law Reform Act, 1969 has lowered the age of majority to eighteen, and the position is now as follows. If either party is under sixteen, there can be no marriage: if a ceremony is performed, it is not valid, and the whole process is void *ab initio* – it is as if there had never been any marriage, as far as the law is concerned. If one of the parties is sixteen or over but under eighteen, any marriage performed will be valid, though the consent of both parents (or the parent who has custody if they are divorced) must be obtained before the marriage is solemnized, unless the infant is a widow or widower. The consent need not be given in any particular form, indeed in the absence of positive dissent it will be implied. This check operates differently for registrar's weddings than for Church weddings after publication of banns: the law demands that the registrar satisfy himself that the necessary consent has been obtained, whereas the only effect on the Church wedding is to make the publication of banns void if anyone whose consent is required 'openly and publicly declares or causes to be declared, in the church or chapel in which the banns are published, at the time of the publication, his dissent from the intended marriage'. If the clergyman has no notice of such dissent, he can celebrate the marriage without fear of censure from his bishop, or any other pain or punishment. (The law relating to parental consent is easily and frequently evaded and the Law Commission believes that the law should be changed.) If the necessary consent cannot be ob-

4. The legal requirements for a valid marriage in England are to be found in the Marriage Act, 1949. The grounds on which a marriage is void or voidable are now set out in the Nullity of Marriage Act, 1971.

tained it may be dispensed with in certain circumstances. If consent is withheld, an application may be made to the High Court, a County Court, or a Magistrates' Court. The hearing is private and informal: in the Magistrates' Court it may be entirely oral and no complaint is necessary. The Court's decision is final, there being no right of appeal.

The Church, which alone for centuries performed the rites of matrimony, has always prohibited marriage within certain prescribed degrees of consanguinity. Until the reign of Henry VIII the state did not interfere in the Church's authority in this matter, but in 1536 for the first time marriage within these degrees was forbidden by statute – in the Ecclesiastical Licences Act, 1536, followed by the Marriage Act, 1540, and confirmed by the Act of Supremacy, 1558 – and this legislation can be seen as part of the process whereby Henry shrugged off the authority of Rome. There have been some changes in the list of degrees in the last fifty years, but it is substantially the same as that laid down by the Catholic Church before the Reformation: intermarriage between persons within the third degree of kindred, or nearer, is forbidden. However, Henry VIII's laws made marriage between first cousins legitimate, whereas before it had been necessary to obtain a dispensation from the Pope for such a marriage. The strict rule admitted no other exceptions until 1908 when the Deceased Wife's Sister's Marriage Act was passed, the title of which speaks for itself: a man could now marry his sister-in-law after his wife's death. At the time it caused violent dissension and sensational forecasts of an immediate increase in wife murder, but it seems to have had no ill effect on society, and it was followed in 1921 by the Deceased Brother's Widow's Marriage Act. The ancient Jewish custom of taking one's dead brother's wife and raising up children from her was thus given statutory approval.

Marriages made in the presence of either of these bars of youth or consanguinity are void if they are contracted in England, whatever may be the race, religion, or domicile of the parties. If contracted abroad, they will be held to be void here if either of the parties is domiciled in England. (As to domicile and recognition of foreign marriages, see pp. 30, 70.)

A valid marriage can only take place between two people of the opposite sex.[5] This seemed a truism until recently; no union between people of the same sex could be regarded as anything more than a pantomime. But with the increased understanding of sexual variants, unfortunates such as the trans-sexuals who do not fit into a simple sexual slot, have been helped in some cases by surgery and hormone treatment to live socially as members of the sex to which their anatomy would not have entitled them. In *Corbett* v. *Corbett*[5a] (the 'April Ashley' case) such an individual, born a male but by treatment made into a convincing female, went through a form of marriage with a man. She (properly so described, as for social and administrative purposes she was now of the feminine gender and was recognized as such for the purposes of the welfare state) contended that the marriage was valid, although unconsummated; but after hearing a mass of medical evidence the judge held that she was a biological male, and had not therefore made a valid marriage with her 'husband'. To come to this conclusion, the judge had to differentiate between gender and biological sex: a person may be female in gender – accepted by society and the state as a woman – yet biologically remain a male, and therefore incapable of contracting a marriage with a male, since marriage is essentially a heterosexual union.

If the rules relating to affinity and age are complied with, and all the formalities are in order, the marriage will not be void but it may be voidable (see pp. 115–24). A marriage entered into without due consent or under duress or mistake as to identity will be voidable; and if a man is so drunk at the ceremony as not to know what he is doing, there can be no consent and therefore the marriage will be voidable. But fraud, apart from deception as to identity, will not have this effect: if a man deceives a woman as to

5. Nullity of Marriage Act, 1971 s.1 (a).
5a. [1970] 2 All E.R. 33.

his fortune or his status, and she marries him relying on the misrepresentation, the marriage will not be voidable. Similarly, if a woman deceives a man into believing wrongly that she is a virgin, and he marries her on that basis, the marriage will not be voidable. Even if the parties contract a monogamous marriage believing it to be polygamous, the marriage is not vitiated.

Mental incapacity negatives consent, and the law was clear on this until 1959: a lunatic as defined by law could not contract a marriage, even in a lucid interval; in other words, there was a presumption that a lunatic was incapable of consent and such a marriage was void. But as the Mental Health Act swept away all classification of the mentally ill, lunatics no longer exist in law and there can be no such presumption. Mental incapacity now only renders the marriage voidable. There must be such mental disorder as to prevent a proper understanding of the nature of the contract. (But marriage during a remission in the mental disorder would be valid, if there was sufficient ability to comprehend the nature of marriage: *Turner* v. *Myers*[6]).

The Law Commission have under consideration the desirability of a prohibition on marriage for persons with serious inheritable defects.[7] The difficulties and dangers of such a provision are obvious, and may well outweigh the advantages. Perhaps the strongest argument against the proposal is the difficulty of limiting the prohibited class to carriers of mental disease: in logic, why then should a transmitter of haemophilia be allowed to marry; and what of the effect of sterilization?

6. (1808) 1 Hag. Con. 414.
7. Law Commission Working Paper no. 20.

Essential validity of marriage

In all these cases, there is a strong presumption of law that any marriage is valid, and the burden of proof on the person trying to set aside the contract is a heavy one. It is particularly difficult to show absence of consent. As Sir James Hannen said in *Durham* v. *Durham*,[8] in 1885, 'The contract of marriage is a very simple one, which does not require a high degree of intelligence to comprehend.' The difficulty of showing that the necessary comprehension was absent was well shown in *Re the Estate of Park, deceased*[9] which caused great interest at the time. A wealthy man of seventy-eight, who had lately suffered a severe stroke, went through a ceremony of marriage one morning, and a few hours later made a will by which his wife benefited to a very modest extent in his £120,000 estate. In a jury action the will was held to be invalid because the deceased was 'not of sound mind, memory, and understanding' when he executed it. He had made a previous will, before his marriage, by which his widow did not benefit at all. Now, the result of the jury action was that the deceased died intestate, since marriage revokes all previous wills, and his widow would then receive much greater benefits than under the invalid will; but if the beneficiaries under the earlier will could show that the marriage was void (as it would have been then) owing to incapacity, the widow would get nothing at all. Since a jury had found the deceased incapable of executing a will on the afternoon of the marriage, the outlook for the widow was not very hopeful, especially as the evidence showed that on the marriage morning the deceased was confused, though the wedding had already taken place, and had to retire to bed at three o'clock in the afternoon after making the invalid will. But the Court held that quite different standards of capacity are required for will-making and marriage, that the marriage was valid, and that the widow took her interest on an intestacy. Nothing could illustrate more vividly the low standard of mental capacity and consent required to form a valid marriage.

8. (1885) 10 P.D. 80. 9. [1945] P. 112.

Duress is obviously difficult to prove in these civilized times, but there have been modern cases where a marriage has been held invalid because the wife was induced to go through the ceremony by force or fear. Now, these marriages would be voidable but not void. Thus in *H* v. *H*[10] a Hungarian woman married a French citizen in her own country, because she was terrified of being taken prisoner by the Hungarian Communist government and simply wanted the protection of a French passport to help her escape. Mr Justice Karminski (as he then was) accepted the evidence that she married only to escape imprisonment, and he held the marriage to be invalid, saying: 'I find that the fears entertained by the petitioner were of such a kind as to negative her consent to the marriage.' In the absence of consent there can be no valid marriage. Again, in *Buckland* v. *Buckland*[11] a Maltese dockyard policeman married a young girl whom he had been wrongly charged with corrupting, in the reasonable fear that he would otherwise be sentenced to a long term of imprisonment. The English Court declared the marriage null and void, but Mr Justice Scarman made it clear that, even if such a fear were reasonably entertained, it would not vitiate consent unless it arose from some external circumstance for which the petitioner was not himself responsible. Thus if a man who has in fact committed a crime married under threat that the police will be informed of the crime, that does not amount to duress sufficient to vitiate the marriage.

A dramatic example of the effect of duress is the case of *Szechter* v. *Szechter*.[12] Nina Karsov, imprisoned in Poland for political offences, escaped by going through a form of marriage in prison with a colleague and friend who had previously divorced his wife in order to rescue Nina by this desperate ruse. The friend and his wife had treated Nina as their daughter and were prepared to carry out this plan to save her from what they believed might lead to her death,

10. [1945] P. 258.
11. [1967] 2 W.L.R. 1506.
12. [1970] 3 All E.R. 905.

and certainly to her social destruction. The English Court granted a decree of nullity, on the ground that the marriage was entered into by Nina under such a fear of immediate danger that her consent was vitiated.

An interesting example of how lack of consent can invalidate a marriage is the case of *Mehta* v. *Mehta*.[13] The Petitioner, an English woman, went through certain rites in Bombay believing them to be part of a ceremony of conversion to the Hindu faith when in fact the ceremony was one of marriage. The Court here held that the marriage was monogamous in its inception, and therefore a 'marriage' within Lord Penzance's definition (see p. 19) but that it was null and void because of the petitioner's lack of intention to marry and the respondent's fraud upon her.

The forms of marriage

The ceremony of marriage itself takes on an infinity of forms in England, from the solemn pomp of a nuptial mass, through the simple service in church or chapel, to the bare declarations before a registrar. But this diversity of forms is a recent development. Up to 1836 the Established Church had the sole authority to celebrate valid marriages, although clandestine marriages were common until stopped by Lord Hardwicke's Act in 1753, which forbade any ceremony except in a parish church and according to the rites of the Church of England. The Marriage Act of 1836 for the first time made it possible for all denominations to marry according to their own forms and ceremonies, and even allowed a type of civil marriage before a superintendant registrar. Whatever the type of ceremony, it must be preceded by certain formalities, and the time and place must be in accordance with the law as set out in this act. Absence of these formalities, however, although a breach of the law, does not in every case render the marriage void (see pp. 20, 30).

Before any marriage according to the rites of the Church of England can take place, either banns must be duly published, or the parties must obtain a licence from the ecclesi-

13. [1945] 2 All E.R. 690.

astical authorities. A marriage may also be celebrated on a certificate from a superintendant registrar (see p. 28), but only if the vicar of the parish is prepared to accept the certificate. Publication of banns is the traditional procedure, honoured by centuries of use but often too slow for the lightning marriages of today. When communities were smaller and more closely knit, and were centred on the parish church, the reading of the banns gave notice to the little world in which the engaged couple lived that a marriage was proposed, and gave an opportunity for impediments to the marriage to be disclosed. Although the procedure has lost a good deal of its point, it remains the cheapest way of initiating Church of England marriage and is still very popular. The parties must give notice to the clergyman who is to publish the banns at least seven days before the first publication, setting out their names and addresses and periods of residence at their present addresses. The banns must be read 'in an audible manner' on three Sundays during morning service (or evening service if there is no morning service on that day) in the parish church of each of the parishes in which the parties reside, and the banns must then be registered in a book 'of durable material' provided by the parish council. Only a clergyman or an authorized lay reader may read banns. The marriage must take place within three months of the publication of banns, otherwise the whole process must start all over again.

Banns may be avoided if a marriage licence is obtained. These licences are 'common' and 'special'. A common licence can be granted in each diocese by the bishop. The application is first made to one of the bishop's surrogates – clergy of some standing in the diocese, whose names can be obtained from any vicar – and is then put forward to the registrar of the diocese, who issues the licence under the seal of the diocesan chancellor. If either of the parties is under eighteen, the surrogate will not support the application unless he is satisfied that the necessary consents have been obtained. This licence, which costs £2.75, permits a marriage in a particular parish, in which one of the parties must have resided for fifteen days immediately before the grant of the licence. It becomes void after three months.

A special licence is granted only by the Archbishop of Canterbury. The procedure is expensive, but it has the advantage that no residential qualifications are necessary. An application, supported by affidavits, must be made through the Master of Faculties at Westminster and the total cost, including legal fees, is likely to be in the region of fifty pounds. This expense is rarely justified, and indeed when people speak of marrying 'by special licence' they usually mean that they have a common licence as opposed to the licence of a superintendant registrar. This latter type of licence is the civil equivalent of the ecclesiastical common licence.

All marriages other than Church of England marriages can be celebrated only on the authority of a certificate of a superintendant registrar. To obtain such a certificate, one of the parties must give notice of marriage to the registrar of the district in which he or she has resided for seven days, stating the names, addresses, and status of the parties, and accompanied by a solemn declaration that he or she believes that there is no impediment to the marriage and, if relevant, that the necessary consents have been obtained. The registrar must then display the notice of marriage in a prominent position in his office for a period of twenty-one days, and thereafter he can issue the certificate. All this costs the sum of five pence.

The three weeks' interval can be avoided by paying the registrar £1.50, over and above the five pence due for the notice, and obtaining from him a licence with the certificate. When a registrar gives such a licence with his certificate, he must enter into a bond of £100 to the Registrar General 'for the due and faithful execution of his office' – a sufficient sanction to make the registrar wary of granting a licence in an improper case. The marriage may take place after one clear day has elapsed from issue of the licence. Notice, certificate, and licence all become void if the marriage is not celebrated within three months of issue. Armed with the certificate, or the certificate and licence, the couple can marry according to any form of ceremony they choose, provided it takes place within a registered building, or the office of a superintendant registrar, or in an Anglican church, or according to the usages of the Jews or Quakers. 'Registered buildings' are in fact all churches or chapels of the different religious sects. Neither Jews nor Quakers need marry in registered buildings, but Quakers must declare when giving notice of marriage that they are both members of the Society of Friends, and a Jewish marriage must comply with Jewish law or it will be void.

The actual ceremony is governed by the usages of religion in Church of England, Jewish, and Quaker marriages, but all marriages taking place in a 'registered building' or at a registrar's office must incorporate somewhere in the ceremony the following declarations by each party to the marriage: 'I do solemnly declare that I know not of any lawful impediment why I, AB, may not be joined in matrimony to CD'; and each must say to the other: 'I call upon these witnesses here present to witness that I, AB, do take thee, CD, to be my lawful wedded wife [or husband].'

However, if the registrar is not present – as will be the case in Roman Catholic and Nonconformist marriages, provided that the minister or priest is duly authorized – the only words that need be said by each party are: 'I, AB, do take thee, CD, to be my wedded wife [or husband].'

Finally, the ceremony must take place in the presence of two or more witnesses, and either the registrar or a person authorized by the trustees or governing body of the 'registered building', except in the case of Jewish and Quaker marriages. Church of England and civil marriages must be celebrated between 8 a.m. and 6 p.m., but Jewish and Quaker marriages can take place at any hour.

The point at which the parties become man and wife is very important. This may be crucial if, for example, the validity of the marriage depends on the hours of birth (as it may where it is necessary to show that both were over sixteen), or if one of the parties should die during the ceremony and questions of inheritance arise. The provisions of the Marriage Act, 1949 would seem to admit of only one interpretation: the marriage contract is complete once the words required by the Act have been said by both parties. Absence of any of the subsequent formalities cannot invalidate the marriage. In general, the omission of the preliminary formalities, although a breach of the law, does not make the marriage void, but certain of them are essential, and if the parties marry knowing full well that these have not been fulfilled no marriage will be contracted. These essential formalities include the due publication of banns, the obtaining of a proper licence where necessary, and the presence of the registrar in office marriages. In other words, although the law lays down many requirements for a valid marriage, few of them are essential, and it is not easy to have a marriage set aside for some technical defect (see p. 113).

Recognition of foreign marriages

A marriage lasts until one of the parties dies, or until there is a decree of a competent court declaring the marriage null or granting a dissolution. It is therefore important to know what marriages are recognized as binding by the Courts of this country. Any marriage contracted here according to law will, of course, be so recognized, but marriages are also contracted out of England, by British subjects as well as by foreigners, and these marriages will only be recognized as valid in England subject to certain rules. Under the Foreign Marriages Acts, 1892 to 1947, marriages where one of the parties is British are valid if they are conducted by an authorized marriage officer – for example, a British Ambassador or some embassy official, a High Commissioner, or a British Consul. Members of the forces can make valid marriages abroad provided they marry before a chaplain to the forces or some person appointed by the local commanding officer. A forces' marriage can also be contracted on board ship in foreign waters, although civilians can no longer marry on board Her Majesty's ships (as they could before 1947).

In other cases, 'foreign' marriages are tested for their validity by the law of the domicile of the parties (see pp. 70–72). Provided that the marriage would be recognized in the country of the domicile, and is conducted according to the formalities required by the country in which it takes place, that is the *lex loci celebrationis*, it will be recognized in England: even a polygamous marriage is binding here in such circumstances, and the children will be regarded as legitimate. However, a polygamous marriage does not give either the High Court or magistrates jurisdiction to make decrees or orders: *Sowa* v. *Sowa*.[14] But where a marriage was at its inception potentially polygamous in nature, yet rendered monogamous by the *lex loci celebrationis*, it will be regarded as monogamous here for the purpose of providing jurisdiction: *Parkasho* v. *Singh*[15] following *Cheni* v. *Cheni*.[16]

If an Englishman marries in a foreign country, the marriage will be recognized if the formalities demanded by the law of that country are complied with, provided that the formalities required are not repugnant to English law: for instance, if the foreign law forbade marriage between white and coloured people, we would not hold a marriage invalid simply because it did not comply with such colour-bar legislation.

But a marriage abroad will also be valid in England if it is celebrated in accordance with the formalities required by the law of the country where it takes place, even if those formalities are quite different from the ones required by English law. This is because it is a principle of international law to test the validity of a contract by the law of the place in which the contract was physically made. It follows that English people who wish to marry, but cannot comply with the formalities required by the law here, can yet make a valid marriage in another country where they do satisfy the local requirements of law. The commonest example

14. [1961] P. 70.
15. [1967] 1 All E.R. 737.
16. [1965] P. 85.

of this is – or was – the Gretna Green marriage. The Scottish law of marriage has always been less strict than the English, and for centuries there were three types of marriage available in Scotland which required no formalities. There was the marriage by promise *subsequente copula* – that is, by the informal exchange of vows followed by sexual intercourse; there was the marriage by 'cohabitation, habite and repute'. There was also the marriage *per verba de praesenti* by which the man and woman merely had to declare in the presence of witnesses that they were man and wife. This was the form most popular with the English. No banns were needed, no priest or registrar had to be present, and – most important of all – Scottish law does not require parental consent to the marriage of a minor. When the English marriage law was tightened up by Lord Hardwicke's Act in 1753, and the scandal of the Fleet marriages[17] was brought to an end, runaway couples notoriously found sanctuary over the border, where they could be married forthwith. The Gretna Green blacksmith did a roaring trade in such 'ceremonies', and at one time it is said that he performed as many as two hundred in a year. The advantages of this type of marriage were not limited only to those who wished to marry under age without their parents' consent; a man could secure the fortune of an heiress within a moment of time if he could abduct her over the border, without the risk of parental intervention during the period of delay required by English law.

These marriages became such a scandal that Scotland passed a law in 1856 making the residence of one of the parties in that country for twenty-one days an essential re-

17. These clandestine unions were made possible by the ease with which marriages could be contracted before 1754. Infamous clergymen, often imprisoned for debt in the Fleet Prison, made 'a very bishopric of revenue' by celebrating marriages between couples whose very names they often did not know, because no sort of licence was then necessary. Many found that they had tied themselves for life during a moment of passion or a drunken orgy: a notable example was the disastrous marriage of the poet Churchill at the age of seventeen which wrecked his whole life.

quirement for a valid marriage. That checked the popularity of the runaway Scottish marriage, since the delay often gave parents time to take some action to prevent the marriage, but they still took place. Then in 1939 all three of the informal types of marriage were abolished by Act of Parliament.[18] It was no longer sufficient for a man and woman to exchange vows or gain a reputation of being a married couple: instead, registrar's marriages were introduced for which a Sheriff's licence is necessary. This licence can only be issued if one of the parties has been resident in Scotland for fifteen days, but although the necessity for some formality has killed the romantic ease of the Gretna marriage, Scotland still provides a useful asylum for certain couples. It is only necessary for the man to live fifteen days in Scotland, and then to be joined by the runaway girl, but this is now only of practical use to those who want to marry without a parent's consent. The abduction of heiresses, no longer so profitable since the Married Women's Property Act (see p. 261) cannot now take the exciting forms of the past – in any case the motor-car and the aeroplane have replaced the lathering post-horses, and the girl is given some days to cool her ardour in the absence of her seducer. Of course, as recent cases have shown, a really determined young couple can still take advantage of the convenient Scottish law, and their parents can do very little to interfere short of kidnapping. No order of the English Courts will stop the marriage, since such an order will not be effective in Scotland: but if the parents should make the minor a ward of Court, and the marriage then takes place without the Court's consent, both husband and wife are in contempt of Court and can be sent to prison if they set foot again in England. A runaway couple may think twice about contracting a marriage which will impose perpetual exile or submission to imprisonment. In fact since the age of majority has been reduced to eighteen, judges will rarely forbid marriage.

It must be emphasized that, although the formalities can be evaded in this way, the essential requirements of a valid

18. Marriage (Scotland) Act, 1939.

English marriage are still necessary. Thus a foreign marriage, even if valid in the foreign country, will not be recognized here if either party is under sixteen, nor if there is lack of mutual consent of the sort we have already discussed. And not all foreign countries take the same view as the English law in regard to formalities. The French Courts, for instance, have held that a marriage between French subjects, valid in England, was voidable in France because the parental consents required by French law had not been obtained: *Simonin* v. *Mallac.*[19]

A curious survival from the past is the 'common law marriage'. Before there were any statutes governing marriage, the law in England was that of the Church – a marriage was valid if performed by a priest if one were available, but if there were no priest to be had, then it could be contracted by the simple consent of the parties. No such marriage has been possible in England for many years, but it can still take place in certain circumstances abroad where the English common law prevails – chiefly the colonies, British merchant ships, and deserted countries where no local law runs. All that is necessary for such a marriage to be valid is that the parties accept one another as man and wife. The theory is that British subjects carry with them to colonies and wild places as much of the English law as can conveniently be applied, a relic of the days when Englishmen were opening up the virgin lands and took with them the civilizing influence of the law of their homeland. An English common law marriage can now be set up only in the most exceptional circumstances, as in times of war and foreign occupation where no operative system of law exists. A Jewish ceremony in Hungary in 1945, without the civil ceremony essential by Hungarian law, was held to be invalid: *Rosenthal* v. *Rosenthal.*[20] The scope for common law marriages on this planet is rapidly diminishing. Perhaps space travel will revive their importance.

19. (1860) Sw. and Tr. 67.
20. (1967) 111 S.J. 475.

2 Sharing a Marriage

Bigamy

The status of marriage is one in which the whole of society has an interest, not just the parties to the marriage; quite apart from the religious and ethical considerations, both economic and social stability depend, to a large extent, on marriage (see chapter 12), and therefore any violation of it is the concern of the law. In a monogamous society, one would expect bigamy to be regarded as a heinous offence. In this country it was at first only an ecclesiastical offence – not that the Church lacked rigour in punishing it – but it became a civil offence in 1603, when an Act was passed making it a felony, described as a crime 'to the great Dishonour of God and the utter undoing of divers honest men's children, and others'. The churchmen no doubt regarded it as the profanation of a solemn ceremony, but Blackstone[1] said that the reason for making it a felony was because it was 'so great a violation of the public economy and decency of a well-ordered state'. As so often with the old lawyers, we find economics put before morals as a basis for the law.

The present law is contained in the great codifying legislation of 1861.[2] Bigamy is committed when a person, being married, goes through a legally recognized ceremony of marriage with another person while the original wife or husband is still living. It is a defence to a charge of bigamy that the first marriage has been dissolved or declared void by a competent court, or that the second marriage was contracted by a person other than a subject of the Crown outside England and Ireland. There is a further defence, merciful but complicated: if the accused can show that the first spouse has

1. Commentaries, IV, 163.
2. Offences against the Person Act, 1861, s.57.

been continuously absent for seven years and has never been heard of by him during that time, he must be acquitted, and for this purpose it is only necessary to establish that the parties have in fact been separated for seven years – it is then for the prosecution to show that within that time the fact of the spouse's being alive had come to the accused's knowledge.

Apart from this last defence, the law of bigamy is strict. It is not enough to have a reasonable belief that your wife has divorced you: if there was no valid divorce, any second marriage is bigamous, however genuine the mistake. That this rule can work harshly is seen in the case of *R.* v. *Wheat and Stocks.*[3] Mr Wheat, a man of little education, instructed solicitors under the Poor Persons' scheme to take divorce proceedings against his wife. There was a long delay and after a year he received a letter from the solicitors saying that they would 'lose no time' over his petition. Another three months passed, and the impatient petitioner sent the solicitors a telegram, to which they replied: 'We have your telegram, and hope to send your papers for signature in the course of a day or two.' Relying on this letter, Wheat believed he was divorced and went off and married Miss Stocks. When they were both charged with bigamy, Wheat gave evidence that he believed the letter meant that he was divorced; the jury found that this belief was held in good faith, but the judge nevertheless directed them to return a verdict of guilty. They appealed, but in spite of the advocacy of their counsel, Norman Birkett, who cited many cases to support his argument that intent was necessary for this crime, the Court of Criminal Appeal upheld the verdict, saying that a reasonable belief in the prior divorce was no defence, but was only a mitigating circumstance to be taken into consideration when imposing sentence.[4] However, bigamy is generally treated leniently by the Courts today; heavy punishments are rare, and often the police hold their hand from prosecuting when there is no public scandal and the crime is unlikely to be repeated.

3. [1921] 2 K.B. 119.
4. This case has now been overruled by *R.* v. *Gould* [1968] 2 Q.B. 65.

Rights and obligations of marriage

At *common law* the husband was always under an obligation to maintain his wife, but this duty was not of any great benefit to her since it was limited to the provision of the bare necessities of life. Only since 1878 has the wife had any *statutory* right to claim maintenance, although since the Vagrancy Act, 1824, the husband could be prosecuted as an idle and disorderly person if he failed to maintain his wife and children. The Poor Law Amendment Acts of 1850 and 1886 gave the local authorities the power to recover from a husband relief paid to his family in certain circumstances. Since the National Assistance Act, 1948, both husband and wife have been under an absolute liability to maintain the other spouse and their children, both legitimate and illegitimate. But a husband is not obliged by these provisions to maintain a deserting or adulterous wife (see *National Assistance Board* v. *Wilkinson*.[5] These laws are and were for the protection of the coffers of the state rather than the good of the parties since they prevent any man, woman or child from becoming a charge on the welfare services while there is an adult member of the family capable of supporting them. In this they differ from the provisions of the specific matrimonial statutes, which give the parties financial protection *inter se*.

The various complicated statutory provisions for mutual maintenance within the family are dealt with later in chapter 12, but here we shall look at the duties imposed by the common law since time immemorial. This law is still important, because it is the law applicable to that vast majority of marriages in which no order has ever been made under any of the statutes relating to maintenance.

It is the duty of every husband to maintain his wife according to his means, and if he failed in this duty she had an implied authority to pledge his credit for all necessaries suitable to his station. This presumption of authority also arose when a man lived with a woman and allowed her to pass as his wife. The effect of this was that anyone who provided the

5. [1952] 2 All E.R. 255.

wife with goods can sue the husband for payment provided they are 'necessaries'. There is a mass of case law which defines 'necessaries', but these need not trouble us here, because the wife's 'agency of necessity', as it was called, was abolished by section 41 of the Matrimonial Proceedings and Property Act 1970.

Nevertheless, the wife may still be an agent of the husband under the ordinary law of agency. If he has allowed her to enter into contracts or to purchase goods as his agent, he will be liable to pay, unless he expressly warns the tradesman concerned that his wife no longer has any authority to bind him. Notices in newspapers making a general denial of liability are not very much use, since in order to avoid paying his wife's debt the husband would have to show that the particular tradesman had seen the notice.

The agency of necessity has left its mark in the orders for maintenance pending suit and security for a wife's costs. Both of these are based on the concept of necessaries; the former remains but the general view is that necessity for costs has gone.

Although wives now have certain legal obligations to maintain their husbands under statute,[6] at common law the obligations were all on the side of the husband – but then, until 1882, he took his wife's entire property on marriage, and it was therefore not unreasonable to expect him to be financially responsible for her. And the law could hardly call on wives to support their husbands when there were virtually no sources of paid employment for women outside the working classes.

We have seen that a husband's liability for his wife's debts, where they were contracted for the purchase of necessaries, was based on the concept of the wife acting as an agent for her husband. No presumption of agency extends to the

6. The Matrimonial Proceedings and Property Act, 1970, gave the Divorce Court power for the first time to order *either* party to maintain the other, or their children, after the filing of a petition for, or on or after making a decree of, divorce, judicial separation, or nullity: see pp. 243–4. Magistrates have had the power to order wives to maintain their husbands in exceptional circumstances since 1960.

wife's wrongful acts, and a husband cannot be liable for his wife's crimes or torts, unless it can be shown that he incited her in the case of crime, or that she did in fact act as his agent in the case of tort. For example, if a man employs his wife as his secretary and in the course of her employment she is driving a motor-car and negligently damages the person or property of another, the husband will be liable in exactly the same way as any other employer. But the wife will be liable too, and the injured person can sue either or both of them as he may choose.

Both husband and wife are under a *legal duty of cohabitation*. In the past this duty was enforced by the Ecclesiastical Courts, which could imprison a spouse who defied the Court's order to return to cohabitation. The Civil Courts recognized the husband's right to his wife's society (and even allowed him to chastise her), but the wife had no corresponding right: hers was the duty to give of her society and services. It followed that a husband could confine his wife against her will, and this view persisted until late into the nineteenth century. But in 1891[7] a deserting wife who had been kidnapped by her husband and confined in his house was granted a writ of *habeas corpus* by the Court, the effect of which was to free her from her imprisonment. The result of this case was that 'the shackles of servitude fell from the limbs of married women and they were free to come and go at their own will'.[8] Until recently, this duty to cohabit could in theory be enforced by an action for 'restitution of conjugal rights', but it was rarely used and was abolished by the Matrimonial Proceedings and Property Act, 1970 s.20 (see p. 88).

But the duty to cohabit still has practical importance, since failure to do so without good cause can be grounds for divorce in certain circumstances, and is a defence to an application for maintenance. 'Cohabit' means living together and treating each other as husband and wife – living together under the same roof is not sufficient – but it does *not* in this

7. *R.* v. *Jackson* [1891] 1 Q.B. 671.
8. *Forster* v. *Forster* (1790) 1 Hagg. Con. 144.

context mean having sexual relations: 'The duty of matrimonial intercourse cannot be compelled by the Court, matrimonial cohabitation may.'[9] But we shall see later (pp. 120, 168) that in certain circumstances refusal of sexual intercourse can now amount to a matrimonial offence, although it never was under the ecclesiastical law.

There are certain curious causes of action arising from this mutual right to cohabitation, of which only one remains. The tort of *enticement*, now abolished by the Law Reform (Miscellaneous Provisions) Act 1970 together with seduction and harbouring (see p. 154) last saw light of day in England in 1958[10] in a case where a husband sued his mother-in-law for enticing his wife away from him and breaking up the marriage. In his judgment Lord Justice Denning stressed that in this country we have no remedy for 'alienation of affections' similar to that available in most States of the United States of America, and that it is contrary to the policy of our Courts to extend the interference of the law into the private lives of husband and wife. 'If a husband is to keep the affection of his wife,' he said, 'he must do it by the kindness and consideration which he himself shows to her.' And he made it clear that he regarded the whole action of enticement as out of keeping with the times, even when brought against a paramour – as indeed it is, being a survival from the days when a wife was little better than a servant, and was protected solely because she was part of the husband's property. It is interesting to note that the husband had exactly the same right of action against a person who enticed away his servant. The action was an atavistic remnant of the support given by the law to the concept of the husband and father as the supreme figure in the family, the wife and children being, like the servants, mere chattels.

9. Mr Justice McCardie in *Place* v. *Searle* [1932] 2 K.B. 497, but matrimonial cohabitation could not now be enforced (see p. 39).

10. *Gottlieb* v. *Gleiser* [1958] 1 Q.B. 267.

The unity of husband and wife

Another survival of a husband's proprietary rights in his wife is the action for loss of *consortium*. Although this is defined as a loss of 'conjugal society', it is really nothing more than a wrong based on deprivation of services; it remains an anomaly of our law that the action only lies at the suit of a husband. In *Best* v. *Samuel Fox and Co. Ltd*,[11] the House of Lords held that a wife could not recover damages for negligence which caused her husband to become impotent. Lord Reid described consortium as 'a bundle of rights' – but it is fairly clear that in the eyes of the law the bundle is only of pecuniary value to the husband. This is one of those actions which revolt the modern mind: the Courts obviously dislike it, and refuse to extend its operation to make it equally available to both sexes, but the right of the husband at least is firmly embedded in our law and cannot be ignored.

'By marriage the husband and wife are one person in law; that is, the very being or legal existence of the woman is suspended during marriage or at least is incorporated and consolidated into that of her husband.'

These words by Blackstone describing the legal fiction of conjugal unity were until very recently as true as they were in the eighteenth century. For centuries this concept of man and wife as a single legal entity – a male *persona* with a female embedded within, like a fly in amber – made it impossible for them to sue each other in contract, but under the Married Women's Property Act, 1882, either party can now apply to the Court for a decision of any question as to the ownership of property in dispute. As we shall see, it was only in 1962 that this unity was abolished in tort. In crime, however, the legal fiction remains, and causes some strange anomalies, ill-suited to the realities of modern life. An idea conceived in the tortuous brains of medieval theologians, and preserved by the respect of ecclesiastical lawyers for

11. [1952] A.C. 716.

antiquity, has lived on into this century with very little change until recently.

Added to this concept there was the notion that a married woman was subordinate to her husband, and therefore might be presumed to be subject to his coercion. As a result of these two principles, there are certain curiosities in the criminal law. Until 1 January 1969 husbands and wives could not be guilty of stealing from each other – unless they were living apart or the taker was just about to leave the other spouse – which had the inconvenient and unjust consequence that the receiver of the goods could not be guilty of any offence. So where a wife took her husband's property and gave it to her lover, the lover was not guilty of receiving stolen goods.[12] But this has all been changed by the Theft Act, 1968, section 30 (1), which provides that the Act shall apply to the parties to a marriage, and to their property, as it would apply if they were not married. Furthermore, either the injured spouse or a third party may bring proceedings for such an offence, but only if the proceedings are instituted by or with the consent of the Director of Public Prosecutions. A husband and wife cannot conspire together, because they are one; yet if they conspire with a third party, all three are guilty of an offence, which seems irrational. Similarly, it is not an offence for a husband or wife to publish a libel against the other spouse. Nor can a wife be found guilty as an accessory after the fact if, after her husband has committed a crime, she gives him shelter, since she is bound to do so by her marital duty.

The idea that a wife was under her husband's subjection led to the rule that where a woman committed a felony (other than treason or murder) in the actual presence of her husband, there was a presumption of law that she was coerced by him, and unless the prosecution could prove that there was no such coercion, she must be acquitted. In the old case of Roger de Fanborne and his wife Agnes, heard in 1226, both were charged with forgery; Roger was hanged but his wife was acquitted, irrespective of her part in the

12. *R.* v. *Creamer* [1919] 1 K.B. 564.

offence, because she was held to be *sub virga viri sui* – under the rod of her husband. This rule remained the law until 1925, when it was changed to the extent that thenceforth there was no *presumption* of coercion, but it remains a good defence. In other words, the burden of proof now lies on the wife to establish that she was in fact driven on to the crime by her husband. It is difficult to imagine what sort of evidence would satisfy a modern jury that this defence had been proved, and there has been no reported case where it has been accepted. But there is authority[13] for saying that in one crime at least there is still a presumption in favour of the wife: where coinage implements are found in a house occupied at the time by a man and his wife, the law presumes that they are in the possession of the husband alone, and the wife cannot be convicted unless there is evidence to show that she was acting separately and without her husband's sanction.

The community of interest between husband and wife is reflected in the rules governing evidence by one spouse against another. Under the common law, no accused person might give evidence in his own defence because of the temptation to commit the cardinal sin of lying on oath, and this disqualification in most cases extended to the wives and husbands of accused persons. This rule led to some curious results. Rush, the Norfolk murderer of 1848, was hanged on the evidence of his mistress, whom he had promised to marry; if he had kept his promise it would have saved his life, since she could not then have testified against him. A tale is told of a man who established an alibi and was acquitted on the evidence of his mistress, who had been at the races with him at the time of the crime: if he had taken his wife, he would have suffered for his fidelity because he could not have proved his alibi. From 1872 onwards the law allowed the accused to give evidence in more and more cases, and in 1898 the whole position was changed by the Criminal Evidence Act and the modern rules were laid down. In all cases the accused may now give evidence on his own behalf – this

13. *R.* v. *Boober* (1850) 14 J.P. 355.

is not always the advantage it may appear to be – and the husband or wife of the accused may also give evidence, *but only if called by the defence*, and only on the application of the party charged.[14] A spouse cannot be compelled to give evidence, even by the defence, and the omission to call such evidence may not be commented on by the prosecution. But there are certain cases in which the spouse of the accused *may* be called, if willing to give evidence, by either prosecution or defence. These include cases of personal violence by one spouse against another, rape and other sexual offences, incest, bigamy, bodily injury to young people under seventeen, and cases where a husband or wife commits an offence against the property of the other. In certain cases – spouses, for instance – the husband or wife is also a *compellable* witness, but as a general rule a spouse can only give voluntary testimony.

Communications between husband and wife should ideally be completely protected from third parties, and it has been suggested from time to time in the cases that at common law a privilege attached to marital confidences. But in *Rumping* v. *Director of Public Prosecutions* (see p. 45) the House of Lords decided that the privilege was entirely a creature of statute. By section 3 of the Evidence (Amendment) Act, 1853, it was provided that:

> No husband shall be compellable to disclose any communication made to him by his wife during the marriage, and no wife shall be compellable to disclose any communication made to her by her husband during the marriage.

The Criminal Evidence Act, 1898, section 1, contained an almost identical provision, thus the statutory privilege applied to both civil and criminal cases. But under section 16 (3) of the Civil Evidence Act, 1968, it was enacted that section 3 of the Evidence (Amendment) Act, 1853, should cease to have any effect except in relation to criminal pro-

14. This still applies even if the husband and wife are judicially separated (*Moss* v. *Moss* [1963] 2 All E.R. 829).

ceedings. The result of this is that husbands and wives are now compellable in civil proceedings, even as to marital confidences, but not in criminal proceedings. Even in criminal cases it was decided, in *Rumping* v. *Director of Public Prosecutions*,[15] that the privilege does not extend to communications which fall into the hands of a third party. In October 1961, a Dutch seaman named Rumping was convicted of the murder of a young woman at Menai Bridge. One of the principal pieces of evidence against him was a letter which he wrote to his wife in Holland on the day after the killing, which contained something very like a confession of the crime, begged for her help, and ended with words of farewell and assurances of love. This letter never reached the wife, but fell into the hands of the police. If the wife had received the letter, she could never have been made to produce it in court; but at the trial the judge admitted the letter, and Rumping was convicted. His appeal, based solely on the admission of the letter, went to the House of Lords, where four out of five of their lordships held that the letter was rightly admitted and dismissed the appeal. However, Lord Radcliffe did not agree: he held that communications within marriage were sacred, and that to accept the evidence of an eavesdropper, or one who accidentally came upon something intended only for the eyes of the other spouse, would violate a principle of the common law.

The former privilege of spouses against compulsion to reveal marital secrets seemed to be the limit of the right, but in 1965 the protection was greatly extended in the case of *Argyll* v. *Argyll and others*.[16] Margaret, Duchess of Argyll, there sought an injunction restraining her former husband and a newspaper from publishing articles which contained confidential communications between the parties during their marriage. Mr Justice Ungoed-Thomas granted the injuction for various reasons, chief among them being that the policy of the law favoured the view that communications between husband and wife during coverture were within the scope of the court's protection against breach of confidence.

15. [1964] A.C. 814. 16. [1967] Ch. 302.

The editor and proprietors of the newspaper were also restrained from publication, Rumping's case being distinguished in that the House of Lords were there dealing only with the admissibility in evidence of marital communications coming into the hands of third parties. The Argyll case is an impressive modern example of the development of an equitable principle to do justice where the common law and statute fail.

Another instance of the survival of the concept of marital unity is *domicile*. Unlike many other systems of law, in the English Courts a wife takes the domicile of her husband, as a legitimate child takes the domicile of his father, wherever the dependant may in fact live (see p. 70). This rule gives rise to injustice and has often been criticized; the problem could easily be resolved by allowing a woman's domicile to be governed by the same rules as apply to men.

Tort and marital unity

In crime and contract law the position of husbands and wives is comparatively well adjusted to modern conditions, but in actions for civil wrongs, or torts, the ancient doctrine of marital unity remained almost inviolate until very recently. Before 1882, husband and wife could in no circumstances sue each other in tort, but in that year the Married Women's Property Act gave to a wife the right to sue her husband for the protection and security of her own property 'as if she were a femme sole'. Husbands were not given this right, and this anomaly remained until August 1962 (see p. 47): a wife whose husband kicked her downstairs could sue him for the damage he did to her clothes, but not for her loss of wages due to the resulting injuries, while her husband could not even recover from her the price of a new suit if she should damage it in spite. However, if a wife suffered injury as the result of her husband's wrongful act committed *before* marriage, she could take proceedings against him *after* marriage, because it has been decided that a wife's legal rights which accrued before marriage are 'things in action', and therefore property, and she was entitled to take legal action for the 'protection and security' of those rights. Naturally, a husband had no similar right to sue for 'ante-nuptial torts', as they are called.

That husbands and wives should not be able to bring their domestic squabbles into court is reasonable enough, but after the motor-car became ubiquitous the principle caused serious injustice. Since a wife could not sue her husband for negligence, his insurers were not called upon to pay damages for any personal injuries she received in a motor accident caused by his bad driving (although she could recover for damage to her own car). A husband's position was worse: since he could not sue his wife in tort at all, his wife could not be made liable for the husband's personal injury or damage to his property due to the wife's negligence, therefore her insurers escaped entirely when the wife drove her husband's car negligently and caused an accident. Other anomalies arose in the field of vicarious liability and for years the judges made it clear that they disliked having to apply such an unjust anachronism (see the words of Mr Justice Devlin in *Drinkwater* v. *Kimber*).[17]

This outmoded doctrine was swept away by the Law Reform (Husband and Wife) Act, 1962, which lays down in section 1 (1) that 'each of the parties to a marriage shall have the like right of action in tort against the other as if they were not married'. Husbands and wives can therefore now sue each other in tort exactly as if they were strangers, with the qualification laid down in section 1 (2) of the Act that the court may stay any action brought by one spouse against the other 'if it appears that no substantial benefit would accrue to either party from the continuation of the proceedings', or that the matter could be more conveniently disposed of under the machinery provided by section 17 of the Married Women's Property Act, 1882 (see p. 262). The qualification is a valuable check on the unseemly litigation of domestic disputes, and the main effect of the Act has undoubtedly been to prevent insurance companies from avoiding payment of certain claims. It does not seem to have brought a new class of matrimonial dispute before the courts. For example,

17. [1952] 2 Q.B. 281.

where a husband sought to get rid of his wife from the matrimonial house by bringing an action in trespass, the judge refused to deal with the case (unreported) because it was a dispute better dealt with under section 17.

Tax and marriage

In one area of living which affects us all – taxation – the law regards husband and wife as one, subject to certain exceptions introduced by the Finance Act 1971. A husband is, in law, primarily liable for the *whole* of the tax payable on the joint incomes of husband and wife so long as they continue to live together. If he fails to pay, the wife then becomes liable for her share of the tax. A *separate assessment* has no effect on the calculation of the total joint tax bill of husband and wife, but if they elect for such separate assessment, each then becomes directly liable for his or her own share of the total tax.

The operation of the assumption that husband and wife are one for tax purposes, combined with the system of allowances, is of considerable benefit to the lower income marriage, but in the past has penalized severely the couple with substantial joint incomes. A married man has a personal allowance of £320 on which he pays no tax, as opposed to the bachelor's personal allowance of £220. This means that if a man marries a woman with no income, he immediately has a small tax advantage. But if the woman has any income, earned or unearned, she will herself have a personal allowance of £220, giving them a total personal allowance of £440 while unmarried, as against the total of £320 when married. But if the wife's income is earned, this tax disadvantage is offset by the impact of earned income relief, and in most cases marriage gives a positive tax benefit to the couple. To take an example, a man earning £30 a week and a woman earning £15 a week will have a joint annual tax bill of about £450 per annum while unmarried. If they marry, their joint annual tax bill will be about £400 – a £50 bonus for propriety.

But the picture is very different for more well to do

couples. Especially if one or the other has a large unearned income, the difference made to their financial position by marriage can be enormous because aggregation of their incomes means that each of them pays surtax on a much larger slice of income than they would have done if single. The impact of this has been particularly great on the professional classes: for example, an accountant earning £7000 a year married to a doctor earning £5000 a year would have a total tax bill of about £4900 if jointly taxed, whereas if they lived together unmarried they would only pay about £3700 on their joint incomes – a premium of £1200 for the advantage of marriage lines.

The Finance Act 1971 has removed this injustice as from the financial year 1972–3. A married couple can now elect to be taxed separately provided the husband forgoes his marriage allowance. Where the joint incomes after deduction of charges (such as mortgage interest and life insurance) is over £6000, the election to be taxed separately can have considerable effect. To take the example already given, the accountant and doctor earning a joint income of £12,000 a year can now expect to pay a total tax of £3750 as against £3700 if unmarried. This must be an encouragement to many professional women to continue with their careers where they were positively discouraged before, since it often costs a woman more in extra expenditure on running her house and caring for her children than she was formerly able to keep after tax.

However, the tax laws in this country still bear heavily on family life in other ways. The limitation of the earned income allowance to the wife who takes employment outside the home is a sore discrimination against the woman who puts all her skill and energy into homemaking, which is not regarded by the law as work of sufficient value to the State to entitle her to equal rights with those who take paid employment. While the legal reason for this is logical – no income is produced, therefore no relief can be given – the practical result is an unhappy one. And we shall see later (p. 250) that our fiscal system subsidizes the broken marriage and repeated divorce and remarriage in a most extraordinary way. It is also arguable that the 'expense account', still with us, although modified in its impact by the Finance Act 1965 which took away its chief fiscal delights, derogates from family unity by facilitating a higher standard of living in the income earner than the homemaker.[18]

Common ownership of property

Husbands and wives are naturally reluctant to consider their individual rights of ownership of objects used in common in the home, but if the marriage breaks down this inhibition melts away like snow in summer. Then the disputes may be bitter, and the law's task a hard one if called upon to decide between the spouses. The details of this problem will be explored in chapter 13, but it is important to understand the broad development of the property rights of married couples at this stage. Until 1882, the matrimonial property, whether acquired by husband and wife either before or after marriage, was to all intents and purposes in the sole ownership of the husband. From then on the wife could hold her own property and keep her own earnings. But she had no claim whatsoever on any property owned, or money earned, by her husband, however much she might have helped him in the acquisition of his wealth. Unless she could show that she had in fact contributed cash to the purchase of the property, could establish a partnership in his business, or could prevail on her husband to settle a share of the property on her in some way, she could not make any claim to it. The Courts tried to mitigate the situation by dealing more generously with a wife than they would with a stranger in disputes over the ownership of the matrimonial home, and by inventing the so-called 'equity of the deserted wife' (see p. 271), the wife was (and still is to some extent) very much at the mercy of judicial discretion in property disputes with her husband.

Since the last war there has been a progression of judicial

18. A further tax disadvantage in marriage is that a husband may only have a 'principal residence' for the purpose of capital gains tax relief on the proceeds of sale.

opinion in favour of some sort of community of property – as well as a good deal of resistance to any such development – and recent legislation has, as we shall see, given wives some modest gains. For example the Married Women's Property Act, 1964, entitles a wife to a half share of any property acquired out of savings from housekeeping moneys provided by the husband. Again, the Matrimonial Homes Act, 1967, gives a wife (or a husband) certain protection in respect of a matrimonial home in which she has otherwise no interest in law (see pp. 270–73).

The wide discretion given to the Divorce Court, by section 4 of the Matrimonial Proceedings and Property Act 1970 (see pp. 277–8), to order transfers of matrimonial property should give scope for redress of financial injustice caused to either party by the breakdown of the marriage. This provision goes a long way towards community of property, to be imposed not by statute, but by the operation of judicial discretion; and it must be stressed that such a sharing of matrimonial property can only be brought about after the marriage has broken down.

Unity after death

The rights and liabilities of the married state do not end with the death of one of the spouses. The rules governing the devolution of their property on death are altered immediately on marriage. In the first place, any will made before marriage is automatically revoked by the act of matrimony, unless the will was expressly made in contemplation of the particular marriage which takes place. Then there are limits on the freedom of married people to dispose of their property by will, and if they die intestate the position is quite different from that of a single person. We shall see later (p. 252) that the Divorce Court may order maintenance for a wife out of her deceased husband's estate. It has always been traditional in this country for a wife to have some rights in her husband's estate, but these were very limited in the past. The widow's right to dower was limited to a life interest in one-third of her husband's lands, provided she could show that issue capable of inheriting the land *might* have been born, and that she had not been expressly deprived of the right to her third – after 1833 she could be deprived by implication if her husband settled a jointure on her. Similarly, if a wife died intestate the husband was entitled to a life interest in the whole of her freehold land 'by the curtesy'. These rights to curtesy and dower were abolished by the property reforms of 1925.

If either husband or wife now dies intestate, the property of the deceased will pass according to a set of rules which depend on what other family survivors are left (see pp. 282–3), but in general the surviving spouse takes most of a modest estate. If there has been a divorce, these rules will of course not apply, as there will not be a surviving spouse. (This is subject to the right of a divorced spouse to claim out of the estate: see p. 252). Judicially separated spouses are not entitled to claim in the intestacy of each other.[19]

Husbands and wives cannot dispose of their property by will as freely as single people. Under the Inheritance (Family Provision) Act, 1938, as amended and supplemented by the Family Provision Act, 1966, a surviving husband, wife, or dependent child who has not been treated reasonably in the will of the deceased can apply to the Court for an order that 'reasonable provision' shall be made for him or her out of the estate. This provision may be by way of a lump sum payment or by periodical payments. The Court must have regard to the deceased's reasons for cutting husband, wife, or children out of the will, and the reasons may be expressed within the will, by written statements, or even orally; but the discretion given is very wide and a mere statement by the deceased setting out the reasons will not necessarily be sufficient. The Court will look at all the circumstances to test the accuracy of that statement. For example, if a husband states that he is leaving all to his mistress because his wife has refused to provide him with the comforts of a home, evidence that in fact the wife was a model of conjugal virtue and her husband was enticed by the blandishments of the

19. Matrimonial Proceedings and Property Act, 1970, s.40.

mistress will prevail, and the Court will make proper provision for his neglected wife. The reasonableness or otherwise of the provision made by the deceased must be judged by the circumstances prevailing at the time of the death. The most important factor is the moral obligation on the deceased to provide for the applicant. In *Re Andrews*,[20] for example, an unmarried daughter aged sixty-nine, in poor health and straitened circumstances, applied for some provision out of her father's estate; this was refused on the ground that the father had no obligation to maintain her since she was living with another man. That the moral obligation is stronger than the legal is illustrated by another case, *Re Joslin*.[21] A husband who had left his wife to live with another woman, by whom he had two illegitimate children, on his death bequeathed the whole of his small estate of £370 on trust for the other woman for life and then to her children. The wife, who had an income of about £190 a year, applied to the Court for provision out of the estate, but was refused because the husband had acted reasonably in providing for his extra-marital family. But a man cannot evade his obligations after death simply because he was bullied into an unwelcome marriage – the wife's right remains until some higher moral claim supplants it.

If a man is determined to exclude his legal dependants from a share of his wordly goods, he can go a long way to securing this end by setting out adequate reasons for doing so. But the only certain method is for him to make sure that he leaves nothing; he can either give everything away before he dies, or he can convey his property to trustees, leaving himself with no more than a life interest.

20. [1955] 3 All E.R. 248.
21. [1941] Ch. 200.

3 Dissolving a Marriage

The broken marriage: changing attitudes

In spite of all the complex problems of sharing a marriage, and in spite of the temptations of the permissive society, the large majority of husband and wives fulfil the marriage contract, and most marriages are unions for life of one man and one woman. But the marriage tie must support the combined human frailties of two people, and inevitably there will be a proportion of cases in which the strain is too great and the nexus goes. If this does happen, one inevitably asks if the policy of the state should be to keep the marriage together at all costs, however much human suffering that must entail, or to allow the couple to wipe out their mistake, and start afresh. In a country like this, where religious tolerance allows an infinity of beliefs, there will be many different answers to this question, but the law has to find one answer only, and inevitably it will reflect the confusion of ideas within society.

There are two excellent reasons why English law should strive to preserve the marriage bond. In the first place, this is a Christian country, and the ideal of Christian marriage as a permanent union must be supported. Secondly, it is in the interests of good order and social security that the family unit out of which society is built should be a stable one. It makes the task of domestic government easier if the family can be relied on to be self-supporting and its members interdependent. A broken marriage often means a scattered family, and neglected wives and children become a burden on the state. During the last 150 years, however, other forces have been at work, and as individual rights have become more widely respected, so claims to personal justice and the right to happiness have pressed more strongly on the legislature. Where a marriage proves unhappy, the ideal of a permanent union can be achieved only by great personal sacrifice, and men have become less and less convinced that such a sacrifice is justified. As a result, the law has compromised between the communal and the personal ideal, and it is this compromise which accounts for much of the ambivalence which we find in the present state of the law. Appreciation of this conflict in the public mind makes it possible to understand a legal system which proclaims on the one hand that marriage is the most solemn contract known to man, yet on the other hand dissolves thousands of marriages a year, sometimes on the most trivial grounds. Even now that 'breakdown' is the sole ground for dissolution, there must still be a full-blown public trial, with judge and advocate wigged and robed in seventeenth century dress; yet when the evidence of breakdown is given, it may well amount to some paltry acts of matrimonial unkindness or disunity such as most people would be prepared to tolerate in the course of a marriage.

This is the inevitable result of a compromise between the ideals of a Christian state and the recognition of the personal right to happiness. The conflict continues daily as the judges quietly strive to hold the balance between the two opposed ideals. It erupts from time to time in cases which cause great legal, and sometimes public, interest because they highlight the resulting anomalies in the law.[1]

This dichotomy is of very recent origin. Before the Reformation the only law relating to marriage, was the law of the Church; consequently there could be no question of dissolution of a validly constituted marriage (except in very rare cases by Papal decree). At that time the interests of society and the ideals of the Church were not on the whole conflicting. Feudalism, based on strict rules of devolution of prop-

1. With divorce by consent a reality, such cases should become less frequent, but will not disappear altogether while men and women continue to quarrel over money and children (but these disputes need not now be in open court.

erty, required a stable family, and therefore permanent marital unions were essential. Individual freedom was subjugated to the need for a rigid, and therefore secure, society in a period when survival was a constant struggle for rich and poor alike. But although the law governing marriage was that of the Church, until the Conquest it was applied by the civil Courts of the shires and hundreds, where the bishops and abbots sat side by side with the magistrates. William I, wishing to increase his royal power and restrict the popular influence of the clergy, removed all ecclesiastical business to a separate Court in each diocese presided over by the bishops' jurisdiction, although they came to some extent under the influence of the Crown in matrimonial causes; but the law became so complex that the bishops then handed over their judicial functions to officers specially trained in law, and there grew up a distinct profession of men specializing in the practice of the ecclesiastical law, both civil and canon. These men, judges and advocates, lived together for hundreds of years in buildings in the city of London which were called 'Doctors Commons': here the Ecclesiastical Courts sat and – by a curious accident – the Admiralty Court also had its home. Doctors Commons remained in existence until 1867, ten years after the revolution in English law which made divorce a practical possibility and sounded the death-knell for the closed system of civil and canon lawyers.

The ecclesiastical law recognized two ways of breaking a marriage, but only one of these was complete in the sense that the parties could remarry. If the marriage ceremony had been deficient in formalities, or if there had been duress, or if the parties were within the forbidden degrees of affinity, then the Courts would declare the marriage utterly void, and each party was restored to the single state. The only other possible decree was that of divorce *a mensa et thoro* whereby the parties were enabled to live apart, although not to remarry. This decree, equivalent to the modern one of judicial separation, was granted where one spouse had committed certain specified matrimonial offences, such as adultery, cruelty, or unnatural offences. This was not much use to people who wanted to remarry, but human ingenuity found a way out. It was the rule of prohibited degrees which gave the ecclesiastical lawyers a way of avoiding the strict rule that there could be no divorce *a vinculo matrimonii* – dissolving the chains of marriage and freeing the parties to marry again – and such elaborate rules of consanguinity were built up that the law became riddled with holes. The doctrine of pre-contract provided the easiest way out of all: if there were proof of a previous binding contract to marry another, the marriage could be annulled. An example of the lengths to which the doctrine of pre-contract could be taken was the case of Roger Donnington who succeeded in having his marriage declared null and void because before the ceremony he had had sexual relations with his future wife's third cousin. Henry VIII's position over Katherine of Aragon, who was formerly betrothed to his brother Arthur, seems somewhat more feasible in such a context.

The Protestant reformers, with their zeal for purity of doctrine and their hatred of hypocrisy, naturally loathed these shifts to evade the divine law, but they equally deplored the church's doctrine that no valid marriages could be dissolved. In their view a decree on the ground of the wife's adultery – not, of course, the husband's – should be *a vinculo*, and the husband should be entitled to remarry. In most Protestant countries, including Scotland, some form of divorce was introduced after the Reformation, and this might well have happened in England if Edward VI had not died so young. During his reign a Commission under Archbishop Cranmer, the Reformatio Legum Ecclesiasticarum, recommended that divorces should be allowed on the grounds of adultery, desertion, cruelty, long absence, and deadly hatred between the spouses – a proposal so revolutionary that even today the last two grounds have not been expressly recognized by the law.[1a] However, nothing came of all this, and the new reign brought no loosening of the divorce law, in spite of the changed climate of opinion.

The Marquis of Northampton tested popular feeling on this matter in 1552 by remarrying after a decree of divorce

1a. Although five years separation, two years with consent, are now grounds to cover such contingencies.

on the ground of his wife's adultery: so strong was Puritan influence at the time that Parliament declared him free to remarry and his new marriage was recognized by a Court of Bishops. But this extreme view was not to prevail against the notorious forces of reaction and in 1602, in *Fuljambe's Case*, the Court of Star Chamber held that an ecclesiastical decree of divorce did not allow the parties to remarry.

This left the position more rigid than before. The evasion of the law by annulments had been damped down by Puritan legislation, and Parliament's recognition of a divorce *a vinculo* had been defied by the ecclesiastical law. But the pressures remained, and where great estates and titles were involved the impossibility of remarriage became intolerable. Tenacious aristocrats, wronged by their wives, were not to be baulked by the church: Parliament, with a new supremacy established by the Great Revolution, was prepared to assist them, and in turn defied the ecclesiastical law by passing, in certain cases, a Private Act of absolute divorce. In 1697 the Earl of Macclesfield, who had been refused a divorce *a mensa et thoro*, obtained the passage of an Act of Divorce from the House of Lords because of his wife's adultery. Then in 1700 the Duke of Norfolk, who had also failed in the Ecclesiastical Courts, was successful in dissolving his marriage in the same way. The words of the Duke of Norfolk's Act make it quite clear that the remedy would only be available to a very narrow class of people and for a very limited purpose – the protection of the inheritance of property and the family succession which would be jeopardized by a wife's adultery:

> For as much as the said Henry, Duke of Norfolk, hath no issue nor can have any probable expectation of posterity to succeed him in his honours, dignities, and estates, unless the said marriage be declared void by authority of Parliament; and the said Duke be enabled to marry any other woman . . . the King's and Queen's excellent Majesties, having taken the premises into their Royal consideration, for divers weighty reasons are pleased that it be enacted . . . [that the Duke and Duchess be no longer married].

Of course marital unhappiness, especially that brought about by the husband's infidelity, was hardly sufficient cause for a Bill of Divorcement at this time. As so often in the history of English law, the rights of property had taken precedence over the Christian ethic. The remedy, although exceedingly expensive, achieved a modest popularity – there were 184 parliamentary divorces between 1715 and 1852. But during that period there were only four such Acts passed on behalf of a wife, and then the husband was found guilty of adultery aggravated by some enormity such as incest or bigamy. However, the women were not entirely neglected: in the House of Commons there was an official with the delicate title of 'The Ladies' Friend' whose duty it was to see that divorced wives were not left destitute by their husbands.

In 1798 the whole process was regularized, and thenceforward it was necessary to obtain both an ecclesiastical decree of divorce *a mensa et thoro* and damages for 'criminal conversation' against the seducer in the common law courts, before petitioning Parliament for an Act of Divorce. That it could never be a popular remedy for the ills of matrimony was ensured by the complexity and expense of the procedure. The ecclesiastical decree itself could cost thousands of pounds if defended, the action for damages as much, and the expenses of a private bill were at least £500. The whole process could not be completed for many months, and might take years.

Advent of judicial dissolution of marriages

In the Age of Reform it was intolerable that there should be such disparity of matrimonial justice, not only between the rich and the poor but also between the very rich and the increasingly powerful well-to-do. It was in this atmosphere of criticism of an outmoded procedure that the first of many Royal Commissions on matrimonial law was set up in 1850.

The terms of reference of this Commission were to inquire into the whole state of the law relating to matrimonial offences, and they had a fine procedural skein to unravel. All cases were heard in the Consistory Court of the diocese in which the person cited in the suit lived[2] (although this requirement as to residence could be waived by the defendant) and the form of pleading was elaborate: allegations, articles, objections, interrogatories, and compulsories could be relied on to drag out the proceedings to the great benefit of the Proctors (as solicitors in ecclesiastical practice were called) and the learned Doctors (who were counsel specializing in ecclesiastical law). Appeals lay first to the Court of Arches in the Province of Canterbury or the Court of Chancery in York, and thence to the Court of Delegates. The Court of Delegates however is reputed never to have allowed an appeal. It gave no reasons for its decisions, and its judges were paid at the rate of a guinea a day by the victorious party!

One can imagine the opposition there must have been from the ecclesiastical lawyers to any reform in this system. It is to the great credit of the Commissioners that when they issued their report in 1853 it recommended reforms so radical that, in the shape of the first Matrimonial Causes Act of 1857, they formed the basis on which modern divorce law has been built up.

The first essential was to take the administration of the matrimonial law out of the hands of the Ecclesiastical Courts. This was done by setting up a new 'Court for Divorce and Matrimonial Causes' to deal with the whole of matrimonial law. The judges were to be the highest legal dignitaries, including the Lord Chancellor and the Lord Chief Justice, the Judge of the Probate Court, and the senior puisne judges, and there was to be a right to trial by jury. The old decree of divorce *a mensa et thoro* was replaced by a decree of judicial separation, and the whole procedure was simplified and thus made quicker and less costly. But the most profound reform of all was that a decree of dissolution of marriage, with the right to remarry, could now be granted, to a husband for his wife's adultery, to a wife for

2. Ecclesiastical Jurisdiction Act, 1531 ('Statute of Citations').

her husband's 'aggravated' adultery – that is, adultery combined with incest, bigamy, sodomy, rape, bestiality, cruelty, or desertion. Equality of justice for the social classes was thus brought in sight, but equality of the sexes before the law seemed no closer.

Such sweeping reforms needed some years to be assimilated. The Act of 1857 expressly laid down that the law must be administered on the same principles as those which had governed the Ecclesiastical Courts, and the reports of the early cases before the new Divorce Court show the thoroughness with which the judges carried out this edict. There was still plenty of work for Doctors Commons at first, since there were the only people who knew the old principles which had to be applied. But it was not long before the common lawyers found their way around the new law and they brought a great draught of sanity from the common law to blow away the musty atmosphere which still clung to the law of marriage. Now that appeals went to the Court of Appeal and thence to the House of Lords, all important decisions were published, and the law was made certain by the growth of precedent.

But there was no great rush to take advantage of the facilities provided by the new Divorce Court. From the beginning, cases in this Court were reported in the same volume as Admiralty and Probate cases (as they are still) and for many years wills and collisions at sea took up much more space than matrimonial suits. In the volume of reports for 1883, the first year after the Courts moved from Westminster to their present Catalonian Abbey in the Strand, of fifty-eight cases reported, only eight were matrimonial; of these one was the divorce suit of a marquis, and five of the others related to the settlement of property or the provision of maintenance. By contrast, out of twenty-two cases reported in 1960, nineteen were matrimonial. Divorce remained a social stigma, and as long as women lost all their property to their husbands on marriage they were discouraged from giving cause to their husbands to divorce them, and from taking proceedings themselves. In 1882 the economic position of married women was radically changed by the Married Women's Property Act (see p. 261), and as henceforth they were able to retain the property they had on marriage and keep their subsequent earnings, they lost much of their dependence on men. Then came the fall of the last bastion of male supremacy in matrimonial law: the Matrimonial Causes Act, 1923 gave wives equal rights with their husbands to petition for divorce on the ground of adultery, without the need to allege any other offence.

The 1937 legislation

Apart from this one change, from 1857 divorce law remained basically the same for eighty years. During all that time adultery was the only ground for divorce, and nullity decrees could only be granted where the marriage was never validly made, or had not been consummated owing to the incapacity of one of the parties. But after the First World War there was a rising tide of feeling that grave injustice was being done to those unhappy people whose marriages had broken up because of desertion or cruelty, or where one of the spouses became insane, or where the marriage had never really begun because one party had wilfully refused to consummate it. The law was felt to be hypocritical: any couple who were sufficiently ruthless could get round the law by one of them committing adultery – or even pretending to – whereas unhappy pairs who were not prepared to twist the tail of the law in this way or to indulge in *ad hoc* fornication could not avail themselves of the law. Sir Alan Herbert canalized this public feeling, and, having exposed the absurdities of the law in *Holy Deadlock,* went on to steer his Matrimonial Causes Bill triumphantly through the House of Commons. But before it became law in 1937, this new legislation caused some of the bitterest controversy of the century. Looking back at the debates of the time, it is difficult to understand how the opposition was ever overcome. Leading churchmen and laymen seemed united in thinking that there would be a complete dissolution of family life, and that universal licence would prevail. But the public mood was for reform, and the loosening of the marriage bond was clearly necessary in the conditions of the modern world. It was argued with some force that keeping a marriage in being at any cost merely encouraged irregular unions; where a young wife was put away for ever in a mental hospital, or had deserted her husband for good, would he not inevitably form some other union, and must the children of that union suffer for ever the stigma of illegitimacy?

There was hard bargaining before the Act was passed. As a solace to the fears of the opposition a clause was included which forbade the presentation of a divorce petition within three years of marriage, except in cases of unusual hardship or depravity. This was a small price to pay – and a wise one – for the reforms which were made by the Act. Henceforth, a divorce or judicial separation could be obtained by either husband or wife not only for adultery, but also for cruelty, desertion for upwards of three years, and incurable insanity for five years or more. New grounds for nullity were introduced: wilful refusal to consummate the marriage, insanity or mental defect or epilepsy at the time of the marriage, pregnancy of the wife by someone other than the husband, or venereal disease in a communicable form in either party at the time of the marriage. Another new provision was for a decree of presumption of death where there are reasonable grounds to suppose that one of the parties is dead. The grounds for divorce, judicial separation, and nullity laid down in 'A. P. Herbert's Act' remained the same until the great changes of 1969, although there were important modifications in the law relating to condonation and collusion which in fact made divorce by consent a legal possibility, even before the Divorce Reform Act came into force.

Jurisdiction in matrimonial suits

Side by side with the development of the divorce law, there has grown up since 1895 a separate matrimonial jurisdiction in the Magistrates' Courts (see p. 86 *et seq.*). The injured husband or wife can today take a choice of Courts – the Court of the justices of the peace, the County Court or the High Court – depending on the remedy sought. The magistrates can make separation orders, orders relating to children and maintenance orders. But magistrates cannot make any order altering the *status* of the parties. The marital status of a person is something which is of interest and importance to society, not only to himself. As we have seen, it was only after many years of attrition by the forces of reform that the legislature reluctantly handed over to the judiciary the power to alter status by breaking the marriage bond, and from 1857 until 1968 only the High Court, on a petition still technically addressed to the Crown by a subject, had the power to dissolve marriages. Even the most straightforward undefended divorce suit was heard by a judge of the Probate, Divorce and Admiralty Division (a curious mixture which derives from the concern of the Ecclesiastical Courts in wills and matrimony, the ships coming in because of the accidental proximity of the Admiralty and Ecclesiastical Courts in Doctors Commons). In addition, on assize, Queen's Bench judges were – and still are – commissioned to deal with divorce. But with the flood of divorce business which followed the introduction of legal aid in 1949 (see p. 143) the High Court bench was quite overwhelmed, and it was necessary to find a way of dealing with the mass of undefended cases. To create enough new High Court Judges would have been impracticable: the expense would have been great, but more important was the difficulty of finding sufficient men of High Court calibre without denuding the Bar. The problem was solved by a practical compromise: divorce was still heard only in the High Court, but certain County Court judges were made *ad hoc* Commissioners of Divorce. Their lilac robes transformed to the sombre black silk of the Probate, Divorce and Admiralty Division, the County Court judges sat once a month or once a fortnight, in the High Court in London or in some designated 'Divorce Town', momentarily endowed with all the puissance of a Queen's Bench judge, and trying most of the undefended and 'short defended' divorce cases.

This judicial charade had one purpose – to preserve the

sanctity of the marriage contract by allowing only the High Court to dissolve it. It is not surprising that many found this a pointless exercise and thought that undefended divorces should be heard in the County Court, especially as costs are higher in the High Court than in the County Court, and most divorces are paid for by the state under legal aid. Also, since only members of the Bar have the right of audience in the High Court, two lawyers had to be employed in even the simplest case, whereas in the County Court, solicitors could conduct their own cases throughout.

County Court jurisdiction

There was a good deal of opposition to a transfer of jurisdiction to the County Court. It was felt that even if the change made divorce easier, quicker and cheaper – and there was no certainty that it would – the solemnity of the occasion would be reduced and divorce would seem less important. In the event, the transition was made by the Matrimonial Causes Act, 1967. Section 1 of the Act gives the Lord Chancellor power to designate *any* County Court as a *Divorce County Court* and lays down that *every* matrimonial cause shall be commenced in a Divorce County Court, Rules of Court to be made to provide for the transfer of causes which cease to be undefended to the High Court and to define the circumstances in which any matrimonial cause is to be treated as undefended. Other sections confer jurisdiction on a Divorce County Court to exercise all the powers relating to ancillary financial relief and children given to a High Court judge by the Matrimonial Causes Act, 1965. The principal probate registry is made a Divorce County Court for the purposes of the Act, and there is provision for the making of rules of court and the fixing of fees. The Matrimonial Causes Rules 1968 were made under the Act, and came into operation on the 11 April 1968, since when all matrimonial causes[3] have been commenced in a

3. 'Matrimonial causes' were defined in the 1967 Act as any action for divorce, nullity of marriage, judicial separation, jactitation of marriage or restitution (the latter no longer exists).

Divorce County Court. These include petitions for divorce, judicial separation, nullity, restitution of conjugal rights, jactitation of marriage, presumption of death, claims for financial relief whether ancillary to a petition or not, applications relating to the custody of and access to children of the family, applications to vary maintenance agreements, applications for maintenance agreements, applications for maintenance from the estate of a deceased former spouse and applications under the Matrimonial Homes Act, 1967, section 7. (These are dealt with in the appropriate chapters of this book. For pages see Index.) As soon as a case becomes defended – that is as soon as an answer is filed – the registrar *must* order the case to be transferred to the High Court, with one exception relating to petitions based on incurable insanity. Intervention by the Queen's Proctor has the same effect. There are other rules which provide for transfer to the High Court, either mandatory or discretionary, in cases relating to settlements and ancillary relief.

High Court jurisdiction

What, then, is left for the eighteen judges of the Probate, Divorce and Admiralty Division to do? Apart from their probate and admiralty jurisdiction, which would certainly not be enough to occupy them, they have to try every matrimonial cause in which an *answer* is filed. This is not quite the same as every *defended* suit: in many matrimonial disputes the petition itself goes unanswered while ancillary matters such as maintenance and the custody of children are hotly contested. With breakdown of marriage now the only ground for dissolution, it is unlikely that there will be more than a handful of genuine defended divorces in a year, that is to say, cases in which a respondent opposes the making of a decree.[3a] But there will undoubtedly be a considerable number of answers filed in order to give the Respondent protection under section 4 of the Divorce Reform Act, 1969, or to obtain the best possible financial provisions. This means that the important jur-

3a. But it seems that cases will still be fought out in open court where the only dispute is over money: see *Porter v. Porter* [1971] 2 All E.R. 1037.

isdiction over children and maintenance – sometimes relating to very large sums of money – has been relegated to the County Court judges, and registrars (whose jurisdiction in civil cases is in general limited to claims not exceeding £750).

However, most such cases involving important issues or relating to large sums of money will finally appear before a High Court judge. The Matrimonial Causes Rules, 1971 give the County Court – either judge or registrar – wide powers to transfer any case relating to children or financial provision to the High Court.[4] In the case of an application for ancillary relief the County Court *shall* make an order transferring the case to the High Court if the Court considers that a contested issue of conduct arises 'which is likely materially to affects the question whether any, or what, order should be made'.[5] If such an order for transfer is made, the application must be heard by a High Court judge.

Orders which may be made by High Court or County Court in matrimonial causes

1. Leave to present a petition for dissolution within three years of marriage (p. 142).

2. Decree of dissolution of marriage (p. 129 *et seq.*).

3. Decree of nullity (see chapter 5).

4. Decree of judicial separation (pp. 85–6).

5. Decree of presumption of death and dissolution of marriage (section 14 of Matrimonial Causes Act, 1965).

6. Order for maintenance on ground of wilful neglect to maintain where no other matrimonial cause pending (p. 248 *et seq.*).

7. Orders for ancillary relief, i.e. maintenance pending suit, periodical payments, child maintenance, permanent alimony,

4. Rules 80, and 97.
5. Rule 80 (1).

lump sum payments, secured provision, avoidance of dispositions, variation of ante-nuptial and post-nuptial settlements, settlements of wife's property (p. 246 *et seq*.).

8. Order for variation of maintenance agreements (p. 84).

9. Order for maintenance from former spouse out of deceased's estate (p. 252).

10. Order under section 7 of Matrimonial Homes Act, 1967 (p. 272).

It is only the *High Court* that can make declarations of legitimacy and of validity of marriage under section 39 of the Matrimonial Causes Act, 1965, or 'bare' declarations as to validity of marriage or of presumption of death or decrees of dissolution under the Rules of the Supreme Court, order 15, rule 16 (see chapter 5).

Jurisdiction of English courts in matrimonial causes

We have seen which Courts now have matrimonial jurisdiction in England, and the sort of decrees and orders they can make. But who can avail themselves of these Courts and benefit by their decrees? In ordinary law-suits, such as an action on a contract or for damages for negligence, anyone who can serve the writ on the defendant in England – and sometimes even abroad – can bring his complaint before the English Courts, and apart from certain narrow exceptions he will be able to pursue his case whether he be a native of this country or not. The jurisdiction of the Magistrates' Courts in matrimonial cases is based on residence, but dissolution of marriage is a different matter. A marriage, unlike a contract, is something which affects not only the parties but also the state. The decree of divorce or nullity is a decree *in rem* – it is intended to bind the whole world – unlike a judgment on a contract, which is *in personam*, and binds only the parties to the contract. Obviously a ridiculous situation would arise if a Japanese could come to England for a flying visit and have his Japanese marriage dissolved, without any regard for the law of his homeland; the English

Courts would be brought into disrepute if the Japanese Courts then refused to recognize the English decree. This problem did not arise before 1857, since the jurisdiction of the Ecclesiastical Courts was limited to suits brought against persons 'inhabiting a dwelling' within the diocese. In other words, jurisdiction was based entirely on residence. The Act of 1857 laid down no rules for jurisdiction, and acting on the principle that the ecclesiastical practice should be followed, the new Divorce Court at first based its jurisdiction simply on the residence of the parties.[6] But as communications improved the civilized world was rapidly growing smaller and the English Courts found that they were out of step with other countries in this matter. It was obviously desirable in the interest of the comity of nations that there should as far as possible be a universal test for jurisdiction in matrimonial cases. As early as 1872 Lord Penzance said in *Wilson* v. *Wilson*:

'It is the strong inclination of my own opinion that the only fair and satisfactory rule to adopt in this matter of jurisdiction is to insist upon the parties in all cases referring their matrimonial differences to the Courts of the country in which they are *domiciled*. . . . An honest adherence to this principle . . . will preclude the scandal which arises when a man and woman are held to be man and wife in one country and strangers in another.'[7]

But it was not until 1895 that the Divorce Court in *Le Mesurier* v. *Le Mesurier*[8] finally accepted that it only had jurisdiction to deal with matrimonial disputes if the parties were *domiciled* in England. The rule in *Le Mesurier* has been followed in numerous cases and must be regarded as settled law[9] with statutory exceptions.

6. *Niboyet* v. *Niboyet* (1878) 4 P.D.1.

7. This case did not turn on jurisdiction and therefore these words were *obiter dicta* ('things said by the way') and not a precedent.

8. [1895] A.C. 517.

9. *Bater* v. *Bater* [1906] P .209 C.A.; *Lord Advocate* v. *Jaffrey* [1921] A.C. 146; *Salvesen* v. *Administrator of Austrian Property* [1927] A.C. at pp. 652, 654–66; and *Herd* v. *Herd* [1936] P. 205.

Domicile

What is domicile? It is an abstract concept of law which is not easy to grasp, partly because it means rather different things in different countries and partly because it may depend on the state of a man's mind. It was well described by Mr Justice Rowlatt, in *Att.-Gen.* v. *Yule*,[10] as a man's 'centre of gravity': it is that place or country, subject to one legal system, considered by law to be his homeland and the centre of his life. It is not necessarily his place of residence, nor his birthplace, nor his parents' country, nor the country of which he is a citizen, although all these factors play a part in determining domicile. Every person has a domicile, and only one, at any one time: not everyone has citizenship or a permanent place of residence, and a man may be the citizen of more than one country at the same time or have more than one place of residence. By English law, every child at birth has 'a domicile of origin' which it inherits from its parents: that is, from the father if he is alive at the date of birth and married to the mother; from the mother if the father is dead or the birth is illegitimate. Foundlings take the domicile of the place where they are found. The territory of the domicile is a unit subject to one law: thus there is no British domicile, only English, Scottish, and Northern Irish, since there are three separate legal systems in Britain. The domicile of origin can be changed later, and a 'domicile of choice' acquired. This change is only brought about by a complete uprooting; there must be an intention to take up permanent residence in a new country, together with a decision not to return to the country of origin, and actual residence in the new country. Residence *by itself* for however long, will not create a new domicile, although it is strong evidence of the intention to change. The case of *Winans* v. *Att.-Gen.*[11] is a striking example of the difficulty of losing a domicile of origin. William Louis Winans was a wealthy American citizen, born in the United States in 1823. In 1859 he came to England and lived here until his death in 1897. Naturally

10. (1931) 145 L.T.G.
11. [1904] A.C. 287.

enough the Crown wanted to show he died domiciled here in order to claim duty on his enormous English estate. Although he had shown no desire to return to his native land, even for a visit, the House of Lords held that he had never lost his domicile of origin in Baltimore, chiefly because he had been engrossed for many years in a scheme to build spindle-shaped vessels, a fleet of which would, he was convinced, restore to America the carrying trade which she had lost and would make it impossible for Britain to wage war against the United States. But it is not always so difficult to change domicile. All that is necessary is the clear intention and the physical change: Byron undoubtedly lost his domicile of origin after he shook the dust of England off his feet and took on Italian domicile the moment he settled in Italy, and those refugees from Nazi oppression who never intended to return to Germany, whatever the outcome of the war, assumed English domicile the moment their feet touched English soil (or even the deck of an English ship). But the domicile of origin is never completely lost – it remains suspended in the background, to be resumed automatically at the moment the domicile of choice is abandoned. The acute difficulty of deciding whether the domicile of origin has been lost is well illustrated in the case of *Henderson* v. *Henderson*[12] where it was held that a man could lose his domicile of origin by settling in another country even though he retained a sentimental attachment to the country of his origin, and a 'floating intention' to return there in the indefinite and uncertain event of retirement.

This, then, is the basis of jurisdiction in *divorce* cases. It matters not where the marriage took place; with certain exceptions, the English Courts will not hear the petition of anyone who is not domiciled in England. A wife takes her husband's domicile, as we have seen (p. 46). There can only be a single matrimonial domicile of the husband and wife; this rule was laid down in *Lord Advocate* v. *Jaffrey*[13] and *Att. Gen. for Alberta* v. *Cook*.[14] When it comes to recogniz-

12. [1967] P. 77.
13. [1921] A.C. 146.
14. [1926] A.C. 444.

ing the jurisdiction of foreign courts to grant decrees, the English courts take a broader view, as we shall see (pp. 75 *et seq.*). A wife is therefore debarred from any relief in the courts of her own country if married to a man of foreign domicile, even if they were married and always lived here. This could cause great injustice, and two modification of the rule have been made in favour of wives. First, in A. P. Herbert's Act,[15] the Court was given jurisdiction in proceedings brought by a wife where the husband, previously domiciled in England, had deserted her or had been deported from the United Kingdom. Then in 1949[16] divorce jurisdiction was extended to allow petitions of wives who have been ordinarily resident in England for three years to be heard, provided that the husband is not domiciled in any other part of the United Kingdom or the Channel Islands or the Isle of Man. (Thus an English woman whose husband takes up a domicile in Scotland must still go to Scotland to divorce him.) The three years residence necessary to qualify for this jurisdiction can include residence prior to the marriage.[17] This provision has been of great value to innumerable deserted wives, particularly those who married foreign servicemen, who would otherwise have been shut out from justice.

Nullity: void and voidable marriages

Nullity cases are subject to rather different rules of jurisdiction, but before discussing these we must know something about the law of nullity which is dealt with in detail in chapter 5. A marriage like any other contract can be 'null and void', simply because it was never properly constituted: if a marriage is null in this sense, it needs no court order to make it so, since it is a nullity by operation of law. This is the case where the marriage was bigamous, or fell within the prohibited degrees, or was entered into under

15. Matrimonial Causes Act, 1937, s. 13.

16. Law Reform (Miscellaneous Provisions) Act, 1949, s. 1 (now Matrimonial Causes Act, 1965, s. 4(1)(b)).

17. *Navas* v. *Navas* (1968) 112 S.J. 110.

duress, or failed to comply with the formalities which are necessary for a valid marriage (see pp. 26–30). The validity of the marriage can be challenged not only by the parties, but also by anyone interested, and even after they are both dead. The Divorce Court is often called on to make decrees that such marriages are void, since there may be some uncertainty and a Court order may be essential to enable the parties to remarry, or to decide the devolution of property. This is one type of nullity decree: it 'pronounces and declares' the marriage to have been void *ab initio* from its very inception. It follows that for almost all purposes the 'marriage' has never existed, and a second marriage contracted by one of the 'spouses' will not therefore be bigamous. The exception concerns the legitimacy of children: since October 1959[18] the child of a void (or voidable) marriage is regarded as legitimate, if at the time of its conception or the date of the marriage both or either of the parents reasonably believed that the marriage was valid.

In addition, the judges of the Divorce Division have the inherent jurisdiction of all High Court judges (see the Rules of the Supreme Court, order 15, rule 16) to make *declaratory decrees*. This power can be used to make bare declarations as to the validity or otherwise of any marriage or divorce, that is to say, declarations as to marital status. But his jurisdiction will only be used sparingly,[19] and is not to be confused with the nullity jurisdiction which derives from the Ecclesiastical Courts. In effect this power is invoked only for declarations relating to marriages or divorces where no other remedy is sought. No orders as to maintenance or children can be made on a bare declaration.

There are other marriages which, while not void, can be made so by decree. These *voidable* marriages are valid for all purposes until the Court pronounces a decree of nullity. Only the parties to the marriage can put its validity in issue: everyone else must accept it until there has been a decree of annulment. The Ecclesiastical Courts would grant such a

18. Legitimacy Act, 1959, s. 2(1).
19. *Har-Shefi* v. *Har-Shefi* [1953] P. pp. 161 and 220.

decree where the marriage had not been consummated owing to incapacity on the part of either husband or wife. Impotence continued to be the only ground until 1937. There are now several statutory grounds for annulment: see Matrimonial Causes Act, 1965, section 9(1), and chapter 5.

Jurisdiction in nullity suits

As we have said, this differs from that in divorce. The jurisdiction dates back to that of the Ecclesiastical Courts, which was based on residence. But superimposed on the old basis of residence is the internationally-recognized test of domicile, so that the Courts will have jurisdiction if the husband is domiciled in England. But in the case of *void* marriages, since they are void *ab initio* the wife's domicile will not necessarily be the same as that of her husband, and the Courts will have jurisdiction if the wife is domiciled here, even if the husband is domiciled abroad. Again, in the case of void marriages, the English Courts will accept jurisdiction if the marriage was celebrated here, even if both parties were domiciled abroad, on the principle that the wrongful act was performed in this country and must be remedied by our Courts. This ground for jurisdiction is not extended to voidable marriages.[20]

Residence of the Respondent in England should, on the basis of the old ecclesiastical practice, give jurisdiction to our courts in all nullity suits, and that now appears to be the case. But for many years a distinction was made between void and voidable marriages in this respect. In 1931 the actress June, Lady Inverclyde, was refused a decree in the English Courts on the ground of her husband's impotence, although she and her husband were both resident in England, because he was domiciled in Scotland, the judge holding that jurisdiction based on residence only applied to void marriages.[21] But this decision was overruled by the Court of Appeal in *Ramsay-Fairfax* v. *Ramsay-Fairfax*,[22] where it

20. *Ross Smith* v. *Ross Smith* [1963] A.C. 280.
21. *Inverclyde* (*otherwise Tripp*) v. *Inverclyde* [1931] P. 29.
22. [1956] P. 115.

was held that the English Courts have jurisdiction to entertain proceedings for nullity of a *voidable* marriage where both parties are resident in England. The present position is bound to be analogous to that set out in the Recognition of Divorces and Legal Separations Act, 1971, as set out below.

Recognition of foreign matrimonial decrees

Confusion has reigned for many years in the field of international recognition of decrees of divorce and separation. Different countries had widely differing rules for jurisdiction in matrimonial suits in their own courts, and just as widely differing rules for recognition of decrees granted by the Courts of other countries. But on 1 June 1970 the United Kingdom and twenty-three other countries signed a Convention at the Hague agreeing to amend the laws of the signatory countries to bring into line their rules governing recognition of foreign decrees. On 27 July 1971 the Recognition of Divorces and Legal Separations Act, 1971 was passed, and its provisions will govern the recognition of all decrees obtained outside the British Isles either before or after 1 January 1971 when the Act comes into force.

The validity of a foreign decree of divorce or legal separation will be recognized if at the date of institution of the proceedings *either* spouse was habitually resident in the country where the proceedings were brought, or *either* spouse was a national of that country (section 3(1)). In those systems of law which, like ours, base jurisdiction on domicile, 'habitual residence' is to include domicile (section 3(2)). These provisions will apply equally to cross-proceedings and to divorces following legal separations.

Furthermore, under section 7, where a decree of divorce or separation is entitled to recognition under this Act, neither spouse shall be precluded from remarriage in Great Britain on the ground that the validity of the divorce would not be recognized in any other country.

This Act, and similar statutes enacted by the signatory countries, will clear away the confusion of differing approaches in various systems of law which led to the great inconvenience and scandal of the 'limping marriage' – that is, one recognized in one country as subsisting and in another country as being at an end as the result of a divorce decree. In a shrinking world, when a man may as soon marry a woman from New York or Sydney as the girl next door, there are increasing numbers of divorces granted in jurisdictions foreign to one of the parties: if there is no consistency of recognition, there will inevitably be anomalous cases where for example the husband finds himself still married under English law, while his wife, domiciled in New York, is free to marry – as occurred in the case of the late Marquis of Milford Haven.[23] The new Act will do away with such cases, but it is not yet law and it is important to understand both the present law of recognition and its development.

Until 1953 our Courts refused to recognize any foreign decrees unless the foreign Court had jurisdiction based on the domicile of the parties, the only exception being decrees which would be recognized by the country of the domicile. This exception is exemplified in *Armitage* v. *Att. Gen., Gilling* v. *Gilling*,[24] where the English Court recognized the binding effect of a decree of divorce of a Court of South Dakota (where the parties were not domiciled and where jurisdiction was based on residence of the Petitioner for ninety days) because the decree would be recognized by the Courts of the husband's domicile (the state of New York.) Thus a Reno divorce, based on twenty-one days' residence of either party, will not be recognized here if the parties are domiciled in England; therefore they could not remarry here without committing bigamy. But if they were domiciled in New York State, since the Courts of that state recognize Reno divorces, the divorce would also be valid here and they could either of them contract a legal marriage in this country.

However, when in 1953 our Courts were given jurisdic-

23. Mountbatten v. Mountbatten [1959] P. 43.
24. [1906] P. 135.

tion to hear a wife's petition when she had resided here for three years, regardless of domicile (see p. 70), it was only reasonable that we should recognize foreign decrees based on a similar residential qualifications. In *Travers* v. *Holley*[25] the Court of Appeal held that a divorce granted by a Court of a country which assumed jurisdiction on three years' residence there by the wife should be recognized by the English Courts, Lord Justice Hodson said in his judgment:

> It must surely be that what entitled an English Court to assume jurisdiction must be equally effective in the case of a foreign Court. . . . It would be wrong in principle and inconsistent with equity if the Courts of this country were to refuse to recognize a jurisdiction which *mutatis mutandis* they claim for themselves.

From that time onwards the English Courts in the interest of international comity extended recognition to any foreign decree where jurisdiction would have been given here according to our rules, for example if the wife Petitioner had been in residence for three years in the country where proceedings were instituted (but the 'comity' basis was frowned on in *Indyka q.v.*)

The attitude of the English Courts to foreign decrees has become less rigid over the past decade or so, and they have even come to recognize divorces effected without judicial intervention. The leading case is *Har-Shefi* v. *Har-Shefi* (no. 2)[26] where a divorce according to the rites of the Jewish religion was effected by the husband handing to the wife a bill of divorcement at the Beth Din which is the Court of the Chief Rabbi. This ceremony was performed in London, but the husband was domiciled in Israel, and the divorce would be recognized there. Similarly, an oral pronouncement of divorce, the *talak* of the Muslems, will be recognized if it had been recorded in the Courts of the domicile,[27] but not

25. [1953] P. 246.
26. [1953] P. 220.
27. *Russ* v. *Russ* [1964] P. 315; or even pronounced and recorded in England in certain circumstances: see *Quershi* v. *Quershi* (1970), *The Times*, October 31.

a mere pronouncement in the absence of the other party and without any such record.[28]

Then came the House of Lords decision in *Indyka*[29] where the whole of the law relating to recognition was reviewed. In that case a Czech national who had acquired a domicile of choice in England was divorced by his wife who was still resident there and who was still a Czech national. On the basis of domicile as the sole test of jurisdiction, such a decree could not be recognized by the English Courts, nor was it recognized by the Judge at first instance or the Court of Appeal. But the House of Lords, accepting the unity of domicile of husband and wife, since that has been given statutory recognition by implication although not expressly, and that up to the present the only grounds for recognition were domicile and long residence, added an entirely new ground for recognition: a 'real and substantial connection' between the person obtaining the decree and the country in which the decree was granted. This new ground can be spelt out of the judgments, although their Lordships relied on different tests for 'real and substantial connection'. For example, while some stressed nationality as the vital factor, Lord Reid preferred 'the matrimonial home' as the test. This is a good example of the House of Lords using their power to extend judge-made law in cases where Parliament is unlikely to intervene. The result has been that many foreign decrees which could not have been recognized under the old law have been accepted by the Courts and many limping marriages have been ended. In *Angelo* v. *Angelo*[30] the extension of recognition was applied to its limit, one would have supposed: An Englishman married a German woman in England; they lived together for two years, then the wife went to her former home in Germany and after another year obtained a decree there; held that she had a 'real and substantial connection' with Germany and the

28. *R.* v. *Hammersmith Superintendent Registrar ex parte Mir-Anwarnddin* [1917] 1 1 K.B. 634. A.C.

29. [1969] 1A.C. 33.

30. [1967] 3 All E.R. 314.

decree should be recognized. Yet in a more recent case[31] the scope of recognition was further enlarged; a German divorce granted to a domiciled Englishman was held to be valid here, on the ground that the Court granting the decree had jurisdiction by reason of the wife's German nationality and residence. The ratio of that decision was that the German decree which was granted by a Court of competent jurisdiction had operated to alter the wife's status and should also be allowed to alter the husband's status.

The borderline of recognition is well illustrated by two other cases. Where a Yugoslav couple who were domiciled in England, the wife having spent all her life in Yugoslavia, obtained joint decrees in Yugoslavia, the decrees were recognized here.[32] But where a Yugoslav couple were domiciled here for fifteen years, and the wife returned to Belgrade expressly to obtain a divorce the decree was not recognized.[33]

It can be seen that after *Indyka* the English Courts were ready for the Recognition of Divorce and Legal Separations Act, 1971, which in section 3(1) gives statutory form to the 'real and substantial connection' test of jurisdiction.

But even if the foreign Court has, by the standard imposed by the English Courts on or after 1 January 1972 by the Act of 1971, jurisdiction to grant the decree, it will not be recognized if it offends our views of substantial justice. In a case where a Maltese Court of competent jurisdiction made a declaration of nullity on the ground that the marriage, celebrated in England, was not a Roman Catholic ceremony, the Court of Appeal refused to recognize the decree.[34] Similarly, a decree obtained by fraud[35] or coercion[36] will not be recognized. But the Courts here did not refuse recognition because there were mere irregularities of procedure,

31. *Mayfield* v. *Mayfield* (1969) 113 S.J. 35.
32. *Tijanic* v. *Tijanic* [1967] 3 All E.R. 976.
33. *Peters* v. *Peters* [1967] 3 All E.R. 318.
34. *Gray* (orse *Formosa*) v. *Formosa* [1963] P. 259 C.A.
35. *MacAlpine* v. *MacAlpine* [1958] P. 35.
36. *Burke* v. *Burke* (1955) L.L.Y. 863.

nor because the grounds for the decree would not be sufficient here, nor because of collusion.[37]

Section 8(2) of the 1971 Act says that recognition of a foreign decree may be refused if, and only if, the following conditions exist.

1. It was obtained by one spouse:
(a) without such steps having been taken for giving notice of the proceedings to the other spouse as, having regard to the nature of the proceedings and all the circumstances, should reasonably have been taken; or
(b) without the other spouse having been given (for any reason other than lack of notice) such opportunity to take part in the proceedings as, having regard to the matters aforesaid, he should reasonably have been given; or

2. Its recognition would manifestly be contrary to public policy.

Recognition in Great Britain of divorces and judicial separations granted in the British Isles

In respect of decrees of divorce and judicial separation granted in the British Isles, section 1 of the Recognition of Divorces and Legal Separations Act, 1971 provides as follows:

The validity of a decree of divorce or judicial separation granted after the commencement of this section shall:
(a) if it was granted under the law of Scotland, be recognized in England and Wales, and, if it was granted under the law of England and Wales, be recognized in Scotland; and
(b) if it was granted under the law of any other part of the British Isles, be recognized in Great Britain.

Effects of dissolution

It is obvious that all members of the family are affected by dissolution of a marriage. These effects are dealt with in detail in other parts of the book, but may usefully be sum-

37. *Davis* v. *Johnson* (1962) 106 S.J. 837.

marized here, provided it is realized that the table is not a statement of the law, for which reference should be made to the relevant chapters.

1. *Both spouses*

No longer bound to cohabit: p. 39.

May re-marry.

Lose protection of Matrimonial Homes Act, 1967: p. 270 *et seq.*

Cannot invoke Married Women's Property Acts in disputes over property after three years have elapsed since decree absolute: Matrimonial Proceedings and Property Act, s. 39.

No longer liable for maintenance of other spouse under National Assistance Act, 1948 (but both still liable to maintain children under that statute): p. 37.

Taxed as separate persons: p. 48.

Compellable as witnesses against each other: p. 43.

Communications between them *after* dissolution no longer protected: p. 44.

No longer able to bring proceedings in Magistrates' Court for maintenance *qua* spouse: p. 244.

2. *Husband*

No longer liable to maintain former wife at common law: p. 37.

Liable to maintain her or the children of the family, or to pay lump sum to either, or to transfer property or vary settlements when so ordered by a Court: p. 246.

No longer liable to pay wife's Income Tax.

3. *Wife*

Liable to maintain husband or children or to pay lump sum to either, or to transfer property, if so ordered by the Court: p. 248.

4 Legal Separation

The duty to cohabit

The first duty in marriage is to live with one's spouse. It is both a moral and a legal obligation, but although the law recognizes the duty to cohabit, it provides little in the way of a positive remedy where one spouse chooses to live apart. And the law does not allow the duty to be enforced by self-help: a husband is not entitled to shut his wife up in the matrimonial home (*R.* v. *Jackson*)[1] nor may he take her back by force. In the past, the Ecclesiastical Courts enforced the right to the *consortium vitae* by ordering the deserter to return, and could send him or her to prison for refusal to do so. The only sanctions the law imposes today are to deprive the deserting spouse of the other rights of matrimony, such as maintenance, and to dissolve the marriage at the petition of the injured party if the desertion continues for long enough. In fact the law is altogether rather lukewarm about this matrimonial duty, and recognizes the right of married couples to live apart if they both agree to do so.

It may seem strange to find a chapter on legal separation in the part of this book devoted to marriage. But since no separation, however 'legal', brings the marriage to an end, the law on this subject is part of the law of marriage and falls logically into place at this point. The way in which numberless couples come to live apart while still remaining married, and the sanctions, remedies, and effects which the law imposes and supplies, will be dealt with in this chapter.

1. [1891] 1 Q.B. 671.

Forms of legal separation

There is a good deal of confusion over the meaning of 'legal separation'. To some it means a deed of separation, signed before witnesses. To others, a legal separation means an order of the magistrates 'that the complainant be no longer bound to cohabit' with the other spouse because of some matrimonial offence. This is by far the commonest form of legal separation. Another is the decree of judicial separation granted by the Divorce Court – rare today, and chiefly resorted to by those whose religion precludes divorce, but sometimes the device of a spiteful wife who wants the advantages of a divorce, while retaining many of the material advantages of marriage such as security of tenure in the matrimonial home and pension rights, without giving her husband the freedom to remarry. All of these are 'legal' ways of avoiding the responsibilities of marriage short of divorce. Probably these remedies will be less attractive since the recent reforms, and in many cases they will be pointless as divorce may be available against the wishes of one of the spouses, and the matrimonial home and other property rights can be safeguarded in proceedings for dissolution (see chapter 13).

The deed of separation

This would seem the most civilized way of legalizing the broken marriage. But such a deed has really no more effect than an oral agreement to live apart: it is stronger evidence than the bare testimony of the parties, since it is less subject to human error and forgetfulness, and it is valuable also for enforcing any financial arrangements, but the really important element is the *agreement* to live apart, not the form it takes. Any agreement to live apart, whether in the form of a deed or otherwise, is a defence to a charge of desertion, and it is in this that the danger of the separation deed lies: it is evidence for all time of such an agreement, and it makes a divorce on the ground of desertion impossible. Many couples have later regretted signing an innocent-looking piece of paper, which seems only to set out their mutual rights to live without molestation and their agreement as to maintenance. Quite apart from this danger, it is of limited effect, since no wife can entirely sign away her right to maintenance. That is a matter for the Courts, and fifty deeds will not oust their jurisdiction. Nor can any agreement as to maintenance be made permanent. If a wife finds that the amount agreed on is insufficient, or if the husband becomes much better off, or if there is any change whatsoever in their relative financial states, either party may apply to a Court for variation of the agreement.[2] Any clause in the deed which purports to contract out of this provision of law is void (although all other parts of the deed remain enforceable).

It can be seen that legal separations by deed are not as effective as they might appear to be, and may have unsuspected dangers lurking within. But they have a certain use in setting out the financial obligations undertaken by the parties; even though they can be varied, the provisions of a deed are strong evidence of what husband and wife were able to offer and prepared to accept at the time of the separation. The Court will only interfere if there has been some marked change of circumstance since the date of the agreement. In any case, such deeds have a moral effect much stronger than their legal content would warrant. To avoid one of the disadvantages of the deed of separation, it is now more usual for couples who wish to live apart to enter into a maintenance agreement, limited to the financial arrangements and omitting any reference to an agreement to live apart. This does not put an end to any desertion, but it can of course be varied by the Court.

In both separation and maintenance agreements it is sometimes difficult to arrive at a figure for maintenance which will do justice to the parties, since the circumstances of either may change. To avoid the necessity of an application to the Court every time there is a change in the relative economic positions of the parties, the device of the 'escalator clause' may be used. This provides for automatic and proportionate variation in the payments, upwards if the husband's income increases, downwards if his earnings decrease or if the wife improves her position.

2. Matrimonial Proceedings and Property Act, 1970, s.14.

Restitution of conjugal rights

Since the first duty of spouses is to live together, it was logical that the Ecclesiastical Courts should try to provide a positive remedy for the deserted wife or husband. The decree of restitution of conjugal rights survived, as a decreasingly useful method of extracting maintenance from a deserting husband, until abolished by section 20 of the Matrimonial Proceedings and Property Act, 1970.

Judicial separation

This is the legal descendant of the old decree of divorce *a mensa et thoro*, and is chiefly of importance today as a remedy for those whose religious views forbid them from seeking a decree of divorce.[2a] The decree absolves the parties from the duty to live together and gives the successful petitioner the same rights as a decree of divorce, save only that there can be no remarriage, since there has been no final dissolution of the marriage bond. Until the Divorce Reform Act, 1969, a petition could be brought on any of the grounds then available for divorce and in addition on failure to comply with a decree of restitution or on any of the grounds recognized by the Ecclesiastical Courts for a divorce *a mensa et thoro*. By section 8 of the 1969 Act the only grounds for a decree of judicial separation are clear evidence of any of the facts required for proof of breakdown under section 2(1) of that Act (see p. 131). In hearing a suit for judicial separation, the court does not have to consider whether the marriage has broken down irretrievably.

There seems no reason why this suit should ever be brought today, except where there is strong religious antipathy to dissolution. The only possible reason (apart from the jurisdiction mentioned in footnote 2a) for using the procedure would seem to be in the first three years of marriage, when a petition for dissolution is impossible in most cases (see p. 141). It might then conceivably be useful as a

2a. Where the husband is domiciled out of England, either husband or wife can petition for judicial separation if both are resident in England.

means of preserving evidence with a view to divorce later. A much simpler method of bringing the marriage to an end would be to separate immediately: divorce would then be available two, or at the most five, years later (see pp. 135–6). Furthermore, now that magistrates have the power to make financial orders without any limit, there would seem to be no cogent reason to preserve this ancient procedure.

Separation in Magistrates' Courts

By far the most important form of legal separation is that brought about in the Magistrates' Courts. Thousands of these separation orders are made every year, and so popular are they that magistrates find that more and more of their time is being given up to matrimonial cases. The grounds for these orders have been extended over and over again, until they were more numerous than the grounds for divorce, even before the recent reforms.

The law relating to matrimonial offences in magistrates' courts is substantially the same as in the High Court and the County Court except that the principle of breakdown has not yet been applied and there is no ground for an order comparable to 'divorce by consent'. This means that lay magistrates are forced to struggle with problems which may puzzle the Court of Appeal and which need both technical knowledge and wide experience. The magistrates perform valiantly their anxious and often distasteful task, and usually manage to do justice to the parties, but inevitably the law is more uncertain in their courts. It is difficult to predict the effect of easier divorce on the jurisdiction of the justices, but probably there will be fewer applications for separation orders and they will be mainly limited to cases where a wife needs a quick financial remedy or an urgent order relating to children, or where a spouse is uncertain about wanting a divorce but needs a temporary remedy of some kind. The County Court divorce jurisdiction will undoubtedly compete strongly with that of the magistrates' courts.

When some small matrimonial jurisdiction was first given

to the justices in 1895,[3] no one could have imagined that it would grow to its present extent. Before that time, none but the rich had any remedies for the ills of matrimony: it is true that there had been a Divorce Court since 1857, but only those who could afford the fees of lawyers could go there – and in those days legal fees were much higher in proportion to the earnings of the working classes than they are today. The very women who had the greatest need for protection from ill-treatment or neglect by their husbands were shut out of the Courts for financial reasons. The statute of 1895 gave these women their charter: they could go to their local magistrates' court and, if they could prove that their husbands had been convicted of assaulting them, had treated them with persistent cruelty, had deserted them, or had failed to maintain them, they could obtain an order releasing them from the duty to live with their husbands, and in addition the men could be ordered to pay them up to two pounds weekly for maintenance. This was indeed a revolution. From these small beginnings grew the present-day jurisdiction of the magistrates. Gradually other grounds for separation orders were added – for example, habitual drunkenness in 1902, compelling to submit to prostitution and insisting on intercourse while suffering from a venereal disease in 1925, adultery in 1937. Finally, the Matrimonial Proceedings (Magistrates' Courts) Act, 1960, codified the whole law, and added several other grounds for orders which can now be made for the benefit of either the husband or the wife.

At first, orders could only be made for the benefit of the wife and on her application, no provision being made for the children. But in 1920, a statute[4] gave the Magistrates power, on hearing a wife's summons against her husband, to order him to pay up to thirty shillings a week maintenance for each of the children of the marriage. In 1902[5] husbands were for the first time entitled to apply for separation orders, but

3. Summary Jurisdiction (Married Women) Act, 1895.
4. Married Women (Maintenance) Act, 1920.
5. Licensing Act, 1902.

only on the ground of the wife's habitual drunkenness, the wife being given a similar right. Then in 1925[6] both husbands and wives were able to obtain separation orders on the ground of persistent cruelty to their children, whether children of the marriage or not. The Act of 1960 put husbands and wives in almost identical positions in the magistrates' court, even to the extent of giving the court power to order a wife to maintain her husband in certain circumstances.

Until recently, an upper limit was imposed by statute on the amount that magistrates could order by way of maintenance, but by the Maintenance Orders Act, 1968, and orders made thereunder the limits have been removed, and the magistrates can make an order for any amount, for either a spouse or a child, or against a putative father in affiliation proceedings.[7]

Procedure in Magistrates' Courts

Anyone can apply to the magistrates and issue a summons, and since the procedure is extremely simple, legal assistance is not essential (although it may make all the difference to the result). The injured spouse merely goes to his or her local court and makes a complaint on oath to a magistrate. If the magistrate accepts the complaint, he signs it and issues a summons, which he also signs. Either the complainant or the clerk to the justices then hands the complaint and summons to the police and they serve it on the defendant. The summons is made returnable for a given day, when the magistrates will adjudicate the matter of the complaint provided there has been service on the defendant. The jurisdiction of the bench is wide: they may hear any complaint where either the complainant or the defendant at the date of the complaint is ordinarily resident within the petty sessions area of their court, or where the cause of the complaint arises wholly or partly within that area. The fact that one of the parties lives in Scotland or Northern Ireland does not

6. Summary Jurisdiction (Separation and Maintenance) Act, 1925.
7. Up to 1968 the limits were £7·50p for a spouse and £2·50p for a child.

prevent the magistrates from having jurisdiction, but they cannot make a separation order – that is, an order that the parties be no longer bound to cohabit – if the defendant lives in Scotland or Northern Ireland. In contrast to proceedings in the High Court, the domicile of the parties is irrelevant to the magistrates' jurisdiction. The fact that the defendant lives abroad does not of itself prevent the magistrates from hearing the complaint, but since the summons cannot be served outside the United Kingdom it is unlikely that they will be able to deal with it unless the summons was served before the defendant left the country. In any case the order could only be enforced if the defendant happened to be living in one of those parts of the Commonwealth with which we have reciprocal arrangements for the enforcement of maintenance orders.[8] Since the Republic of Eire has no such agreement with us, the best and most accessible sanctuary for a husband who wishes to escape his liabilities to his wife and family is Southern Ireland.

The difficulties that magistrates encounter can be seen from some of the cases that go to the Divisional Court on appeal. There have been many cases where magistrates have been criticized for leaning too much upon their Clerk – often the only legally-qualified person in the Court – and even the maxim *audi alterem partem* has sometimes been honoured more in the breach than the observance. It is particularly important that the processes of justice should be meticulous when, as so often happens in Magistrates' Courts, the parties are not legally represented. In matrimonial cases, it has been said,[9] the justices should always hear both sides before coming to a decision, and not dismiss a complaint at the end of the complainant's evidence because no case has been made out. That is to say, the complainant is to be given the opportunity to establish a case on the defendant's evidence and cross-examination, something quite alien to the practice in the Divorce Courts and indeed to that followed in criminal cases before the justices.

9. Maintenance Orders (Facilities for Enforcement) Act, 1920.
8. *Waters* v. *Waters* [1956] P. 344 and *Bond* v. *Bond* [1967] P. 39.

Contrary to the procedure in the Divorce Court, where a petition can be brought at any time after three years of marriage, in the magistrates' court the summons must be taken out within six months after the last act relied on. Desertion and wilful neglect to maintain being continuing offences, the six-months rule does not apply. But in the case of assault, cruelty, adultery, and other offences the last act complained of must fall within the six months immediately preceding the date of the complaint, although evidence may be given of earlier acts if they are relevant, as in the case of persistent cruelty where the course of conduct may have continued for years. The cause of complaint in adultery arises when the act of adultery first *became known* to the complainant, not necessarily when it was actually committed; and if the complainant was serving with the forces abroad, or on board a British ship, during the six months following the discovery of the adultery, he or she may make the complaint at any time within three months of returning to the United Kingdom.

The magistrates will not normally deal with any summons if a matrimonial suit between the parties is pending in the Divorce Division of the High Court: see *Craxton* v. *Craxton*.[10] By analogy, the magistrates will presumably not deal with the summons if a petition has been filed in the County Court. And they have the power to refuse to deal with any complaint if they believe the matter in question would be 'more conveniently' dealt with by the High Court: Matrimonial Proceedings (Magistrates Courts) Act, 1960, section 15. One would sympathize with an impatient bench, faced with a lengthy and difficult case, if they construed 'more conveniently' widely, applying it especially to their own convenience, and packed the parties off to the High Court to resolve their conflicts. But the Divorce Division can send the case back to the magistrates if the Court does not agree that it should have been sent up in the first place (ibid. section 5) which no doubt checks any temptations which justices face to rid themselves of troublesome litigation.

10. (1907) 71 J.P. 399.

There can be no doubt, however, that lay benches *are* being required to deal with complex questions of law which would be much more suitably decided by judges, and the extension of legal aid to summary cases has added to their burden. As long ago as 1906 in *Dodd* v. *Dodd*,[11] when the jurisdiction of magistrates was very much more restricted than it is today, the then President of the Divorce Division, Sir Gorell Barnes, questioned the wisdom of throwing such a burden on laymen. 'It may be doubted,' he said, 'whether these summary proceedings are suitable for the determination of matters which affect the whole future life of the parties and their children.' It is a further disadvantage that appeals from magistrates, to the Divorce Divisional Court of the High Court, are not by way of re-hearing. This makes it more difficult for the High Court to interfere, and to right any injustice that may have been done. These are some of the factors which make the establishment of Family Courts in one form or another so necessary if matrimonial law is to be consistent.

Grounds of complaint in Magistrates' Courts

The grounds on which spouses may make complaint to the magistrates are now so numerous that they must be listed.[12] Either husband or wife may make complaint that the other, during the course of the marriage,

1. has deserted the complainant;

2. has been guilty of persistent cruelty to –
(a) the complainant
(b) the complainant's infant child
(c) an infant child of the defendant who was, at the time of the cruelty, a child of the family (that is, a child who had been accepted as one of the family by the spouse other than the parent);

3. has been found guilty –
(a) on indictment (that is, by a Court of Quarter Sessions or Assize), of any assault on the complainant;

11. [1906] P. 189.
12. Matrimonial Proceedings (Magistrates' Courts) Act, 1960, s.1.

(b) by a Magistrates' Court, of unlawful wounding, an assault causing bodily harm, or aggravated assault on the complainant, whatever the sentence – or of common assault if sentenced to prison for not less than one month;
(c) of a sexual offence (or an attempt to commit such an offence) such as rape, intercourse with young girls, incest, and unnatural offences; or of an act of gross indecency with an infant child of the complainant or an infant child of the defendant who was a child of the family at the time;

4. has committed adultery;

5. has insisted on sexual intercourse with the complainant while knowingly suffering from a venereal disease, or has permitted such intercourse without the complainant being aware of the disease;

6. is a habitual drunkard or drug addict.

A *wife only* may make complaint that her husband

7. has compelled her to submit to prostitution;

8. has wilfully neglected to provide reasonable maintenance for her or any child of the family.

A *husband* may also make complaint that his wife

9. has wilfully neglected to provide, or to make a proper contribution towards, reasonable maintenance for the husband or any child of the family who is a dependant

in a case where, by reason of the impairment of the husband's earning capacity through age, illness, or disability of mind or body, and having regard to any resources of the husband and the wife respectively which are, or should properly be made available for the purpose, it is reasonable in all the circumstances to expect the wife so to provide or contribute.

Desertion in the Magistrates' Court is the same as in the High Court or County Court, and this is discussed in chapter 9. But the desertion need not last for two years to be a cause for complaint before the justices: however short – even for a few days – desertion is a matrimonial offence for which a remedy is available, although of course separation for a very short period is unlikely to satisfy the tests required to prove that an offence has been committed. The order in such a case should not usually be a separation order – that is, it should not contain the 'non-cohabitation clause' since such an order by the magistrates brings desertion to an end and would therefore prevent divorce proceedings being brought later on that ground. A complaint of desertion is brought almost always by a wife, in order to get maintenance and custody of the children. In rare cases a husband may make such a complaint in order to have a finding of desertion against his wife which will enable him to divorce her later without calling any more evidence.[13]

Cruelty, which is no longer of itself a ground for divorce (although it will almost certainly amount to conduct such that 'the Petitioner cannot reasonably be expected to live with the Respondent') remains a ground for separation in the Magistrates' Court. The legal definition of cruelty is the same as it was previously in divorce suits (see chapter 8) save that the element of *persistence* is necessary in the Magistrates' Court; this suggests that a higher standard of cruelty is necessary for a Justices' order than was previously required for a divorce, but this is not strictly the case. It is true that magistrates generally take a robust view of marriage and are often reluctant to make separation orders, especially when a couple are young, and they may therefore find no cruelty proved where the evidence would have been quite adequate to found a petition for divorce on cruelty in the High Court in the past. But the word 'persistent', which is a relic from the Act of 1895, now simply means that there must be more than one act of cruelty. There is a question whether the acts may occur on one day, or must be widely separated in time: as Mr Justice Barnes said in *Broad* v. *Broad*,[14] 'If there is cruelty on one day, why should it not amount to persistent cruelty? Is the wife to wait until she is half murdered?' Only the last act of cruelty need fall within

13. See Matrimonial Causes Act, 1965, s.3(2).
14. (1898) 78 L.T. 687.

the six-month period; the evidence in these cases frequently covers the whole of the married life, and mud is dredged up from the past and slung by both sides in a nauseating fashion, small incidents which passed almost unnoticed being inflated to get the charge of persistent cruelty off the ground.

Where there is only one act of violence, however, there is still a remedy: the injured party can take out an assault summons and if there is a conviction for one of the offences set out in (3) above (and imprisonment also in the case of common assault), the complainant will be entitled to a separation order without any further evidence. In cases of physical cruelty this would seem the best way of ensuring that the order is granted: although technically there are two sets of proceedings, the magistrates can be asked to issue a matrimonial summons immediately after the conviction for assault, and if the defendant agrees, the matter is dealt with straight away and the separation order is granted without more ado. This by-passes the wide discretion which the magistrates have when deciding on an allegation of persistent cruelty, since they are unlikely to refuse an order where there has been an appropriate conviction. The disadvantage is that the assault summons, being a criminal matter, must be heard in open court and the press are free to publish the facts. A wife who is quite prepared to denigrate her husband in comparative privacy before a magistrate may well jib at branding him a criminal in the Magistrates' Court; and a man must sink his pride a good deal before going into the witness-box to complain publicly that his wife assaulted him and he needs the law's protection. Furthermore, legal aid cannot be granted to the informant for a criminal prosecution.

It remains to be seen what effect the new divorce legislation will have on the decisions of magistrates. Now cruelty has been replaced as a ground for divorce by conduct of such a nature 'that the Petitioner cannot reasonably be expected to live with the Respondent', it would be reasonable to assume that magistrates will make separation orders more readily, and on the basis of conduct which a spouse could not reasonably be expected to tolerate – something very different from the old test of 'persistent cruelty', and a lower standard even than that imposed by the Courts in the interval since the House of Lords decision in *Gollins* v. *Gollins*.[15]

Adultery is of course the same in the Magistrates' Court as in the Divorce Courts, and is dealt with in chapter 7. *Intercourse while suffering from venereal disease* is not a separate matrimonial offence in the Divorce Courts, although it may well be proof of breakdown under section 2(1)(b) of the Divorce Reform Act, 1969. To prove the offence in the Magistrates' Court, it must be shown that intercourse took place – an attempt is not sufficient – and that the defendant knew that he or she was suffering from a venereal disease at the time. The definition of a venereal disease is given in the Venereal Disease Act, 1917, as 'syphilis, gonorrhoea, or soft chancre', and presumably one of these three diseases must be the subject of a complaint under this section. The communication of crabs has been held to be cruelty, but infestation with these creatures does not strictly constitute a 'venereal disease' and therefore in such a case the summons would have to allege persistent cruelty rather than sexual intercourse while suffering from a venereal disease.

Habitual drunkenness and *drug addiction* are also separate offences only in the Magistrates' Court, not being grounds for divorce of themselves, although they amounted to cruelty in the Divorce Court (see p. 169) and they would now be evidence of intolerable conduct. A habitual drunkard or a drug addict is defined as a person (not being a mentally disordered person within the law) who

> by reason of habitual intemperate drinking of intoxicating liquor [or] by reason of the habitual taking or using, otherwise than upon medical advice, of any drug to which any of the provisions of the Dangerous Drugs Act, 1951, for the time being applies – (a) is at times dangerous to himself or to others, or incapable of managing himself or his affairs; or

15. [1964] A.C. 644.

(b) so conducts himself that it would not be reasonable to expect a spouse of ordinary sensibilities to continue to cohabit with him (1960 Act, Section 1b(1)).

(b) was added only in 1960, and it gives the magistrates a wide discretion, but it is still necessary to prove that the drunkenness or drug addiction are 'habitual', which may not be easy. Medical evidence is almost essential in such a case. Magistrates have the power to order the complainant spouse, whether husband or wife, to pay maintenance to the spouse against whom the order is made (section 2(2) of the 1960 Act).

Compelling to submit to prostitution cannot be excessively rare, but there are no reported cases of this offence being made the ground for a separation order. Perhaps most of the wives who could make this complaint have either reconciled themselves to the profession, or are too frightened of their husbands to bring them to court.

Wilful neglect to maintain on the part of the husband is one of the oldest matrimonial offences and has its roots in the common law. The wife's right to support is, as we have seen (chapter 3), one of the fundamental rights of marriage, but in the past the husband had no claim on his wife for maintenance. Recent statutes[16] have, however, made a wife liable to maintain her husband if she is able and he is in need – one rather unexpected result of the growth of equality between the sexes which has developed over the last hundred years. But orders for maintenance in favour of a husband are likely to be rare, the provisions being intended to relieve the state of the burden of maintaining a man who for some reason is incapable of work and who has a wife with adequate means. The sort of case where such an order would be made is that of a sick husband whose wife is earning more than she needs for her own support and that of the children, or has substantial private means. The whole question of the right to support within the family is dealt with in chapter 12;

16. National Assistance Act, 1948, s.42; Matrimonial Causes Act, 1950, s.19(4), now Matrimonial Causes Act, 1965, s.16(3); Matrimonial Proceedings (Magistrates' Courts) Act, 1960, s.2(1)(c) and s.2(2).

but it must be emphasized here that an order on the ground of wilful neglect to maintain in the magistrates' court is based on the commission of a *matrimonial offence* – the failure to maintain must be wrongful, in the sense that there must be some breach of duty. It is therefore necessary to show first of all that the husband (or in certain cases the wife) has not provided *adequate* support – and this is a question of fact, based on the particular financial circumstances of both spouses – and secondly, that he had the *capacity* to provide such support. Even if both these elements are proved, the failure to support will still not be wrongful if there was some good excuse: for example, the adultery or desertion of the party claiming maintenance will be a complete defence to such a claim (in the Magistrates' Court, but see p. 237 for the different approach in the Divorce Court).

Powers of Magistrates in matrimonial proceedings

The magistrates now have very wide powers on the hearing of any matrimonial complaint. The most far-reaching of these is the power to make a *separation order*, that is an order containing a provision 'that the complainant be no longer bound to cohabit with the defendant'. Since this order has exactly the same effect as a decree of judicial separation, it alters the legal position of the parties and to all intents and purposes brings married life to an end (apart from the right to re-marry). It is a valuable defence to a wife who has been cruelly dealt with by her husband (although a magistrate has no power to grant an injunction to prevent one spouse from molesting the other to obtain such an order, divorce proceedings must be commenced), but as we have said a separation order should never be made where the charge is desertion, since it brings the desertion to an end and thus prevents divorce proceedings on that ground. However, if it can be shown that the non-cohabitation clause was put into the order by mistake, the Divorce Court may ignore it and hold that desertion ran during the subsistence of the order (*Cohen* v. *Cohen*[17]). Also, if the order is later varied

17. [1947] P. 147.

and the non-cohabitation clause is struck out, the period of separation before the original order was made may be added to the period of separation following the variation, and when these two periods together amount to three years a petition for divorce on the ground of desertion may be presented (*Green* v. *Green*[18]).

A separation order will only be made, of course, if the complaint is proved, but the other orders which magistrates have power to make – those relating to custody, maintenance, and supervision of children – can be made irrespective of any specific finding of a matrimonial offence. Even if the justices do not complete the hearing of the complaint they are entitled to make an order for the welfare of the children of the family. But a separation order is not granted as of right on the proof of one of the matrimonial offences listed in the statute: the complainant must come to the court with clean hands, and must not have forgiven the wrong complained of. Thus the magistrates are expressly prohibited from making a separation order, or an order for maintenance, if the complainant has committed an act of adultery during the marriage, unless the court is satisfied that the adultery was condoned, connived at, or conduced to by the defendant's conduct. Nor may they make an order on the ground of adultery unless they are satisfied 'that the complainant has not condoned or connived at, or by wilful neglect conduced to, that act of adultery'. (The legal meaning of condonation, connivance, and conduct conducing is discussed in chapter 6.) In this respect the Magistrates are in a different position from the Divorce Courts, since there adultery is no bar to divorce: before 1971 it was in the discretion of the judge to decide, on the particular facts of each case, whether a petitioner who had been guilty of adultery shall be allowed a decree. Now it is only of relevance in defended suits and maintenance proceedings. That adultery should be an absolute bar in the magistrates' court proceedings, while it is almost irrelevant in the Divorce Court, seems to be very wrong. A woman who commits one act of adult-

18. [1946] 1 All E.R. 308.

ery, perhaps in circumstances which go far to excuse her lapse, is for ever shut out from obtaining an order against her husband in the Magistrates' Court, however badly he may have treated her; yet if she should elect to take divorce proceedings, her adultery will be no bar at all unless her conduct was particularly reprehensible or obviously contributed to the breakdown of the marriage and her husband raises it as a defence. This is an injustice which should be remedied.

Maintenance is frequently the main object of a summons in the Magistrates' Court. Now that magistrates have the power to make unlimited orders, this jurisdiction is even more important. The magistrates have a wide discretion to order such sums as they think proper in all the circumstances, but they must act judically and apply the proper principles of law. These are dealt with later in chapter 12, but there are certain principles which apply particularly to families where there is only a small total income for distribution. In many cases, the wife and children will be receiving supplementary benefits, and no order that can be made will improve their lot, but this is no reason for the magistrates to refuse to make an order.[19] Indeed, the wife often only makes a complaint to the magistrates at the instigation of the Ministry of Social Security. The way in which the court should approach the problem of the small income was dealt with by the Divisional Court in *Ashley* v. *Ashley*.[20]

Orders relating to children: One of the most important aspects of the justices' jurisdiction is in relation to children. Under the Guardianship of Infants Act, 1925, section 7, Magistrates' Courts were given power to make custody, guardianship and maintenance orders under the Guardianship of Infants Act, 1886, in respect of children under the age of sixteen (see p. 209). This was an important step forward in child welfare, as it gave to those with small means an opportunity to seek a Court's intervention in disputes about children.

19. *Ashley* v. *Ashley* [1968] P. 582 and see *National Assistance Board v. Parkes* [1955] 2 Q.B. 506.

20. *Kershaw* v. *Kershaw* [1966] P. 13 and *Ashley* v. *Ashley* [1968] P. 582.

The powers of magistrates are now very much wider. Where a court has *begun* to hear any matrimonial complaint, whether for separation, maintenance or even for variation or revocation of an existing order, then the Court may, whether or not it proceeds to make the order asked for in the complaint, make a wide range of orders:

1. A provision for the legal custody (not limited to one of the spouses) of any child of the family under sixteen years.

2. A provision committing any such child to the care of a specified local authority if the Court finds exceptional circumstances which make it impracticable for it to be entrusted to either of the parties or any other individual.

3. An order that any child committed to the custody of any person shall be under the supervision of a probation officer or a specified local authority.

4. Provisions for access.

5. Provisions for maintenance by either parent to the other or to the local authority having custody.

Furthermore, the Court is specifically enjoined not to dismiss or make a final order on any complaint where the above powers are exercisable until it has decided whether or not, and if so how, those powers should be exercised.[21] This means that once a party to a marriage brings a domestic dispute to the justices, the question of their children's welfare *must* be investigated, whether the complainant likes it or not. And the Court is given the power to call for a report on any such child from a probation officer or officer of a local authority – which report must be given by oral evidence or read aloud in Court so that the parties have an opportunity to challenge any of its contents. It is probable that through this jurisdiction the Magistrates' Courts do their most important work in the domestic field, and it is work to which the wise and experienced layman is particularly well suited.

Effect of Magistrates' Orders

A separation order in the Magistrates' Court is not final. It may in certain circumstances cease to have any effect, or it

21. Matrimonial Proceedings (Magistrates' Courts) Act, 1960, s.4.

may be revoked on the application of either party. Although such an order may be made while the spouses are still living together, its effect is suspended until they separate; and if they are still living together three months after the date of the order, it becomes altogether nugatory. However, any provisions in the order relating to the children are unaffected by the parties continuing to live together. On the application of husband or wife the magistrates may at any time vary the provisions of the order – this applies to maintenance, custody, and access only – or they may revoke the order altogether. The main grounds for revocation are that the parties have started to live together again, or that the original complainant has committed adultery. The adultery may have occurred before the date of the order, but provided it was unknown to the defendant at the time, the order will be discharged on proof thereof – again, only if the adultery was not condoned, connived at, or conduced to by the defendant's conduct. The order is not automatically brought to an end by a subsequent divorce – indeed, many wives prefer to rely on a Magistrates' Court order for maintenance rather than apply to the Divorce Court, since enforcement of the former is much simpler – but it is a ground on which justices *may* revoke an order. Where a wife complainant remarries the order ceases to have effect save in relation to any arrears due at the date of her remarriage.[22]

One of the advantages of a magistrates' order is that it can be relied on in a Divorce Court as evidence of the matrimonial offence which the justices found proved. If, for example, a wife obtains a separation order on the ground of cruelty, she can at any time petition for divorce on the ground that the marriage has broken down under section 2(1)(b) of the Divorce Reform Act, 1969, and need produce no other evidence than her own testimony and a copy of the magistrates' order certified by their clerk: she need not call witnesses all over again. The same applies to orders on the grounds of adultery or desertion. This does not mean that the party against whom the order was made cannot defend the divorce proceedings; the Divorce Court is in no way

22. Matrimonial Proceedings and Property Act, 1970, s.30.

bound by the magistrates' findings, but they inevitably have strong evidential value, since the justices will have seen and heard both parties nearer to the date of the offence alleged. Even when the ultimate object is divorce, husbands and wives are sometimes well advised to start the proceedings in the Magistrates' Court. The complaint is heard promptly, so that evidence can be called which might later be unobtainable; it is cheaper to call witnesses there than in the Divorce Court and an easily enforceable order for maintainance can be obtained without delay. These advantages are not so marked now that undefended divorces are heard in the County Court, but where there is likely to be a contest the Magistrates' Court may still be the better tribunal in order to obtain quick relief.

The magistrates may *vary* or *discharge* any order on hearing fresh evidence. If the complainant is proved to have committed adultery, which the defendant has not condoned, the maintenance order must be discharged. But where a wife continues to rely on a Magistrates' Court order after divorce, and then has sexual intercourse with another man, the justices are not obliged to discharge the order, since she has not committed adultery *vis-à-vis* the defendant. They should only discharge or vary the order in such circumstances if the financial position makes it just to do so: for example if she is being maintained by the man with whom she is associating.[23] The order ceases to have effect on her remarriage.

Appeals from Magistrates

It is obvious that justices will sometimes decide wrongly in matrimonial cases; however conscientious they may be, prejudice may influence their evaluation of the facts, or ignorance their application of the law. But happily they are not the final judges: an appeal lies in any matrimonial case to the High Court, where it will be heard by a Divisional Court of the Probate, Divorce, and Admiralty Division, usually consisting of the President of the Division and one other divorce judge. And from this Court there is a further

23. *Stead* v. *Stead* [1968] 1 All E.R. 989.

right of appeal to the Court of Appeal, and thence to the House of Lords, but in each case only with the consent of the Court from which it is wished to appeal. There is a time-limit of twenty-one days for lodging an appeal to the Divisional Court, but it is not difficult to obtain leave for extra time. The Court decides the appeal after consideration of legal argument on the evidence – a note of which must be supplied by the Clerk to the Justices – and on the reasons given in writing by the magistrates for their decision. No evidence is usually allowed, but where the clerk's notes are deficient in some way, affidavits can be read by leave of the Court, and in rare cases evidence which has become available since the hearing is admitted.

Enforcements of Magistrates' Court orders

The popularity of separation orders in the Magistrates' Court is undoubtedly due to three advantages which they have over actions for divorce: expedition, freedom from publicity, and ease of enforcement. It is this last virtue which is paramount: money payable under maintenance orders in the Magistrates' Court is collected by the Clerk of the Court, who has a powerful sanction in that he can bring a husband who is in arrears before the Court and have him committed to prison. The Clerk can do this without any action on the part of the complainant, although he almost invariably does not do so except at her request. Thus the money is collected by the Court without the necessity to instruct a solicitor every time there are any arrears. It was hoped that the provisions for attachment of earnings orders (see p. 258) would be an important step in avoiding arrears of maintenance payments, consequent supplementary benefit payments to wives and families, and husbands lingering in gaol for non-payment of maintenance. The idea is obviously an excellent one. Money payable under an order is diverted to the wife before it reaches his pocket, whence it may rapidly disappear into thin air and never be recoverable. It is little consolation to a wife whose husband has fallen into arrears with his maintenance to have him thrown into prison, where he is effectively prevented from earning anything with which to pay what he already owes, and may lose his job so that he will be unable to keep up payments when he is released. But unhappily the idea has not worked out in practice. Husbands have found ways of changing their jobs with such speed and frequency that the order served on their original employer does not catch up with them. It seems as if imprisonment for maintenance debts is to remain a big problem, although imprisonment for other types of debts has now been abolished.[24]

It may be questioned whether lay justices are really suited to the task of deciding the rights and wrongs of broken marriages, when their findings can have such profound legal effect. Jurisdiction in matrimonial matters was given to magistrates at a time when the High Court was the only divorce tribunal and was inaccessible to any but the rich: it was a cheap way of bringing rough justice to the masses, but is it really the right answer in times of greater equality? Now that legal aid is available to all, surely the serious disputes should find their way to the Divorce Court, and husbands and wives should be discouraged from airing their petty domestic squabbles before a Court of men and women who have more urgent calls on their time. There will always be the cases where the injured spouse is not interested in divorce, or judicial separation, and only wants maintenance, but there is jurisdiction for the High Court to hear disputed claims for maintenance even where no divorce suit is pending,[25] and this would seem a more suitable forum for a protracted dispute than the Magistrates' Court.

One of the disadvantages of hearings before the justices is that they tend to be diffuse and lengthy, because the issues between the parties are not usually clear at the outset, especially in cruelty cases. There are no pleadings, as there are in the High Court, and as it is not usually possible for the defence to obtain particulars before the hearing of the charges to be brought, much time is often wasted on irrele-

24. See the Administration of Justice Act, 1970.
25. Matrimonial Causes Act, 1965, s.22.

vant matters. (An exception to this is a charge of adultery: where this allegation is to be made, whether by the complainant or the defendant, particulars of the adultery must be given to the other side before the hearing.) Where there are lawyers on both sides and the charges and counter-charges are set out in advance, the points at issue can often be narrowed down and the case shortened, but this does not usually happen before the justices, and all this leads to protracted hearings. Adjournments are often necessary, sometimes for long periods, and this may militate against a proper judicial consideration of the points at issue. Magistrates have quite enough to occupy them with crime and juvenile delinquency; matrimonial quarrels, if not profound enough to demand a divorce or judicial separation, would be better conducted within the privacy of the home, if necessary with the help of probation officers, marriage guidance counsellors, or other trained social workers. It is to be hoped that the reconciliation provisions of section 3(1) of the Divorce Reform Act, 1969, may be an example to those who deal with matrimonial cases in Magistrates' Courts, but the great stumbling-block is the shortage of qualified workers.

Part Two **The Divorce**

Introduction

Like any other contract, marriage can be avoided, varied or terminated in certain circumstances. But marriage is not like other contracts known to the law: the rules governing marriage are not determined by the contracting parties, but by the law of the land. The parties cannot agree on the rules governing the formation of the contract, since these are laid down by law (see p. 26 *et seq.*); nor can they agree on what is to amount to a breach of the contract, nor what compensation shall be paid for any such breach, nor how the contract may be brought to an end. The reason for this distinction was set out in 1878 in the judgment of Lord Justice Brett, in *Niboyet* v. *Niboyet*:[1]

'Marriage is the fulfilment of a contract satisfied by the solemnization of the marriage, but marriage directly it exists creates by law a relation between the parties and what is called a status of each. The status of an individual, used as a legal term, means the legal position of the individual in or with regard to the rest of a community. That relation between the parties, and that status of each of them with regard to the community, which are constituted upon marriage are not imposed or defined by contract or agreement but by law.'

This passage bears close study, as it is the starting-point of the whole law relating to relief. This section will deal with the manner in which our own community regulates the recognition of the validity of the contract and the way in which it may be terminated. We have already seen how the Courts of this country decide whether or not they have jurisdiction to determine such questions (see p. 68 *et seq.*).

1. [1878] 4 P.D. 1.

But once the English Court accepts jurisdiction, wherever the marriage was made and whatever the religious persuasion, nationality or residence of the parties, the personal laws of England will be applied in granting relief.

There are three classes of case with which the Courts are concerned when granting relief. First there is the 'marriage' which never existed in law, and thus does not strictly require any intervention by the Courts, but may nevertheless come before them for consideration; such a marriage is *absolutely void*, and it has never existed for any purpose (but see p. 193 for effect of void marriage on legitimacy of children).

Second, there is the marriage which has such defects in the formation or performance of the contract that it will be recognized by the law as a nullity when a Court has declared it to be so, but not before. This is a *voidable* marriage: that is, a marriage which has never got off the ground as a marriage, but will remain legally binding on the parties until one of the spouses obtains a declaration of nullity.

Third, there is the marriage which is a completely constituted contract, unimpeachable in its formation and institution, but which is brought to an end by the Courts at the instigation of one or both of the parties according to certain rules of law. This is dissolution, a *divorce*, and it is a comparatively new branch of the law which has only been available to ordinary people in this country for just over a hundred years.

When studying this part of the law, relating to relief, it will be helpful to keep in mind that the jurisdiction of the Matrimonial Courts is inherited from the Ecclesiastical Courts. Before 1857 the Bishops in the Diocesan Courts had the sole jurisdiction over matrimonial disputes: they alone could pronounce decrees of nullity, or order deserting spouses to return (with the sanction of imprisonment), or make orders of divorce *a menso et thoro* (judicial separation: see p. 85). They could not dissolve a marriage *a vinculo* – that is, with freedom to remarry – but this, the only exception to the ecclesiastical jurisdiction, could be effected only by an Act of Parliament (see p. 58). Even today, whenever a difficult point of law arises, and no guidance can be found in statute or case law, the Courts will look back to the Canon law and the practice of the Ecclesiastical Courts (the history of matrimonial jurisdiction is dealt with earlier in chapter 3). With an understanding of the roots of English divorce law, the anomalies become explicable and the relevance of old decisions can be better appreciated.

5 Nullity

Nullity is much less important than divorce, at least numerically: in 1966 there were 41,081 decrees of dissolution, but only 764 decrees of nullity. It may be thought that now breakdown has become the sole ground for divorce, nullity will fade into insignificance; if a marriage is such that it can be declared null and void, it can equally be said to have broken down. But there are important distinctions between nullity and divorce as we shall see, and it seems likely that there will continue to be a steady stream of nullity petitions running at an average of just under 900 a year, and resulting in an average of 675 decrees a year.

One reason why nullity declarations will continue to be sought is religious: those whose religion forbids divorce, or remarriage after divorce, and who are faced with broken marriages, will wish to have them annulled rather than dissolved. There is another important difference between nullity and divorce: a nullity petition may be presented at any time after marriage, whereas a divorce petition cannot be presented until three years have elapsed, unless the leave of the Court is gained. This is only granted on grounds of exceptional depravity or exceptional hardship (p. 141).

A nullity decree is made, as we have said, where there is a defective marriage. Defects may make the marriage either *void* or *voidable*. The distinction is important.

A *void* 'marriage' does not require a decree of a Court to bring it to an end, since it has never existed. The parties can 'remarry' with impunity, provided they can satisfy the registrar or priest that their former 'marriage' was void. They do not commit bigamy by 'remarriage'. A void 'marriage' can be challenged by anyone – not only the parties – at any time, even after the death of the parties.

A *voidable* marriage is a valid and subsisting marriage until a decree of a competent court pronounces it to be void. The parties will therefore commit bigamy if they remarry before they obtain a decree absolute of nullity. A voidable marriage cannot be impeached when one of the parties has died, and in general no one but a party to the marriage can challenge it (but a person having a financial interest may possibly seek the annulment of a marriage to which he is not a party).[1]

The present law relating to void and voidable marriages and decrees of nullity is contained in the Nullity of Marriage Act, 1971 which gives statutory form to the old Ecclesiastical law and makes some important alterations. The principal provisions only apply to marriages which take place after the Act comes into force on 1 August, 1971.

Void marriages

There are now only three grounds on which a marriage is void:

1. that it is not a valid marriage under the provisions of the Marriage Acts 1949 to 1970 (that is to say where
(a) the parties are within the prohibited degrees of relationship;
(b) either party is under the age of sixteen; or
(c) the parties have intermarried in disregard of certain requirements as to the formation of marriage);
2. that at the time of the marriage either party was already lawfully married;

3. that the parties are not respectively male and female.

1. *Invalid under provisions of the Marriage Act 1949 to 1970*

The grounds on which a marriage is invalid under these Acts are as follows:
(a) Consanguinity and affinity. Any marriage between parties

1. *Ray* v. *Sherwood and Ray* (1836) 1 Curt. 193.

within the prohibited degrees of relationship is absolutely void. These degrees were set out in 1563 but were modified in 1907 and 1921 to allow marriages with a deceased wife's sister or a deceased brother's widow.[2]

The prohibited degrees now are:

For a man	*For a woman*
mother	father
daughter	son
grandmother	grandfather
grand-daughter	grandson
sister	brother
wife's mother	husband's father
wife's daughter	husband's son
father's wife	mother's husband
son's wife	daughter's husband
grandfather's wife	grandmother's husband
wife's grandmother	husband's grandfather
wife's grand-daughter	husband's grandson
grandson's wife	grand-daughter's husband
aunt	uncle
niece	nephew

Relationship by the half-blood, whether legitimate or illegitimate, is a bar within the prohibited degrees. Adoption brings a child within the degrees as if he were a natural child of his adopter.

The abhorrence of intermarriage which gave rise to these prohibited degrees seems to be derived partly from a fear of the results of inter-breeding – this can only apply to the degrees of consanguinity – and partly from fears of the social and moral effects within the family. Modern scientific opinion seems to incline to the rejection of the biological dangers of intermarriage, but even without such dangers the social and moral problems remain. Affinity is a different matter, since these degrees were based on the concept of husband and wife as one person, and this has almost disappeared from our law. The Law Commission is considering

2. Marriage Act, 1949, 1st Schedule, and the Marriage (Enabling) Act, 1960.

this subject, especially as it applies to the adopted child, and may well recommend changes.

In the case of a foreign marriage, the English Courts will hold it to be void only if the parties come within the prohibited degrees according to the law of their domicile.[3]

(b) Marriage under the age of consent. Any marriage between persons either of whom is under sixteen is void by the Marriage Act, 1949, section 2. The age of consent was raised to sixteen by the Age of Marriage Act, 1929: before that time it had been fourteen for a boy and twelve for a girl. (This has not been affected by the alteration in the age of majority made by the Family Law Reform Act, 1969.)

(c) Parties intermarried in disregard of certain formalities. We have seen (p. 26) that there are certain forms which are required for marriage in England. The Marriage Act, 1949 makes certain of these formalities essential, in that lack of them will render the marriage void. Other defects in formality do not invalidate the marriage. The more important formalities which are essential to a valid marriage are as follows:

(i) Where a marriage is according to the rites of the Church of England, it will be void, unless banns have been duly published, or a special licence or common licence or duly issued Superintendent Registrar's certificate has been obtained. Publication of banns in a false name, with the knowledge of both parties with the intention of concealment, makes the marriage void.

(ii) A marriage purporting to be by licence is void if no proper licence was in fact in existence, but only if both parties knew of the irregularity.

(iii) A marriage celebrated under a Superintendent Registrar's Certificate without due notice is void if both parties knew of the irregularity.

In the case of *foreign marriages* the English Court will apply the *lex loci contractus* in determining whether the essential formalities have been complied with and thus

3. *Cheni* v. *Cheni*, [1965] P. 85.

whether the marriage is valid.[4]

2. *Prior marriage of either party*. English law recognizes the Christian definition of marriage as the voluntary union for life of one man and one woman to the exclusion of all others, the definition given by Lord Penzance in *Hyde* v. *Hyde* (see p. 19). If at the time of the ceremony of marriage one of the spouses was already a party to a valid and subsisting marriage, wherever contracted and in whatever form, the second marriage will be declared null and void. Even if the prior marriage was polygamous, if it was valid by the Courts of the domicile of the parties, the second will be held to be void.[5]

But the English Courts will not adjudicate on a polygamous or potentially polygamous marriage. Any foreign marriage will be held valid here if, at the time of its inception, it precluded the spouses from marrying any other person, or even if at the time proceedings are taken it is monogamous.[6] A change in personal law may make a potentially polygamous marriage a monogamous one.[7] The question of whether there is a prior subsisting marriage may involve difficult questions or recognition of foreign marriages and also of foreign divorces, but the decision of the House of Lords in *Indyka* (see p. 79) simplified the latter problem and it is now covered by the Recognition of Divorce and Legal Separation Act, 1971 as from 1 January, 1971 (see p. 75–81).

3. *Parties not respectively male and female*. This has already been dealt with on p. 22.

Voidable marriages

Since the Nullity of Marriage Act, 1971 there are six grounds on which a marriage may be voidable:

1. *Non-consummation due to the incapacity of either party*. Until 1937, this was the only ground on which a voidable marriage could be declared null. The Divorce Court in-

4. *Kenward* v. *Kenward* [1951] P. 124.
5. *Kassim* v. *Kassim* [1962] P. 224.
6. *Cheni* v. *Cheni* [1965] P. 85.
7. *Ali* v. *Ali* [1966]2 W.L.R. 620.

herited the powers of the Ecclesiastical Courts to pronounce a decree of nullity on the ground of non-consummation due to incapacity of either husband or wife, and the remedy is the same as it has been for many centuries. Either party can petition, but the impotent spouse may only petition if he or she did not know of the defect at the time of the marriage. The failure to consummate may be due to a physical defect, which must be either incurable or only curable by treatment which the impotent party has refused to undergo; or it may be due to some mental or moral disability which prevents intercourse with the particular man or woman concerned – an insurmountable repugnance or a psychological disturbance which makes it impossible for the man to produce or sustain an erection, or which produces such spasm on the part of the woman as to prevent intercourse.

Such a personal cause for impotence was not always good ground for an annulment. The old rule was *qui aptus est ad unam aptus est ad aliam*, and it seems that the first Petitioner to succeed in obtaining a decree of nullity because of this type of impotence was the Countess of Essex in 1613. The Countess alleged that she and the Earl had for three years 'lived together at bed and board, and lain both naked and alone in the same bed' and that she had 'again and again yielded herself to his power, and as much as lay in her offered herself and her body to be known'; that the Earl again and again 'did try to have copulation, as with his lawful wife, which she refused not, but used the best means she could', yet he never succeeded. The allegation continues: 'Yet before the said pretended Marriage, and since, the said Earl hath had, and hath power and ability of body to deal with other women, and to know them carnally, and sometime have felt the motion and pricks of the flesh carnally'. Despite this averment that the Earl was impotent only with Lady Frances Howard, the Court of Delegates, after much learned argument drawn from the scriptures and the early fathers of the Church, pronounced a decree of nullity – the Archbishop of Canterbury dissenting, since in his view there had been insufficient almsgiving and fasting to appease the wrath of God which surely must have been the cause of the failure of the marriage.

At one time the Courts required cohabitation for three years – the *triennalis cohabitatio* – before granting a decree, but this is no longer necessary. And before the introduction of wilful refusal to consummate as a ground for nullity, the Courts would infer incapacity on the part of a wife who had continued her refusal for several years. This legal fiction, which provided a nice example of the Court bending the law to assist an injured party shut out from any remedy on the strict interpretation of the law, was abandoned as soon as the true cause of the failure to consummate was recognized by statute as a ground for nullity.

When is a marriage consummated? Sexual intercourse is obviously necessary, but what exactly amounts to intercourse capable of consummating marriage? It is certainly something more than the connection necessary to base a charge of adultery or rape. Many legal battles have been fought around this point through the centuries and the lists are not yet closed. The doctors of civil law begged the question by putting it into Latin: there must, they said, be *vera copula*. Perhaps the best, and certainly the most quoted, definition was made in the middle of the nineteenth century by the great Dr Lushington in *D.* v. *A.*[8]

> Sexual intercourse, in the proper meaning of the term, is ordinary and complete intercourse; it does not mean partial and imperfect intercourse; yet, I cannot go to the length of saying that every degree of imperfection would deprive it of its essential character. There must be degrees difficult to deal with; but if so imperfect as scarcely to be natural, I should not hesitate to say that, legally speaking, it is no intercourse at all.

He went on to say that if the wife is not and cannot be made capable of more than 'an incipient, imperfect and unnatural coitus', he would pronounce the marriage void.

The difficulty arises as to the meaning of 'imperfect' and

8. (1845) 1 Rob. Eccl. at p. 299.

'unnatural'. How far must the male organ penetrate? For how long must intercourse be prolonged? These questions have never been exactly answered, but there have been several cases which give some indication of the standards required. In *B.* v. *B.*[9] where a wife who had been born with certain male organs and without a vagina, had been provided, as a result of plastic surgery, with an artificial vagina which permitted penetration for a distance of at least two inches, the Court held that this was not sufficient to consummate a marriage, but the judge based this decision on the artificiality of the organ rather than the degree of penetration. In *S.Y.* v. *S.Y.* (*orse W.*)[10] the reasoning in *B.* v. *B.* was disapproved. In that case the wife had no uterus and only a short cul-de-sac in place of a vagina. The medical evidence was that the rudimentary vagina could be lengthened by a plastic operation which would then allow full penetration. The Court of Appeal held that coitus in these circumstances would amount to *vera copula* sufficient to consummate the marriage, and refused the husband a decree of nullity. (The wife had been willing to undergo the operation, but the husband left before she could do so.)

Such cases as these are rare and difficult, and each will turn on its own facts, especially on the medical evidence. But it is clear that advances in plastic surgery have modified the definition of Dr Lushington.

One thing is certain: it is the possibility of normal intercourse, and not the ability to conceive children that is the test of consummation. It is quite possible for a woman to conceive without having intercourse at all – sperm deposited outside the vagina may find their way up to fertilize the egg-cell – and she may therefore have a child without consummating her marriage.[11] Artificial insemination with the husband's seed, even if resulting in pregnancy, does not amount to consummation.[12] The use of contraceptives was at one

9. [1955] P. 42.
10. [1963] P. 37.
11. *Clarke* (otherwise *Talbot*) v. *Clarke* [1943] 2 All E.R. 540.
12. *R.E.L.* (otherwise *R.*) v. *E. L.* [1949] P. 211.

time believed to prevent true intercourse, but in 1947 the House of Lords in *Baxter* v. *Baxter*[13] decided once and for all that consummation can take place even if such methods are used. In that case the wife had refused to have intercourse unless her husband wore a sheath; it was argued for the husband in nullity proceedings that the wife had refused to consummate the marriage, since the use of a sheath by the man, as in this case, or a cervical cap the woman, prevented the emission of semen into the vault of the vagina which was necessary for true and complete intercourse. The House held that such emission was not necessary and the Lord Chancellor, Viscount Jowitt, adopted the words of a seventeenth-century lawyer, Lord Stair:

> So then it is not the consent of marriage as it relateth to the procreation of children that is requisite; for it may consist, though the woman be far beyond that date; but it is the consent, whereby ariseth that conjugal society, which may have the conjunction of bodies as well as of minds, as the general end of the institution of marriage, is the solace and satisfaction of man.[14]

It follows from this decision that the practice of *coitus interruptus* cannot prevent consummation. (But the use of *any* contraceptive method may be ground for a divorce if it amounts to 'unreasonable behaviour; see p. 168.) This is one of the points at which the law seems to be divided from the standards of ordinary men and women by a great gulf. Most people would regard sexual relations which stop short of ejaculation as incomplete, yet pentration of the vagina on one solitary occasion, without even the possibility of sexual satisfaction on either side, is sufficient to consummate the marriage for the purpose of the law.

Impotence may be a ground for a decree even if it be *quoad hunc* or *quoad hanc* – that is, limited to the particular partner.

Sterility of either party is not in itself a ground for a decree of nullity.[15]

13. [1948] A.C. 274.
14. Quoting Lord Stair's 'Institutions', 1832, 1 tit. 4 para. 6.
15. *Baxter* v. *Baxter* [1948] A.C. 274.

2. *Wilful refusal to consummate.* This and the next four grounds for relief were introduced by the Matrimonial Causes Act 1937.[16] Only the injured party, that is the one who has been refused, may petition, and the burden of proof is on him or her to show that consummation has been proposed with reasonable tact, persuasion and encouragement[17] and that the refusal amounts to a settled and definite decision arrived at without just excuse. The whole history of the marriage must be looked at to see whether or not these conditions have been fulfilled. It is not necessary for either the proposal or the refusal of consummation to be in words,[18] but the refusal must persist up to the date of the petition.[19] Mere neglect to comply with a request is not necessarily tantamount to refusal. Where one spouse puts himself or herself in such a situation that consummation is not possible, as by refusing to cohabit, the refusal will be inferred.

If the parties have had intercourse before marriage, even if a child has been born, there may be wilful refusal after the marriage.

What amounts to consummation is discussed above under 'Impotence'.

3. *Lack of consent.* A marriage is not voidable unless both parties validly consented to it. Such consent may be vitiated by duress, mistake, unsoundness of mind 'or otherwise'. The consent must be both to marry and to marry a particular person.[20] We have already seen how fear, duress and mistake can operate to vitiate consent (see p. 25). It is important to appreciate the limitations of lack of consent in making a marriage void. The imperfection of the analogy of marriage with an ordinary commercial contract is shown clearly here: the sort of lack of consent which would invalidate an ordinary contract will usually not affect a marriage. The words of Sir Francis Jeune in 1897 are still the law:

16. Now Matrimonial Causes Act, 1965, s.9.
17. *Baxter* v. *Baxter* [1948] A.C. 274.
18. *Ponticelli* v. *Ponticelli* [1958] P. 204.
19. *S.* v. *S.* (otherwise *C.*) [1956] P. 1.
20. *R.* v. *Mills*, [1844] 10 Cl. and Fin. 534.

No fraudulent concealment or misrepresentation enables the defrauded party who has consented to it [the marriage] to rescind it [. . .] There must be the voluntary consent of both parties [. . .] but when in English law fraud is spoken of as a ground of avoiding a marriage, this does not include such fraud as induces a consent, but is limited to such fraud as procures the appearance without the reality of consent.[21]

Insanity is a particular form of lack of consent. Until recently anyone who was a lunatic so found by inquisition was unable to make a valid marriage but, since all classification of mental defect was abolished by the Mental Health Act, 1959, the only test is whether or not a spouse has sufficient understanding at the time of the ceremony. As we have seen the degree of understanding required is not very high.[22] A person is regarded as being capable of giving consent if he is capable of understanding the nature of marriage, which involves a mental capacity to appreciate the responsibilities normally attaching to marriage. Strong medical evidence will normally be required to invalidate a marriage on this ground.

Proceedings must be instituted within three years of the marriage.

4. *Mental disorder at time of marriage.* If either party at the time of the marriage, though capable of giving a valid consent and therefore not within section 2(c), was suffering from a mental disorder within the meaning of the Mental Health Act, 1959 the marriage can be voidable, provided that such disorder made that party unfitted for marriage. (This replaces the awkward provision of the Matrimonial Causes Act, 1965 section 9(1)(b).) 'Mental disorders' is defined by section 4(1) of the Mental Health Act, 1959, as 'mental illness, arrested or incomplete development of mind, psychopathic disorder, and any other disorder or disability of mind'. This is a very wide definition – on 25 November, 1971, Sir Jocelyn Simon P. (as he then was) granted a

21. *Moss* v. *Moss* (*orse. Archer*) [1897] P. 263.
22. *Re Park* [1954] P. 112 C.A.; and see p. 24.

decree[23] to a wife petitioner on the ground that the husband, although by no means insane or even incapable of working, was suffering from chronic alcoholism at the time of the marriage, Cogent medical evidence however will be required to establish the fact of such mental disorder. And it should be noted that the mental disorder, while it need not be permanent or continuous, must be present at the time of the marriage. Proceedings must be instituted within three years of the marriage.

5. *Venereal disease at time of marriage.* If at the time of the marriage the Respondent was suffering from venereal disease in a communicable form, that is a ground for a nullity decree. Venereal disease is defined by the Venereal Disease Act 1971, as 'syphilis, gonorrhoea or soft chancre', but 'crabs' have also been held to be a venereal disease for the purpose of establishing a *prima facie* case of adultery[24] and would probably so be held for the purpose of this section. Communicable has been held to include communicable to a child of the family.

A nullity decree will not be granted under this subsection unless proceedings are instituted within three years of the marriage, and the court is satisfied that the Petitioner was at the time of the marriage ignorant of the facts alleged.

6. *Pregnancy by another at time of marriage.* This speaks for itself, but it is often very difficult to prove, especially where the parties had intercourse before marriage. If blood tests can be taken with the consent of the parties it may be possible to exclude the husband from paternity.[25] It was decided in *Re L*[26] that the High Court has power to order blood tests now[27] but would not do so unless it is in the interests of the child; (generally it will not in these circumstances as the tests could bastardize the child but could only

23. *Carnegie* v. *Carnegie* (unreported).
24. *Stead* v. *Stead* [1927] 71. S.J. 391.
25. *Stocker* v. *Stocker* [1966] 1 W.L.R. 190.
26. *L.* [1968] 1 All E.R. C.A. P. 20.
27. *M.* v. *M.* (1968) 112 S.J. 840.

rarely establish legitimacy; see pp. 196–7). But in two recent cases[28] the House of Lords has decided that while the Court must protect the interests of the child when considering whether or not to order blood tests, it is entitled to look at all the evidence available including that of a blood test and need not be satisfied before ordering such a test, that the outcome will be for the benefit of the infant.

The burden of proof on the petitioner has always been a heavy one but under section 26 of the Family Law Reform Act, 1969, the question of legitimacy is now to be determined on the balance of probabilities.

Bars to nullity decree where marriage is voidable

Apart from the qualifications of time and knowledge imposed on proceedings brought under (c) (d) (e) and (f) above, no decree of nullity on the ground that a marriage is voidable shall be granted if the Respondent satisfies the court of the following:

1. The Petitioner, with knowledge that it was open to him to have the marriage avoided, so conducted himself in relation to the Respondent as to lead the Respondent reasonably to believe that he would not seek to do so.
2. That it would be unjust to the Respondent to grant the decree.

This statutory provision replaces the old defences of approbation ratification and insincerity. Such defences are analagous to a plea of estoppel on the ground that facts and circumstances exist which make it inequitable or contrary to public policy to grant a decree of nullity, although the marriage would otherwise be voidable.[29] It is clearly inequitable to permit a husband who has allowed his wife to adopt a child, for example, later to turn round and say that there was no marriage. There must be some conduct or overt acts which show recognition of the existence and validity of the marriage – such as the adoption of a child – without

28. *S.* v. *S.* & *W.* v. *W.* [1970] 3 W.L.R.366.
29. *G.* v. *M.* [1885] 10 A.C. 171.

reference to 'any intention the Petitioner might have had which remained locked in his own bosom.'[30] But a spouse will not be held to have approbated the marriage by taking advantage of the marriage situation unless he was ignorant of both the facts and the law; as for example where a wife applied for maintenance at the behest of the National Assistance Board and not because she had accepted the marriage.[31] Artificial insemination by a donor might well amount to approbation, but not in the absence of prior knowledge of the legal right to an annulment,[32] nor if the step was taken in the hope of bringing about normal sexual relations.[33]

Delay can be evidence of approbation or lack of sincerity, or it can make the granting of a decree inequitable because the other spouse has been allowed to act in the belief that the marriage was accepted. A premarital agreement to live with a wife *tamquam soror*, without sexual relations, will defeat a nullity petition for wilful refusal.

Collusion was a bar to a nullity decree even after it ceased to be a bar to divorce. But by section 5 of the Nullity of Marriage Act, 1971 collusion is no longer a bar to the granting of a decree of nullity whether the marriage took place, or the proceedings were instituted, before or after commencement of the Act.

30. *W.* v. *W.* [1952] P. 152.
31. *Tindall* v. *Tindall* [1953] P. 63.
32. *Slater* v. *Slater* [1953] P. 235.
33. *R.E.L.* v. *E.L.* [1949] P. 211.

6 Divorce in General

Until 1969, the law of divorce was founded on the doctrine of the matrimonial offence. That is to say, a divorce would only be granted to the 'innocent' party to a marriage who could prove that the other party had been guilty of some wrongful conduct such as adultery, cruelty or desertion (an exception was incurable insanity, added as a ground by the 1937 Act). This derived from the punitive approach of the ecclesiastical law to the spouse who caused the breakdown of a marriage and it has coloured public attitudes to divorce up to the present day. Because divorce is the final rupture of the marriage bond, it is a violent deed which even people who believe that the balance of good is in favour of divorce where a marriage has completely broken down, must find sordid. Where there are children, the deed can well be tragic: the selfishness with which some parents use their children as sticks to belabour each other is horrible, but even when they behave in the most civilized fashion their children must either suffer the complete loss of one parent or endure a heartless shunting from one to the other. But slowly the realization has developed that it is the breakdown of the marriage, not the resulting divorce, which is the tragedy; it is the cancer, not the removal of the affected organ, which destroys the patient's health.

A growing realization of this has taken much of the sting of shame out of divorce in the last thirty years. While very few approve of divorce, most people accept it as part of the social scheme and are only too glad to avail themselves of it when their own marriages become unhappy.

Since nearly seven per cent of marriages (even before the new Act) ended in divorce, most people in this country have at least one relative or close friend who has been divorced, and therefore cannot ignore the possibility that they themselves might one day end up in the Divorce Court.

The increase in divorce over the last hundred years has been the most startling social change in a century of social revolution. Divorce was, as we have seen, available only to the very rich before 1857, but even after the Divorce Court was established it was not exactly popular. In the five years between 1876 and 1880 there were on an average only 460 petitions for dissolution – including both divorce and nullity – every year; between 1921 and 1925 the average yearly figure was 2848; between 1946 and 1950 the figure was 38,901. This rapid increase in dissolution of marriage had several causes, some practical and obvious, others less clear. Between 1857 and 1925 the Courts were still open only to people of means; although the procedure had been greatly simplified and cheapened, the fees of counsel and solicitors still had to be met, and these put divorce quite out of reach for the working classes. Furthermore, the only ground for divorce was adultery, and in the case of a husband the adultery had to be accompanied by some other offence. So the annual figure during those years only crept up to something less than 3,000. Then two things happened: in 1923 women were given the right to petition on their husband's adultery, unaggravated by any other enormity; and in 1925 a very limited form of legal aid was introduced whereby the really poor were enabled to take divorce proceedings at the expense of the state, counsel and solicitors giving their services for charity. Even these two factors only raised the annual rate to about 4,700. It was the Act of 1937, which introduced desertion, cruelty, and incurable insanity as grounds for divorce and enlarged the grounds for nullity, that opened the sluce-gates. By the beginning of the Second World War the number of petitions yearly was about 7500 and during the war it rose to 16,000. By this time divorce was available on the grounds open to petitioners today, and the effects of the separations and loosening of morals brought about by a great war were having their effect. In 1945, 25,711 petitions were filed; in 1947 there were 48,501, but this was the result of a back-log of wartime broken marriages and was quite untypical. Most of these cases were financed by the Law Society's Service Divorce Department.

But there were still many who wanted divorce and could not afford it: only the very indigent could avail themselves of the 'Poor Persons' divorce facilities, and the great mass of the people could only hope for a decree if they could beg, borrow, or save the substantial sum necessary to take proceedings. In divorce there was in reality one law for the rich and the very poor, and another for the poor.

This injustice was removed when the Legal Aid Scheme was introduced in 1949.[1] Then the true demand for divorce showed itself: in 1951 no less than 38,382 petitions for divorce and nullity were filed. This figure settled down to a steady average of around 30,000 a year after the back-log had been dealt with; in 1959 there were 25,689 petitions, and in 1960, 27,870.[2] The average now runs at over 45,000 divorce petitions a year, and it seems likely that this figure will be greatly increased in the first few years of the operation of the new Act.

Curiously enough, the growing fashion for divorce has been accompanied by an increase in the popularity of marriage. People marry younger than ever today, and apparently with less preparation and forethought – perhaps because they realize that marriage is no longer necessarily permanent – and nearly 70 per cent of divorced people remarry. It looks as if there has been a complete change of attitude to the married state: it is now probably regarded by many, if only subconsciously, as an *attempt* at finding a life-partner – an attempt which can be abandoned if it fails. A

1. Legal Aid and Advice Act, 1949.

2. The figures given here, it will be noted, are for the number of *petitions filed*, not for the *decrees granted*, since this gives a truer picture of the trend of divorce at any particular period. And of course the increase must be related to the population figures and the number of existing marriages: the ratio of marriages dissolved to those contracted was 0·2 in 1911, 6·7 in 1954 and 8·9 in 1968.

mistaken selection may bring some years of unhappiness, but it does not entail a life sentence of misery. This is no place to discuss whether the change is a good or a bad one, but it must be recorded as a great social shift in family life directly brought about by operation of law, though of course deeper causes made changes in the law inevitable.

Largely because the public is cut off from its usual source of information – the newspapers – by a law which prevents the reporting of any but the barest details in matrimonial cases, there is widespread ignorance in England about divorce law. It is a principle of English law that justice must not only be done, but must be seen to be done; it is for this reason that all courts of law are open to the public except in very special circumstances. This rule applies equally to divorce cases; anyone can listen to any divorce or nullity case, subject only to the judge's discretion to clear the court when evidence of an intimate or revolting nature is being given. The court is always so cleared in nullity cases where medical evidence is given, and usually when the fate of children is being canvassed, but otherwise the discretion is very sparingly used. The freedom of the Press to report cases is part of this principle of open justice, but it is obvious that matrimonial suits can provide such scurrilous matter that the freedom might well be abused, as it certainly was when divorce first became common. In 1926 an Act[3] was passed which limited the publication of the particulars of a matrimonial case to the names, addresses, and occupations of the parties and the witnesses, a concise statement of the allegations made and the defences raised, submissions on points of law and the decision of the court on them, the summing-up of the judge, the findings of the jury (if any), and any observations made by the judge in the course of his judgment. In effect this means that the judge can decide just how much of the facts of the case shall be released to the press; by wording his judgment carefully, he can keep out anything which he thinks should not be published. In the ordinary undefended case nothing can be published save the

3. Judicial Proceedings (Regulation of Reports) Act, 1926.

names and addresses of the parties and the grounds for the divorce, since the judge usually says nothing in his judgment except to give the ground on which the decree nisi is granted and any orders he makes relating to children, property and maintenance.

Breakdown as sole ground for divorce

With an annual figure of over 40,000 divorce decrees by 1966, public opinion showed signs of change. Reformers had been urging for years that the demand for divorce made nonsense of the law. The necessity to prove a matrimonial offence, generally on one side only, meant that the Court was often asked to make a finding quite inconsistent with the true facts. Even the Royal Commission on Divorce in 1956, which recommended that the matrimonial offence should remain, recognized this:

> The law of divorce as it at present exists is indeed weighted in favour of the least scrupulous, the least honourable, and the least sensitive, and nobody who is ready to provide a ground of divorce, who is careful to avoid any suggestion of connivance or collusion and who has a cooperative spouse, has any difficulty in securing a dissolution of the marriage.

It is safe to say that in 1956 public opinion would not have accepted wide reforms in divorce. Yet as early as 1943 Viscount Simon in *Blunt* v. *Blunt*[4] had recognized the importance of breakdown. In that case the House of Lords laid down the principles on which the courts should exercise discretion to grant a decree even where a Petitioner had committed adultery, and his Lordship said that a primary consideration was 'the interest of the community at large, to be judged by maintaining a true balance between respect for the binding sanctity of marriage and social considerations which make it contrary to public policy to insist on the maintenance of a union which has wholly broken down.' In the ten years following the report of the 1956 commission there must have been a fundamental change in our attitudes to divorce, for in

4. [1943] A.C. 517.

1966 a committee set up by the Archbishop of Canterbury, under the Bishop of Exeter, published a report which suggested the most revolutionary reforms ever contemplated except by those of extreme views.[5] The most sweeping of these was the substitution of breakdown of marriage for the matrimonial offence as the only ground for divorce. The reasoning behind this suggested reform was simple and attractive: we know that when a marriage breaks down a couple can, if they wish, obtain a divorce; why then make them drag up some real or imaginary 'matrimonial offence' to provide a ground for divorce within the law, when the true reason for the divorce is the breakdown itself? The logic of this can only be answered by the argument that anything which makes divorce easier loosens the marriage bond. The advocates of the case for breakdown replied that divorce was already easy, especially for those who were prepared to twist the tail of the law; this reform would make it not easier, but more decent, more realistic and more just. The Bishop of Exeter's committee would have liked to see a full judicial inquiry into the marriage in every case before a decree was granted, but this was felt to be too wasteful of judicial time and wholly impracticable. When the Law Commission reported on divorce law reform in November 1966[6] they defined the objectives of a good divorce law as first to buttress rather than to undermine the stability of marriage and second when, regrettably, a marriage has irretrievably broken down, to enable the empty legal shell to be destroyed with the maximum fairness, and the minimum bitterness, distress and humiliation. The commission came out strongly in favour of breakdown as the sole ground for divorce but against the judicial inquest.

It was against this background, and based on this evidence of informed opinion, that the Divorce Reform Act, 1969,

5. *Putting Asunder: A Divorce Law for Contemporary Society*, the Report of a Group appointed by the Archbishop of Canterbury, under the Bishop of Exeter, SPCK, London, 1966.

6. *Reform of the Grounds of Divorce*, 'The Field of Choice', Cmnd. 3123.

after one false start and thirteen sittings at the Committee stage, made the revolutionary change from matrimonial offence to breakdown. It also incorporated some of the other reforms suggested in the report and by the Law Commission. Probably this measure would not have reached the statute book, at any event not so soon, if it had not been for the clear indication given by the Bishop of Exeter's committee that even churchmen were anxious for reform. Certainly opposition in Parliament was directed mainly to the details of the Bill rather than to the change in principle. Since January 1971 it has been the law that 'the sole ground on which a petition for divorce may be presented to the Court by either party to a marriage shall be that the marriage has broken down irretrievably' (section 1 of the Act). By section 8 of the Act breakdown is also made the only ground for judicial separation, save that the court need not consider whether the marriage has broken down irretrievably before granting a decree. If a suit is undefended, it may perhaps be inferred that the breakdown is 'irretrievable', but a decision on this point may prove extremely difficult in defended cases. The Act goes on to lay down the tests of breakdown,[7] saying that the court shall not hold the marriage to have broken down irretrievably unless the Petitioner satisfies the court of one or more of the following facts:

1. Since the celebration of the marriage the Respondent has committed adultery and the Petitioner finds it intolerable to live with the Respondent.
2. Since the celebration of the marriage the Respondent has behaved in such a way that the Petitioner cannot reasonably be expected to live with the Respondent.
3. The Respondent has deserted the Petitioner for a continuous period of at least two years immediately preceding the presentation of the petition.
4. The parties to the marriage have lived apart for a continuous period of at least two years immediately preceding the presentation of the petition and the Respondent consents

7. s.2(1).

to a decree being granted.

5. The parties to the marriage have lived apart for a continuous period of at least five years immediately preceding the presentation of the petition.

A duty[8] is imposed on the Court to inquire, so far as it reasonably can, into the facts alleged by the Petitioner and into any facts alleged by the Respondent – a faint echo of the matrimonial inquest proposed in *Putting Asunder*.

Proof of breakdown

The old matrimonial offences linger on in the 'facts' which the petitioner must establish before the Court can find breakdown and these will be dealt with in detail in later chapters. (These offences are of course still the grounds for orders in the Magistrates' Courts, where breakdown is not of itself a ground for any order.) But in the Divorce Court there are some significant modifications in the law relating to those 'offences' which should be mentioned here.

1. Adultery is no proof of breakdown unless in addition the other spouse finds it intolerable to continue to cohabit. This is intended to avoid dissolution based on the single act or 'temporary' adultery, and needs some comment. A spouse who files a divorce petition clearly finds something in the marriage intolerable, even if the cause for the intolerability be his own adultery. It should be noted that the words of the section make it clear that the 'intolerable' element is disjunctive and need have no connection with the Respondent's adultery,[8a] it may be something quite separate, such as prolonged marital unhappiness which culminated in the adultery: or even something more trivial. Sincc the test of intolerability must necessarily be a subjective one, the judge should in most cases have no difficulty in accepting the petitioner's evidence on this point. But if the Court does investigate the question more fully (pursuant to the duty imposed by section 2(2) of the 1969 Act), and discovers that the Petitioner has himself been committing adultery, or has con-

8. s.2(2).
8a. *Goodrich v. Goodrich* [1971] 1 W.L.R.1142.

nived at the Respondent's adultery, or is continuing to have intercourse from time to time with the Respondent, then it may be difficult to hold that the Petitioner finds it intolerable to live with the Respondent. Thus the old bars to divorce may arise in a new form (see p. 139) and the provisions of section 3(3)(b) of the Act, dealt with on p. 140.

However, it seems unlikely that any such difficulties will arise, and the general view seems to be that even a single act of adultery will be sufficient, in all but the most exceptional cases, to entitle a petitioner to a decree as of right. The proof of adultery and its legal consequences are dealt with in chapter 7.

A decree will not be granted on the ground of adultery if, after the adultery became known[9] to the Petitioner, the parties lived together for a period or periods totalling more than six months. This is the bar of condonation in a modified form. But if the parties came together, after the adultery had become known, for a period or periods of a total length of six months or less, this cohabitation shall be disregarded in determining whether the Petitioner finds it intolerable to live with the Respondent. This latter provision – together with those relating to cohabitation and its effect on a finding of separation 'unreasonable' conduct and desertion (see pp. 135 and 139) is intended to encourage parties to come together in an attempt at reconciliation.[10]

2. A Petitioner cannot reasonably be expected to live with a Respondent who behaves with cruelty to him or her, thus any conduct which falls within the definition of legal cruelty, as laid down in the case-law, will establish this 'fact' (for this see chapter 8). But the new provision obviously includes conduct falling short of legal cruelty as defined in *Russell* v. *Russell* (see p. 157). Ill-treatment other than physical violence is only cruelty if it caused injury to health or reasonable apprehension of such injury.[10a] But even without any danger to health, there may well be ill-treatment which makes it un-

9. Neither suspicion nor belief amount to knowledge (see *Burch* v. *Burch* [1958] All E.R. 848).

10. s.3(3).

10a. And still is in the Magistrates' Court.

reasonable to expect one spouse to continue to live with the other. It is already clear that the courts will be satisfied with the sort of conduct which has been regarded as sufficient to cause a spouse to leave the matrimonial home – that is, the standard required for constructive desertion (see p. 175), which will now rarely be grounds for a petition since the aggrieved spouse will bring a petition under section 2(1)(b) without waiting for two years desertion to elapse. But it will still be relied on in an answer and cross-petition. Such offences as rape, bestiality and sodomy, previously grounds in themselves, will fall under section 2(1)(b). Homosexuality or lesbianism, until now not matrimonial offences *per se*,[11] could no doubt be sufficient reasons for breakdown under 2(1)(b). Drunkenness, drug-taking, nagging, neglect, or any other aberration of conduct could fall within this wide definition, but the test of whether the conduct is of sufficient degree to qualify must be to a certain extent objective, since the judge will have to decide what it is reasonable to expect a spouse to tolerate. However, this cannot properly be assessed without some consideration of the Petitioner's capacity for endurance and the judge will still have to ask himself whether the conduct of *this* man to *this* woman is tolerable in all the circumstances.[12] The burden of proof is on the Petitioner to show that the Respondent behaved in such a way that he or she could not reasonably be expected to live with the Respondent, on the balance of probabilities: but in *Blyth* v. *Blyth*[13] the House of Lords laid down that in proportion as the offence is grave, so ought the proof to be clear.

Again, as in the case of adultery, provision is made to encourage reconciliation attempts, and any period or periods of cohabitation up to a total of six months is to be disregarded in determining whether the Petitioner cannot reasonably be expected to live with the Respondent.[14] But

11. Although they could be considered as cruelty (see p. 170).

12. See *Jamieson* v. *Jamieson* [1952] A.C. 525 and *Gollins* v. *Gollins* [1964] A.C. 644.

13. [1966] A.C. at p. 664.

14. s.3(4).

note that there is no question of approbation in respect of this cause of breakdown (see above under 'Adultery').

3. Desertion without cause for a continuous period of at least two years is subject to the same criteria in respect of the inception and termination as before (see chapter 9), save that it need now only last for two years. But the provisions of section 3 of the 1969 Act, which are designed to encourage reconciliation have a profound effect on the continuance of desertion.

In considering for the purposes of section 2(1) of this Act the period for which the Respondent has deserted the Petitioner or the period for which the parties to a marriage have lived apart, and in considering whether the desertion or the last mentioned period has been continuous, no account shall be taken of any one period (not exceeding six months) or of any two or more periods (not exceeding six months in all) during which the parties resumed living with each other (section 3(5)).

This means that a man can leave his wife in June 1968, come back to her in June 1969, leave her again in May 1970, and she will be able to petition for divorce the following month. There will still have to be proved both the *animus deserendi* and the *factum*, but a second parting, against the will of one spouse, even when the couple have spent nearly half of the requisite two years together, and not apart, may lead to some curious situations. It seems inevitable that we shall see parties divorced for desertion, who have been living together up to a few months before the hearing or even at the date of the hearing.

4. Separation for two years represents the first real breakthrough to divorce by consent. This will undoubtedly be the commonest type of 'breakdown' to be brought before the courts. In New Zealand, where a three-year period of separation is necessary, forty-six per cent of decrees are granted on this basis. Since, as we have seen, the period of separation can include one or more periods of cohabitation not exceeding in all six months, anyone who leads the sort of life quite common today in occupations ranging from travelling

sales representatives to diplomats may be able to establish grounds for divorce under this head at almost any moment of time. Unlike desertion, consent to the separation is no bar, but this is not necessarily the same thing as consent to the divorce.

The proviso that 'the Respondent consents to a decree being granted' does not require the Respondent to give any formal consent. The petition must be served on the respondent spouse, and the accompanying notice explaining the right to object, but thereafter silence will suffice. Section 5 of the Act gives a protection to the consenting Respondent:

> Where the court on granting a decree of divorce held that the only fact mentioned in Section 2(1) of this Act on which the Petitioner was entitled to rely in support of his petition was that mentioned in paragraph (d), it may, on an application made by the Respondent at any time before the decree is made absolute, rescind the decree if it is satisfied that the Petitioner misled the Respondent (whether intentionally or unintentionally) about any matter which the Respondent took into account in deciding to consent to the grant of a decree.

This provision makes it imperative for the Petitioner to make full disclosure to the Respondent of any fact which might affect the giving of consent. For example, it may be wise to inform the Respondent of the Petitioner's adultery.

5. Five years' separation as proof of breakdown, resulting in a divorce even without the consent of the other spouse, has been the most controversial aspect of this legislation. Because of this provision it has been dubbed both a 'Casanova's Charter' and a 'Jezebel's Justification': for the first time in our history a completely innocent 'spouse' may be divorced by the 'guilty' partner, without even the necessity for collusion. The provision is intended to assist those who leave the marriage and set up a second, illicit, establishment, often with children, and are unable to legalize their second union because the deserted spouse refuses to take divorce proceedings and has done nothing which would entitle the deserter to relief.

The meaning of 'separation', 'continuous period' and

'living apart' in this Act will have to receive judicial consideration, but help may be found in the case-law of some Commonwealth countries. New Zealand has had divorce on the ground of separation since 1920, Australia since 1961.[15]

Financial sanctions

The introduction of unilateral divorce, against an innocent and unwilling spouse, is intended to be counterbalanced and checked by the financial sanctions given to the court by section 4 of the 1969 Act:

> The Respondent to a petition for divorce in which the Petitioner alleges any such fact as is mentioned in paragraph (e) of Section 2(1) of this Act may oppose the grant of a decree nisi on the ground that the dissolution of the marriage will result in grave financial or other hardship to him and that it would in all the circumstances be wrong to dissolve the marriage. The Court can dismiss the petition if of the opinion that it would be wrong to dissolve the marriage.

On the face of it, this very wide discretion might be expected to prevent a divorce being granted against the will of a Respondent wherever it would be unjust to give the Petitioner relief. But it is doubtful whether many decrees will be refused under this section. When a man has been living for five years with another woman, and has three children by her, the interests of one of the parties to the marriage, of the illegitimate children and of the other woman concerned, will generally outweigh the somewhat dubious interest of the wife in having the shell of her marriage preserved. What the section should do is to give the judge a powerful weapon to extract proper financial provision for the first wife and family – where there is any money available to make such provision. But in the large majority of cases there will not be enough money to go round: what then is the judge to do? Should we preserve the marriage and prevent the man from legalizing his second family? Or will he not in most cases

15. A useful review of the Commonwealth cases appears in the eleventh edition of *Rayden on Divorce*, pp. 270–78.

decide that, in the words of Lord Simon in *Blunt* v. *Blunt*[16] 'it is contrary to public policy to insist on the maintenance of a union which has utterly broken down'. In the past, wherever a discretion has been given to a divorce court to withhold a decree, it has always come to be exercised in the Petitioner's favour and no doubt this discretion will operate in much the same way.

Further financial protection for the Respondent to a petition based on separation for two or five years under section 2(1)(d) and (c) is given by section 6 of the Act, which gives the court power to hear an application after decree nisi relating to financial arrangements, and the court shall not make the decree absolute unless satisfied either 'that the Petitioner should not be required to make any financial provision for the Respondent' *or* 'that the provision made by the Petitioner is reasonable and fair or the best that can be made in the circumstances.' The court must consider all the circumstances of both parties, including age, health, earning capacity, resources and obligations, and also the likely position of the Respondent after the death of the Petitioner. Thus the court will be able to make sure that a Respondent wife does not lose her pension rights, or is if possible compensated for her loss, before the decree is made absolute. But if there are circumstances making it desirable that the decree should be made absolute without delay, and the Petitioner has given the court a satisfactory undertaking to make such financial provision as the court may approve, the court can proceed to make the decree absolute without any such enquiry.

Encouragement of reconciliation

It has always been a ground for criticism of our law that large amounts of time and money are spent on breaking up marriages that have failed while almost no attention is paid to preventing breakdown or salvaging marriages that have gone on the rocks. 'To buttress, rather than to undermine, the stability of marriage' is a fine ideal, but one which it is

16. [1934] A.C. 517.

difficult to weave into divorce law. The 1969 Act makes some attempt at the introduction of reconciliation machinery into the law of divorce. Under section 3(1) rules of court may be made 'requiring a solicitor acting for a Petitioner for divorce to certify whether[16a] he has discussed with the Petitioner the possibility of a reconciliation and given him the names and addresses of persons qualified to help effect a reconciliation between parties to a marriage who have become estranged'. This seems a peculiarly useless provision. Any conscientious solicitor already does just this, unless he can see that reconciliation is hopeless, when going through the motions of inquiry, and the furnishing of a list of names of marriage guidance counsellors would be a farce.

A more useful provision is made by section 3(2) which gives the court, if it appears that there is a reasonable prospect of reconciliation, power at any stage of divorce proceedings to adjourn the proceedings once for such period as it thinks fit to enable attempts to be made to effect a reconciliation.

Much more important is the abolition of the bars of condonation, connivance, collusion and delay by the repeal of section 5(1) to (4) of the Matrimonial Causes Act, 1965. Under the old doctrine of the matrimonial offence, it was a complete defence to a charge of adultery or cruelty that the petitioner had *condoned* – that is forgiven and remitted – the offence by resumption of cohabitation, and in an undefended suit evidence of such forgiveness was a bar to the granting of a decree. The principle was sound: a husband should not be allowed to complain of his wife's adultery when he had reinstated her and taken her back to bed and board, especially as by resuming sexual relations with her he might have made her pregnant and it would be inequitable to reject her thereafter. The principle was applied to wives who forgave their erring husbands with less harshness and certainly with less cogency. Obviously this rule militated against reconciliation: a husband would think many times before running the risk of condoning his wife's faithlessness,

16a. Many solicitors certify that they have *not* discussed reconciliation.

when he was unsure that the experiment would work. *Connivance* – encouragement of, or complacency at the Respondent's adultery – was also an absolute bar; while *collusion* between the parties, once an absolute bar, had become a discretionary bar since 1963. *Delay* in bringing proceedings was always a discretionary bar. The existence of these bars inhibited experimental reconciliation and civilized communication between estranged spouses, and encouraged an injured party to hasten to the court to seek a remedy.

By section 3(3)(b) no party may rely on adultery if the parties have lived together for six months or more after the adultery was discovered. Further to encourage reconciliation, sections 3(3) and (4) of the new Act provide that the court must disregard any period or periods of resumption of cohabitation not exceeding six months in all whether the Petitioner finds it intolerable to live with the Respondent. Intolerable or the other conduct such that the Petitioner could not reasonably be expected to live with the Respondent. We have already seen the effect of section 3(5) on desertion and separation.

Agreements or arrangements between parties

The doctrine of the matrimonial offence required a Petitioner to come to the court to seek his remedy with an urgent sense of injury. If the parties agreed between themselves the manner in which the suit should be presented, or even the financial arrangements for wife and children after decree, they were in effect ousting the jurisdiction of the court, and asking the court to put an official stamp on their own bargain. The court frowned on such conduct (less sternly of late it is true) and collusion was a dreaded word among divorce practitioners. This made civilized negotiations between the parties a risky and inhibited process. The situation was relieved by legislation in 1963 making collusion a discretionary bar, and providing machinery for parties to bring proposed agreements before the court for leave to implement them at an early stage in the proceedings. Now although such a procedure is unnecessary to satisfy the court in respect of collusion, under section 7 of the 1969 Act, provisions may be made by rules of court for enabling agreements or arrangements for financial provision to be brought before the court and for enabling the court to express an opinion on the reasonableness of the agreement or arrangement and to give directions thereon. This continues the useful practice, under section 5 of the Matrimonial Causes Act, 1965, of bringing arrangements before the court for consideration quite separately from, and before, the hearing of the petition, so that the parties can know how their proposals are regarded by the court, and can put them into effect with confidence and expedition.

Petitioner's adultery, cruelty or other misconduct

Until the traditional bars to a divorce decree were abolished by the 1969 Act, the court had a discretion to refuse a decree to a Petitioner who had been guilty of adultery or cruelty, or, where the ground was adultery or unsoundness of mind or desertion. had been found guilty of such wilful neglect or misconduct as conduced to the adultery or unsoundness of mind or desertion. 'Conduct conducing' had been a dead letter for many years before it was formally abolished as a bar, and a Petitioner's own cruelty very rarely prevented him from obtaining a decree. But a Petitioner's adultery was a very different matter, since he was obliged to make full disclosure of it to the court, in the form of a discretion statement, and had to include a prayer for discretion in his petition, thus revealing to the Respondent that he had committed adultery. It is true that after *Blunt* v. *Blunt* (see p. 138) not many decrees were refused for this reason, but from time to time a judge would baulk at granting a decree to a Petitioner whose discretion statement revealed that he had been grossly promiscuous or had himself broken up the marriage.

The discretion statement is now a thing of the past, and a Petitioner need no longer disclose adultery to the court. But it remains a factor in determining whether the Respondent's adultery is 'intolerable', or whether his conduct has been such that the Petitioner cannot reasonably be expected to live with him. In this way it will no doubt feature in some defended divorces. Even in the undefended case, in deciding whether the Respondent's adultery was intolerable or whether conduct was bad enough to cause breakdown, a judge may have to take into consideration the Petitioner's own adultery, or any other misconduct, in the unlikely event of his knowing that there was such conduct on the part of the Petitioner.

No petition within three years of marriage

We saw in chapter 3 that the extension of the grounds of divorce made by A. P. Herbert's Act of 1937 were accompanied by a new restriction on divorce: henceforth no petition might be presented within three years of the marriage, unless the Petitioner could show exceptional depravity on the part of the Respondent, or that the Petitioner would suffer exceptional hardship if not allowed to start proceedings immediately. This remains the law.[17] Proceedings to obtain leave to petition within three years are commenced in a Divorce County Court by way of an originating application, accompanied by an affidavit setting out the grounds of the application, particulars of hardship or depravity, whether any, and if so what, attempts at reconciliation have been made, and details of any children. The application is heard by a County Court judge if undefended; if defended, it is transferred to the High Court. Some hardship and depravity are features of many divorce cases but the judge must be satisfied that they are really 'exceptional' before giving leave. Examples of hardship which would be regarded as exceptional are cruelty of such a nature that there is serious danger to life or to health, or adultery by a wife resulting in pregnancy, which would involve the husband in maintaining another man's child if he took her back. 'Exceptional depravity' can only be established if there is something particularly obnoxious about the offences alleged: for

17. Matrimonial Causes Act, 1965, s.2.

instance, a husband's adultery within a few weeks of the marriage, or with a servant in the house, or cruelty coupled with perverted lust. The judge will take into account the possibility of reconciliation, especially if there is a child, and will only give leave if there is absolutely no hope for the survival of the marriage. The principles on which the discretion is exercised were set out by the Court of Appeal in *Bowman* v. *Bowman*.[18]

The cost of divorce

It is difficult to tell yet what effect the changes in divorce law will have on the cost of the divorce. The transfer of jurisdiction from the High Court to the County Court appears to have made no difference to costs in non-legally aided cases. For a straightforward case with no inquiries to be made and no witness to be traced, the present minimum is about £100. Of this, something less than twenty pounds goes to counsel for preparing pleadings and appearing at the hearing,[19] and about fifteen pounds is absorbed by court fees and incidental disbursements. The balance is the solicitor's gross profit, but as his overheads are likely to be between sixty-five and seventy-five per cent the net profit to his firm will be around £20. If the solicitor conducts the case he may be able to reduce the fees, since he will not be employing counsel; but if he is a senior partner and very experienced, who values his time so that the loss of half a day in court away from his office is higher than counsel's fee, he may well charge more for doing the case himself. It must be stressed that it is uncommon for a divorce case to be completely straightforward, and also that the figures given are rough estimates; if the solicitor has to make investigations or employ agents, or has difficulty in serving papers on the Re-

18. [1949] P. 353.

19. The minimum brief fee in the County Court agreed between the Law Society and the Bar Council is nine pounds in London, or wherever there is a Local Bar, and eleven pounds elsewhere with a conference fee of three pounds in each case. These figures are likely to be increased. There is of course no maximum fee in non-aided cases.

spondent or Co-respondent, then the disbursements he has to make will necessarily be reflected in the total costs. And naturally solicitors vary in their charges; like anyone else with services to sell they can put their own price on these services, within certain limits defined by the profession. Defended divorces of course cost very much more; even so, the astronomical figures sometimes mentioned in newspaper reports are only incurred in cases of great length, where the parties are willing to pay extravagant fees to fashionable lawyers, and in any event are usually wildly inaccurate guesses by ill-informed reporters. When no figure is agreed at the outset, a client can always ask for a detailed bill of costs if he is dissatisfied, and he can ask for this bill to be referred to the Law Society. If he is dissatisfied with this reference, he may appeal to the Court. Thus no one can be required to pay exorbitant costs unless he himself agrees at the outset that no expense shall be spared.

A successful Petitioner will in many cases recover a substantial proportion of his costs from the Respondent or the Co-respondent. Where the wife is Petitioner she will almost always be awarded costs, but a husband is unlikely to get costs against his wife unless she has substantial means. In cases of adultery he will always get an order for costs from the Co-respondent, unless the latter can show that he had nothing to do with the break-up of the marriage as, for instance, where the wife was promiscuous; but the fact that he did not know that she was married will not generally exempt him, since he should have found this out. (Of course, if the wife is living as a prostitute, he cannot be expected to inquire into her married state, and he will not have to pay the costs.) An order for costs is by no means always satisfied.

Legal aid in divorce

For those of modest means, legal aid is readily available and has completely changed the divorce scene. Anyone whose disposable income – that is, what he has left after paying certain unavoidable expenses and after making allowance for his dependants – is £750 per annum or less can obtain assistance. This does not mean that litigation will be free. The Law Society, who run the Legal Aid Scheme, make themselves responsible for all costs, but fix a maximum contribution from the litigant after investigation of his means and require payment of this sum by instalments over a period of time. If the costs come to less than the contribution, the balance is returned. Often costs are recovered against the Respondent, or Co-respondent, and then the legal aid fund, after paying solicitor and counsel, reimburses the Petitioner with the balance. The great virtue of this scheme is that a man knows before he goes to law the most that he will have to pay; its disadvantage is that his opponent, even if successful, cannot, except in rare cases, recover more than nominal costs against him. The Legal Aid and Advice Act, 1949, section 2(2) laid down that a legally-aided litigant's liability under an order for costs made against him 'shall not exceed the amount (if any) which is a reasonable one for him to pay having regard to all the circumstances including the means of all the parties and their conduct in connection with the dispute'. In practice, this means that the order for costs is almost always limited to his maximum contribution for legal aid. The Legal Aid Act, 1964, made it possible for the Courts to award costs out of the Legal Aid Fund in certain cases, but it is unlikely that this will be done very often.[20] By and large legal aid has been a vast success, and it has certainly made divorce possible for innumerable unfortunate couples who were previously shut out from justice.

20. See *Nowotnik* v. *Nowotnik* [1965] 3 W.L.R. 920; *Gooday* v. *Gooday* [1969] P. 1; and *Hanning* v. *Maitland* [1970] 1 Q.B. 586, and *Povey* v. *Povey* [1971] 2 W.L.R. 381.

7 Adultery

Even in a period of undoubted sexual licence, adultery remains the greatest single cause of matrimonial breakdown. But it is the adultery of the wife, rather than that of the husband, which has traditionally been regarded as the great danger to the family. This is understandable since the practical results are likely to be more serious: whereas a man's unfaithfulness will, at the worst – that is, if it is discovered by his wife – cause pain and loss of love and trust, a woman's unchastity may saddle her husband with illegitimate children to support. Now that contraception is almost universal, the risk of 'confusion of progeny', which Dr Johnson took to be the great disadvantage of adultery, is much less, and properly tends to be personal rather than tied to the family by settlements and devolution on death. Thus the reasons for imposing different standards on men and women have almost disappeared. Yet the feeling remains that adultery is a more heinous offence in a woman: although adultery is no longer regarded by individuals as an offence against property, the bias is still there.

The development of the law reflects society's horror of the adulteress and her seducer, and easy tolerance of the husband's infidelity. Until very recently, discovered adultery in a woman meant social death, and even when divorce was not generally available, her husband was able, if rich enough, to divorce her by Act of Parliament for a single act of adultery. In spite of expense, many such Bills of Divorcement were brought by wronged husbands. But in all the reported cases, from the Reformation to 1857, there are only four in which a marriage was dissolved on a wife's petition, and in those cases the husband's adultery was committed in circumstances of 'aggravated enormity' – that is, the adultery was combined with incest, bigamy, rape, or some other beastliness. The Matrimonial Causes Act of 1857 perpetuated this distinction: while a husband could divorce his wife for a single act of adultery, she could not succeed unless the husband's adultery were aggravated by incest, rape, sodomy, cruelty, or desertion. It was not until 1923 that women were given equal rights with men in this respect. Furthermore, until 1857, as we have seen, adultery was an actionable wrong or tort, known as 'criminal conversation', for which the husband could obtain damages from his wife's seducer – an action which, needless to say, was not available to an injured wife. No Bill of Divorcement could be presented until the husband had brought a civil action for this tort. Although the tort of criminal conversation has been abolished, its shadow lingered on until 1971 in the award of damages against a co-respondent (see p. 155).

For the purposes of divorce, adultery can be defined as voluntary sexual intercourse between a married person and someone of the opposite sex other than the spouse during the existence of the marriage. The voluntary aspect is important: if a woman is raped, she is not guilty of adultery, although her ravisher is; similarly, if either party should be insane, or under the influence of drink or drugs so as to be incapable of understanding the nature and quality of their actions, the intercourse will not be adultery in the case of the person so affected. Then we have to consider what is meant by sexual intercourse. It seems clear from the cases that there must be some penetration of the vagina to amount to intercourse for this purpose, although possibly not as much as is required for consummation (see p. 118). In one case,[1] both the wife and the other man admitted to desiring intercourse, and indeed to attempting it for a long period, but since the man was unable to effect penetration the Court held that there had been no act of adultery. Again, it has been held that masturbation of a co-respondent by a wife is not

1. *Dennis* v. *Dennis* (Spillett cited) [1955] P. 153.

adultery.[2] But where acts of sexual indecency short of adultery are proved, the Courts will almost inevitably draw the inference that adultery was committed; the only defence which could conceivably succeed would be that the woman with whom a husband indulged in such practices was *virgo intacta*[3] (see p. 151); even that is not necessarily sufficient if the judge concludes that what Lord Birkenhead called 'some lesser act of sexual gratification' than full intercourse had occurred.[4]

Whether artifical insemination with semen from a donor other than the husband (AID) amounts to adultery has never been decided in this country. In Scotland, it has been held not to be adultery,[5] although in some American states the Courts have given a different answer. In this country, since the definition of intercourse requires penetration by the male organ, it is difficult to see how the injection of semen, even that of a stranger to the marriage, through medical intervention could amount to adultery. In any case there would usually be such consent by the husband that he could hardly be heard to say that the 'adultery' was itself intolerable.

Standard of proof and evidence of adultery

Adultery, although not a crime in English law as in New York and some other American states, was regarded by the Ecclesiastical Courts as a crime and by the civil courts as a serious tort ('criminal conversation'). Until recently the burden of proof was the same as in a criminal case. That is the judge had to be satisfied beyond reasonable doubt that the offence had been committed.[6] The less stringent test applied in civil proceedings,

2. *Sapsford* v. *Sapsford and Furtado* [1954] P. 394.
3. See also the passage from Lord Merriman's judgment in *England* v. *England* quoted on p. 150 below.
4. *Rutherford* v. *Richardson* [1922] P. 144.
5. *Maclennan* v. *Maclennan* (*or Shortland*) [1958] S.L.T. 12.
6. *Ginesi* v. *Ginesi* [1948] P. 179.

the balance of probabilities, was not enough for this serious offence although it was applied to the proof of other matrimonial offences. But in *Blyth* v. *Blyth*[7] the House of Lords, reviewing the whole question of burden of proof in matrimonial cases, altered this. It was held that so far as the grounds for divorce are concerned, the case, like any civil case, may be proved by a preponderance of probability but the degree of probability depends on the subject matter. In proportion as the offence is grave, so ought the proof to be clear. The word 'satisfied' in section 4(2) of the Matrimonial Causes Act, 1950, does not import a criminal standard of proof. Thus proof of adultery need not be beyond reasonable doubt, but it must be 'clear'. The burden of proof is always on the party alleging adultery, and there is no duty on the parties accused to disprove the allegation. The results of this proposition can be curious, and a situation sometimes arises which makes the law look foolish if it is not fully understood. It frequently happens that the evidence against the Respondent spouse fulfils the requirements of law and adultery is found proved, while the evidence against the person with whom adultery is alleged to have taken place is insufficient and he or she is dismissed from the suit. This does not occur so often since the Civil Evidence Act, 1968, made out-of-court statements admissible as evidence.

In the nature of things it is rare to find direct evidence of adultery. Indeed, an assertion by one spouse of having found the other *in flagrante delicto* is so unlikely as to be regarded with considerable suspicion. The nearest thing to direct evidence that is commonly available is a confession of adultery, and this is regarded by the Courts with even greater suspicion. For what could be easier than for parties who desired a divorce to put a spurious confession before the Court? It is therefore important for the Court to look at the circumstances in which the confession was made. If it is contrary to the interests of the party making it, as in the case of a wife

7. [1966] 1 A.C. 643.

who has everything to lose by such a confession, or where she is anxious for forgiveness, it will be accepted, if necessary without any supporting evidence; but where the confession is clearly made with an eye on the Divorce Court, and with a desire to marry someone else, then the confession must be corroborated. The usual corroboration is that of an enquiry agent who took the confession and speaks of the limited sleeping accommodation, the articles of man's and woman's clothing to be seen there, and possibly the presence of a child of the illicit union.[8] Where a co-respondent indicates in the form of acknowledgement of service of a divorce petition that he does not intend to deny the allegation of cruelty by defending the suit, this statement is not admissible against him as evidence of the adultery.[9]

In the absence of a confession, the evidence will be what is known as 'circumstantial'. In the case of adultery this means evidence of guilty passion and the opportunity to indulge it. Thus if a man and woman have shown the outward signs of desire, even with a persistent and unexplained seeking-out of each other's company, and it can also be shown that they have had the opportunity to commit adultery, then the Court will draw the natural inference. But this inference of adultery can be rebutted, and if the respondent goes into the witness-box and denies it he is entitled to be believed. In *England* v. *England*[10] a man and a woman, who admitted to being in love and wishing to marry, and to having discussed committing adultery, spent one night together in the woman's apartment. But they both gave evidence on oath that they had not committed adultery on that or any other occasion, that the woman had been ill, and that the man had sat by her bedside nursing her. They were believed: which is not to say that every such denial would be accepted by the

8. In *Comrs. of Customs and Excise* v. *Harz* [1967] 1 All E.R. 177 the House of Lords dealt with the admissibility of confessions in criminal cases. Much of the reasoning there applies to adultery cases.
9. *Inglis* v. *Inglis and Baxter* [1968] P. 639.
10. [1953] P. 16.

Courts. In his judgment in that case Lord Merriman summed up the law on inclination and opportunity as evidence of adultery in the following words:

'I decline to hold that there is any rule of law that the conjunction of strong inclination with evidence of opportunity leads to an irrebuttable presumption that adultery has been committed. That it affords very strong *prima facie* evidence is indisputable, but that is quite another thing. I am reluctant to drag in my own experience as a judge . . . but I should say from my own recollection that I have known several cases where, although the circumstantial evidence from which an inference of adultery has been sought to be drawn has been very strong – at least as strong as in this case – nevertheless one has been persuaded that the evidence of the parties denying that adultery had been committed must be accepted. I cannot believe that there is any law which obliges a Court to decide in a contested case, where there is strong *prima facie* evidence on the one side, and, maybe, strong circumstantial evidence supporting a denial on the other side, that, contrary to its own belief, adultery has been committed. I put to counsel, by way of testing how far this proposition went, the question whether, if a denial in the same terms as in this case was supported by the circumstantial evidence, supposing the alleged paramour to be a woman, that she was proved by medical evidence which left no doubt to be *virgo intacta*, it could still be said that the fact that the parties had spent a night alone in a room was not susceptible of an innocent explanation.'

A more recent case,[11] *Christian* v. *Christian and another*, illustrated the difficulty of proof in some cases, and showed that even the most experienced judges may disagree on the evidence required to satisfy the court. A wife charged her husband with adultery, the evidence being that he had written amorous letters to a girl, had been found in bed with her, and admitted that he had been guilty of indecent assaults on her (he had been convicted of the assault and sent to prison for twelve months). But he denied that he had actually committed adultery, although he had done everything short of the sexual act. There was equivocal medical evidence: the

11. (1962) 106 S.J. 430.

girl was still technically a virgin, her condition being consistent with some, but not complete penetration. The trial judge dismissed the wife's petition, finding that the adultery had not been proved beyond reasonable doubt. This decision was upheld on appeal, but only by a majority of two to one; Lord Justice Willmer dissented, saying there was abundant evidence of inclination and opportunity, and that adultery could, and should, be inferred from the husband's conduct.

Where the only evidence of adultery is that the respondent has stayed the night with an unnamed man or woman at a hotel, the Court's suspicions are always aroused, and the case is unlikely to succeed unless there is some background of adulterous inclination. For example, where a man has been in the habit of spending unexplained nights away from home, or has come home with lipstick stains on his shirt, or carried contraceptives of a type never used with his wife, the court may be satisfied on 'hotel evidence' even if the woman is not named. But there should always be an attempt to find out the name of the other man or woman in such a case, and there should be evidence that they did in fact occupy a room together.

Evidence that one spouse contracted venereal disease from the other is sufficient evidence of adultery, and for this purpose 'crabs' or 'the itch' has the same significance as syphilis or gonorrhoea – wrongly, some doctors might think. Visiting a brothel has been held to be evidence of adultery, but as in other cases where the Court draws an inference of adultery from a man's actions, he is entitled to deny it, and if his evidence is believed the inference will be rebutted.

Birth of a child when the husband could not possibly have been the father is proof of the wife's adultery, but the burden of proof has always been a heavy one, since the result is to bastardize the child; the burden of proof was altered by the Family Law Reform Act, 1969 section 26: it is now the balance of probabilities. However, if the child was conceived after a decree of judicial separation or a Magistrates Court separation order, there is a presumption of law that the child is a bastard. The difficulty in these cases is to know *when* the child was conceived; although the average period of gestation is 280 days, the court cannot accept this as a fact without expert evidence, and medical witnesses have proved difficult to tie down to either a minimum or a maximum period. In *Preston-Jones* v. *Preston-Jones*[12] the House of Lords refused to hold that the birth of a child 360 days after the last possible date of marital intercourse was of itself proof of adultery. This seems to be the legal high-water mark of prolonged pregnancy. The shortest period of gestation which has been accepted by the Courts is 174 days.[13] All such decisions would have been different after section 26 came into force.

Blood tests as proof of adultery

In certain cases a husband will be able to prove that a child born to his wife, and conceived at a time when he was having intercourse with her, must have been the result of an act of adultery because the child's blood-group is inconsistent with the husband being the father. In many cases the experts will be able to say positively from examination of the blood of the child, the husband, and the wife that the child cannot possibly have been fathered by the husband,[14] and adultery has been found proved on such evidence. However, blood tests can only exclude, never prove, fatherhood: scientists now claim that in nearly eighty per cent of cases where the man is *not* the father, paternity can be excluded beyond doubt by these tests. Where two men have had intercourse with a woman at the time of the conception of a child, it is said that there is a ninety per cent chance that blood tests will eliminate one man, thus showing the other must be the father.

In some cases, the scientist will be able to give useful statistics as to the probability of a man with a particular

12. [1951] A.C. 391.
13. *Clark* v. *Clark* (no. 1) [1939] P. 228.
14. *Hing* v. *Hing and Clifte* (1962) 106 S.J. 264; *F.* v. *F.* [1968] P. 506.

blood-picture being the father of any given child, but only in a relatively small number of cases will the degree of probability be sufficient to satisfy the court.

The importance of blood tests in elucidating paternity led the House of Lords in *Re L, an infant*[15] to rule that a judge of any division of the High Court might order a blood test on a child, if it is in his interests. But no such tests could be ordered on an adult, since a test done against the person's will would be an assault, and this severely limited the scope of blood-testing. However, the Family Law Reform Act, 1969[16] provides that a court may, in any civil proceedings, direct the use of blood tests. Consent is required, but the court may draw 'such inferences if any party does not comply as appear proper in the circumstances' (section 21).

The *timing of adultery* is important. Only adultery which has taken place since the marriage and before the date of the petition can be a ground for divorce, although it is always possible to file a supplemental petition setting out adultery which took place after the date of the original petition. But evidence of other acts of intercourse, either before marriage or since the petition, may in certain cases be admitted at the hearing. If, for example, a man asserts that his wife has committed adultery with a certain man during the marriage, but the only evidence is of opportunity, he could call evidence showing that she had had intercourse with that particular man before the marriage. But the fact that the wife had been incontinent with quite different men prior to marriage would probably be regarded today as irrelevant, and therefore inadmissible as evidence. Evidence of adultery after the date of the petition may always be given to show what inference should be drawn from earlier acts of familiarity, but in such a case the usual course would be to file a supplemental petition setting out the new adultery.

15. [1968] p. 119 and see p. 194. See also *W.* v. *W.* and *S.* v. *McC.* [1970] 3 W.L.R. 366.

16. S.20 of part 3 of the Act, which is not yet in force.

Damages for adultery

The common law action for damages for the tort of criminal conversation was abolished in 1857, but survived rather uneasily as the claim for damages for adultery until it was finally abolished by the Law Reform (Miscellaneous Provisions) Act, 1970, section 4. The claim had become increasingly anachronistic with the growth of the freedom of women and greater equality in sexual relations. It passes into legal history, together with the torts of seduction, enticement and harbouring, all based on the concept of wife and children as the husband's property (see p. 40).

Claims for damages made in petitions filed before 1 January 1971 are not affected and in such cases damages may still be awarded.

8 Cruelty and Unreasonable Behaviour

Legal concept of cruelty

Although cruelty as such is no longer a ground for divorce (see pp. 33–5) the legal concept of cruelty remains of great importance. It remains a ground for a separation order in the Magistrates' Court (where most matrimonial disputes are still heard) and it remains the basis of the test of conduct such that the petitioner cannot reasonably be expected to live with the respondent under section 2(1)(b) of the Divorce Reform Act, 1969 (this will be referred to henceforth as 'unreasonable behaviour'). It is therefore necessary to inquire into the present legal meaning of cruelty, and this can only be understood by looking at its history as a matrimonial offence.

Cruelty and love, especially sexual love, are closely intertwined in human nature. Cruelty is in fact the negative manifestation of an emotion of which love is the positive. Love of another induces the desire for power, and that power can be exerted by tenderness and the ties of affection or by bullying and violence. That cruelty and love are very close can be seen most vividly in the sexual act. All sexual intercourse contains an element of sadism: the desire to hurt the other partner is linked with the desire to please and satisfy even in the most normal unions (whatever they may be), while in perverted sex either the tenderness or the cruelty may prevail. If the gentler aspects of sexual love gain the upper hand in either the man or the woman, impotence or frigidity may result; if violence wins, the sexual act may be made intolerable and even dangerous.

The law has always recognized the possibility of this distortion of the sexual bond and has given some sort of protection to husbands and wives. The Ecclesiastical Courts granted a divorce *a mensa et thoro* to any spouse who could prove that the other had behaved with cruelty, but as we have seen there could be no dissolution of marriage on the ground of cruelty until 1937 (see pp. 62–3). Cruelty excused the injured party from the duty of cohabitation: the Courts would not make a decree for restitution of conjugal rights where the petitioner was shown to have been guilty of cruel conduct. When the newly constituted Divorce Court took over matrimonial causes in 1857, the same principles governed the granting of decrees of judicial separation, and when cruelty became a ground for divorce in 1937, the law relating to cruelty remained the same, save that a decree of dissolution was now possible in place of a separation decree.

Cruelty has never been defined by statute: all the law on cruelty is judge-made, and must be extracted from the cases. Since judges are human and live in society, they are affected by the prevailing social mood, and the law has developed accordingly. What would have been accepted as justifiable behaviour in the eighteenth century may well be regarded as intolerable today, so that acts which would not then have amounted to a matrimonial offence may now be held to be cruelty. But the basic principles relating to the law of cruelty have been extraordinarily consistent, and remain today unchanged from those governing the Ecclesiastical Courts, even though cruelty as a matrimonial offence is no longer a ground for divorce. While every case must be judged on its own facts – and it is here that social change has its effect – there are certain tests which must be applied to all cases, and it is these which have remained unaltered throughout the history of cruelty as a matrimonial offence. These tests were set out with clarity and authority in the case of *Russell* v. *Russell*,[1] the first of the modern authorities and still the basis of the law of cruelty.

In 1897 the House of Lords was called upon to decide whether the Countess Russell was guilty of cruelty such as would entitle the Earl to a judicial separation. The marriage had been short-lived and bitter: a few months after the wed-

1. [1897] A.C. 395.

ding the Countess petitioned for a judicial separation on the ground of the Earl's cruelty, alleging that he had been guilty of 'an odious crime in concert with one Mr R.'. Her counsel does not appear to have been greatly impressed with the evidence, since at the hearing of the suit he withdrew all charges of impropriety, and the jury acquitted the Earl of cruelty. But only four days after her petition had been dismissed there appeared in a newspaper a statement by the Countess that she had in her possession evidence of the Earl's guilt, which she had not produced at the trial partly out of regard for his family and partly from misapprehension of the course of the proceedings (or so she said). Since her counsel was the famous Sir Edward Clarke, it seemed highly unlikely that all available evidence was not brought before the Court, and the first reason she gave was belied by her subsequent conduct. Since she persisted in her allegations and followed them up by petitioning, somewhat inconsistently, for restitution of conjugal rights, the Earl was constrained to defend himself by cross-petitioning for a decree of judicial separation on the ground of his wife's cruelty. At the trial of the Earl's suit his wife's case was that, although she now realized her allegations to be unfounded, her conduct was excusable because she had based her charges on evidence in her possession. It turned out that she had never had any such evidence, and that her whole campaign against the Earl was a series of falsehoods. The jury found her guilty of cruelty, but the Court of Appeal held that there was no evidence of legal cruelty and set the decree of judicial separation aside. Eventually it fell to the House of Lords to hear the Earl's appeal and to decide whether or not his wife's persecution of him amounted to cruelty in law. In order to come to a decision, the House examined thoroughly the leading cases in the Ecclesiastical Courts, and drew from them a conclusion which governs the limits of legal cruelty to this day. In the words of Lord Davey:

'The general idea which, I think, underlies all those decisions [of the Ecclesiastical Courts] is that, while declining to lay down any hard and fast definition of legal cruelty, the Courts acted on the principle of giving protection to the complaining spouse against actual or apprehended violence, physical ill-treatment, or injury to health.'

In the Court of Appeal this had been put in rather different words, meaning much the same thing: it was said that the conduct must have caused 'danger to life, limb, or health, or given reasonable apprehension of such danger'. The Earl had suffered no physical violence nor had reason to apprehend any injury, and there was no evidence that his health had suffered, therefore his wife was not guilty of cruelty.

Although the law remains unchanged, the result would probably be different today: no doubt the Earl would be able to call medical evidence that he was suffering from nervous irritability, sleeplessness, loss of appetite, and incipient anxiety state, thus satisfying the requirement of 'injury to health'. But the decision in *Russell* v. *Russell*, although it remains the authority on cruelty, was only a majority one: out of the nine Law Lords sitting, four refused to impose so narrow a definition, and if they had had one more supporter, the whole of the law on cruelty would have developed differently. There was clearly a feeling at that time for a broadening of the ecclesiastical concept of cruelty, but once the House of Lords had made this momentous decision, it was final since by the rule of precedent it is binding on all lower courts and (in general) on the House of Lords itself.

This, then, is the nearest to a definition of cruelty that the law will come. Although it derives from the principles on which the Ecclesiastical Courts acted, those Courts were much more reluctant than the modern Divorce Court to find cruelty proved. One case is sufficient to illustrate this. In 1755[2] a wife proved that her husband had deserted her, taken her money, abused her, and sworn at her, and had finally locked her in a room with two men and in their presence threatened that these men would hold her down while he had forcible intercourse with her; on her escaping through the window and into a neighbouring house he fol-

2. *Holmes* v. *Holmes* (1755) 2 Lee 90.

lowed her and dragged her back by the hair. The Court of Delegates held that this was not legal cruelty:

She had charged nothing but words, except the single fact of dragging her by the hair, which happened after she had separated herself from him, and that was not a cruelty sufficient to entitle her to a divorce.

Today, such conduct would undoubtedly be held to be cruelty, even without the hair-pulling; thus does the law change, even while the principles remain the same.

Of course, the *Russell* v. *Russell* definition was not the end of the matter, since there is ample scope for argument as to the meaning of 'apprehended violence', 'ill-treatment', and even 'injury to health'. Conduct which would cause fear of violence or danger to health in one person might have no effect on another, sturdier temperament. Should the test then be objective or subjective? Must the conduct be such that it can be called cruel irrespective of the recipient, or must it be judged entirely by the reactions of the party against whom it is directed? The Courts have not shown any certainty on this, although the subjective test was favoured until recently. In *Jillings* v. *Jillings*,[3] where a strong, healthy husband complained of his wife's nagging for ten years yet could prove no injury to his health, Lord Justice Hodson said:

What may be cruelty to one person may not necessarily be cruelty to another. But I think it is clear that the test is not wholly subjective. When one talks about reasonable apprehension of injury to health, it is necessary to apply some objective test.'[3]

While it is not clear what Lord Hodson meant by those words, it is probably fair to say that the subjective test must be applied, but only so far as it seems reasonable to do so: in other words, the test is, 'Did this particular man's conduct cause injury (or fear of injury) to this particular woman?' but if the woman's sensitivity reaches beyond the bounds of reason, then it need not be taken into account. It is obvious

3. (1958) *The Times*, December 11.

that this gives a good deal of scope for variation in the judges' views of what is beyond reason, and indeed one finds in practice that judges do vary in their assessment of cruelty: this is a human problem, and a judge cannot, nor should he, leave behind any of his humanity when he sits on the bench.

In deciding whether or not conduct falls within the general definition of cruelty, different considerations will apply depending on whether or not there is an element of physical violence. Violence, unless very mild, must be cruelty, since it either causes danger to life or limb or reasonable apprehension of such danger. When cruelty was still a ground for divorce, even one act might be enough, if serious, although usually more was required. In the Magistrates' Court, since there the cruelty must be 'persistent' more than one act is always required. In the Divorce Court it was said that if there had been one assault of sufficient severity, and there was reason to believe the violence might be repeated, there was no obligation to await the repetition.[4] No doubt this principle will be followed in assessing what is tolerable. The true test with physical violence is whether it is of such a nature as to make it intolerable for the injured party to go on living in the married state, and this of course will depend on the capacity for endurance of the victim. To some husbands and wives the exchange of blows is part of the stuff of marriage, and it would be ridiculous to hold that a few bruises inflicted in a scuffle were sufficient to justify a divorce. But among more highly civilized people, or those who regard violence with horror, even one blow struck in anger may be sufficient to make married life unendurable for fear of a repetition of the injury. Sir J. Nicholl in *Westmeath* v. *Westmeath*[5] in 1827 put the position thus:

'A blow between parties in the lower conditions and in the highest stations of life bears a very different aspect. Among the lower classes blows sometimes pass between married couples who are in the main very happy and have no desire to part; amidst very coarse habits such incidents occur almost as freely as rude or

4. *Meacher* v. *Meacher* [1946] P. 216.
5. (1827) 2 Hag. Eccl. Supp. 61.

reproachful words: a word and a blow go together. . . . If a nobleman of high rank and ancient family uses personal violence to his wife, his equal in rank, the choice of his affection, the friend of his bosom, the mother of his offspring – such conduct in such a person carries with it something so degrading to the husband and so insulting and mortifying to the wife as to render the injury far more severe and insupportable.'

Although class distinctions have largely disappeared, and refinement of conduct is by no means universal in the 'highest stations', differences of temperament still remain, and must be taken into account. The real test is whether the violence was resented *at the time*; and it is obvious that a blow struck with the intention of hurting will cause more suffering than the same blow struck in an explosion of temper. This must be particularly true when deciding whether conduct has been such as to make it unreasonable to expect one spouse to continue to live with the other. But these cases of physical violence cause little difficulty, and here at any rate the layman and the lawyer have much the same standards of what is and is not cruelty.

It is in what is loosely called 'mental cruelty' that the difficulties arise. Greater suffering can probably be inflicted by one human being on another by a course of conduct calculated to injure the feelings than by any degree of physical violence. The greatest evil one spouse can do to another is to erode all confidence and destroy all quietness of mind by repeated nagging, abuse, or calculated neglect. Most people would willingly exchange the drawn-out misery of life with a husband or wife who is determined to humiliate at every opportunity for the odd outburst of violence. The law has long recognized that there can be cruelty without violence, but sensibilities become more acute as life becomes easier, and the standards of 'mental cruelty' have changed a good deal over the last thirty years. The subjective test should be much more important here than in cases of physical injury, and the attitude of the judge is therefore more important. But the sympathy of the Court cannot be the test, or there would be no certainty and as we have already seen certainty of the law is one of the first essentials of justice. The law must limit the definition of such cruelty without ever closing the classes of conduct which may from time to time be held to be grounds for divorce. This has proved to be one of the most difficult tasks ever imposed on the English Courts. On the one hand, the law must be kept flexible, since cruelty is a matter of personal feelings and these must change in changing circumstances. On the other hand, new grounds for divorce, never intended by Parliament, could not be allowed to creep in under the guise of variations of cruelty. (The fact that Parliament has now opened the door much wider is another matter.)

How then have the Courts solved this problem? What is 'mental cruelty' in the eyes of the law? Baron Channel said as long ago as 1870 in *Kelly* v. *Kelly*:[6]

'It is obvious that the modes by which one of two married persons makes the life or health of the other insecure are infinitely various, but as often as perverse ingenuity may invent a new manner of producing the result, the Court must apply the remedy by separating the parties.'

To answer the questions posed, therefore, we have to try to extract some principles from the cases – there can be no hard and fast rule, and there is no branch of the law where experience of the Courts is so vital in advising on any particular set of facts. Examples of decided cases may to some extent take the place of experience, but individual decisions are sometimes misleading and it is better to rely on the principles which run through the whole of the case-law.

The first of these principles we have already referred to: one test of whether any conduct is cruel is whether or not it caused suffering in the particular person against whom it was directed. In other words, the capacity for endurance of the victim must be taken into account. Another principle is that the conduct must be looked at as a whole, and its cumulative effect be considered. Acts which could never amount to cruelty if taken by themselves may, if repeated or added to

6. (1870) L.R. 2 P. & D. 59.

other conduct, add up to grave injury. Lord Reid said in 1952 in *Jamieson* v. *Jamieson*:[7]

'there can hardly be a more grave matrimonial offence than to set out on a course of conduct with the deliberate intention of wounding and humiliating the other spouse and making his or her life a burden... Such conduct may consist of a number of acts each of which is serious in itself, but it may well be even more effective if it consists of a long-continued series of minor acts no one of which could be regarded as serious if taken in isolation.'

These words include and describe the sort of conduct presumably envisaged by section 2(1)(b) of the 1969 Act.[8]

The third principle governing mental cruelty, and the most complex, is that of motive. If a man strikes his wife, unless it is an accident or he is insane, he will be assumed to intend to hurt her; but if he nags her, neglects her, tyrannizes her, or abuses her, the assumption of motive is not so easily made. He may be domineering, feckless, or ill-tempered by nature; how far is his conduct part of what his wife accepted 'for better or worse', and how far is an intention to injure relevant to a finding of cruelty? Over the past ten years the divorce judges have been divided on this question of motive, and there have been several shifts of judicial opinion. It would seem reasonable to require evidence of some sort of intention to injure, since it is, on the face of it, illogical to describe as cruel the conduct of a person who does not know what he is doing. As we shall see (p. 167) it has now been finally decided that it is unnecessary to prove *intent*, but judicial opinion was long divided on this point. Lord Denning, for example, always took the view that the intention must be clearly shown by the manner in which the injury is inflicted: the conduct must in some sense be 'aimed at' the injured spouse, and not merely be a defect of temperament.

7. [1952] A.C. 525.

8. See also *J.* v. *J.* (1967) 111 S.J. 792, and *Walker* v. *Walker* (1967) 111 S.J. 463.

Other judges, led by a former President of the Divorce Division, Lord Merriman, took a broader view: a man must be taken to intend the natural and probable consequences of his acts, they said, and if those acts did cause injury to health, then they would amount to cruelty, whatever he intended the result to be.

The Denning school of thought was clearly expressed by his Lordship in the Court of Appeal in *Kaslefsky* v. *Kaslefsky*.[9]

'If the door of cruelty were opened too wide [he said], we should soon find ourselves granting divorce for incompatibility of temperament. This is an easy path to tread, especially in undefended cases. The temptation must be resisted lest we slip into a state of affairs where the institution of marriage itself is imperilled.'

Two cases which followed this – one a Scottish case in the House of Lords[10] and one an appeal from New South Wales in the Privy Council, *Lang* v. *Lang*[11] – were soon to dispose of the 'for better or for worse' school of thought: the principle that a man was to be presumed to intend the natural consequences of his actions became firmly entrenched in divorce law, and it seemed that Lord Denning's worst fears might be realized. The application of this principle could make almost any conduct 'cruelty', provided there were injury to health, and some Courts allowed through cases which fall far short of what Parliament had envisaged when making cruelty a ground for divorce. The section says that the respondent must have 'treated' the petitioner with cruelty, and surely this imports something in the nature of an intent to injure? The injustice which can result from this development in the law was vividly shown in *Alway* v. *Alway*:[12] the husband there showed that his health had been injured by his wife's fanatical devotion to cleanliness, which ruined their domestic life and interfered with his

9. [1951] P. 38.
10. *Jamieson* v. *Jamieson*, above.
11. [1955] A.C. 402.
12. (1961) 105 S.J. 725.

work. She insisted on elaborate rituals of dressing and undressing and preparation of food; their diet was eventually reduced to biscuits and frozen food because she would only admit packaged food to the house; when her husband brushed against a coloured man in the street he had to bath and change his clothes before coming into the living-room. There was medical evidence that the wife's conduct was entirely due to an obsessional neurosis, apparently incurable. Since she was not legally insane (see p. 171) she must, the Court held, be taken to intend the natural and probable consequences of her actions; *ergo*, she was guilty of cruelty. That this was the law at that date there can be no doubt and no one could have taken greater care than the judge who tried the case. That the result was a great blessing to the husband is also beyond question, but could there be anything further from the commonly accepted meaning of 'cruelty'? The unfortunate wife no doubt suffered as much as her husband: to stigmatize her as cruel is surely a mockery of the law, but it follows inevitably from the neglect in subsequent decisions of Lord Denning's words in *Kaslefsky* – 'The presumption that a person intends the natural consequences of his acts is one that may – not must – be drawn.'

But soon after this there were signs that the law might be veering back to the stricter interpretation of cruelty. The late President of the Divorce Division, Lord Simon, showed that his sympathies were with the school of thought which required some evidence of intent in conduct which was to be labelled as 'cruel'. However, Lord Justice Danckwerts said in the Court of Appeal in *Hall* v. *Hall*[13] that there was too much talk in matrimonial cases of one party accepting the other 'for better or for worse', or about behaviour which a party 'bargains to endure'; such phrases might have some sense in countries which did not recognize divorce, but within the jurisdiction of the English Courts they seem to be 'something of a cynical jest'.

This uncertainty was deplorable. People do not usually

13. [1963]. P. 178 This was a case of desertion but the same principles apply as in cruelty and unreasonable behaviour.

enter into bargains without knowing what they are taking on, but until recently even a judge of the Court of Appeal could not be certain of what the law required him to put up with in marriage. However, in *Gollins* v. *Gollins*[14] the House of Lords finally laid down (but only by a majority of three judges to two) that it was unnecessary to show any malevolent intention in order to prove cruelty. That case went a very long way to establish that *any* conduct, however brought about, which causes injury to health or apprehension of injury, is cruelty. In other words, the nature of the act scarcely matters, only its result.

It seemed as if this would be the end of judicial doubt about the nature of cruelty. But subsequent cases (especially *McEwan* v. *McEwan*[15] and *Le Brocq* v. *Le Brocq*[16] showed that there were still two schools of thought. The Court of Appeal refused to apply some of the tests laid down by the House of Lords in *Gollins*; Lord Justice Harman went so far as to say (in *Le Brocq*) that 'cruelty is what it always was', and that some of the things said in *Gollins* 'set the ball rolling down that slippery slope which may end in the last resort in absurdity'. The safest view at present is that 'cruel' still *means* cruel: before a charge of cruelty can be made out there must be some misconduct, of a grave and weighty nature, which an ordinary man, or a jury, would describe as cruel in the ordinary and natural meaning of that word. But cruelty as such is only important now in the Magistrates' Court (see p. 94) where it must be persistent and there must be injury to health. Where a divorce is sought on the ground of breakdown under section 2(1)(b) there will be no necessity to prove injury to health, although such injury would be strong evidence of unreasonable behaviour. In the light of these still somewhat conflicting principles we can now look at examples of conduct which may, in certain conditions, amount to legal cruelty, and *a fortiori* as unreasonable behaviour. But it must be

14. [1964] A.C. 644.
15. (1964) 108 S.J. 198, C.A.
16. [1964] 3 All E.R. 464.

remembered that in most cases the conduct complained of is not confined to one particular matter, but is an accumulation of different offences, and the allegations must be looked at *as a whole*. And it must also be emphasized that, in the absence of physical violence, there can be no legal cruelty unless injury to health, or danger of such injury, is proved.

Nagging is perhaps one of the chief causes of matrimonial unhappiness, but in its common form it can hardly be cruelty. It must be something outside the ordinary wear and tear of married life; if long-continued, it may well affect health, and it will then amount to cruelty. Mr Justice Henn Collins in *Atkins* v. *Atkins* described this sort of conduct vividly:

> 'One knows that dropping water wears away the stone. Constant nagging will become completely intolerable, and though in the case of married life you may be able to point to no single instance which could possibly be described as, in common parlance, 'a row', yet nagging may be of such a kind, and so constant, that it endangers the health of the spouse on whom it is inflicted. Then this Court intervenes, as it always will intervene, for the protection of the person.'[17]

False accusations of infidelity, *threats*, and *vulgar abuse* fall into the same category as nagging, and must be tested in the same way. *Domineering conduct* may also be cruelty: the classic case is an old one, *Kelly* v. *Kelly*, where the husband, who was a religious fanatic, believed it to be his duty to make his wife subservient to him; he accordingly forced her to eat and sleep apart from him, censored her correspondence, and accused her of apostasy. Her health suffered, and the Court held that he had treated her with cruelty, although not intending to harm her.[18]

Neglect and *lack of affection* by themselves can hardly amount to *cruelty*, but where a man caused injury to his wife's health by consistently failing to work and provide for her he

17. *Atkins* v. *Atkins* [1942] 3 All E.R. 248.
18. *Kelly* v. *Kelly* (1870) L.R. 2 P. & D. 59.

was held to be guilty of cruelty, although there was no suggestion that he *intended* to injure her: he was simply incorrigibly and inexcusably lazy.[19]

Drunkenness can be cruelty, especially if long-continued and accompanied by particularly revolting features, always provided that it has caused injury to the other spouse's health.[20] For example, where a man insists on driving his wife in a motor-car when he is drunk, he is cruel because he endangers her life.[21] Drug addiction is similar to drunkenness: where it is persisted in with full knowledge of its ill-effects on the other spouse, it can be cruelty.[22] *Crime* will only be cruelty if it involves the other party in some way – as for instance where a husband is convicted of an indecent assault on the wife's child[23] – or if a life of crime is persisted in after remonstrances from the wife and broken promises to reform. Cruelty to the children of the family, or the petitioner's children, can be cruelty,[24] and indecent assaults on the children will almost certainly be cruel.[25]

Philandering, whether to the lengths of adultery or not, may be cruelty if it is carried on with a deliberate intention of hurting the other spouse, or without caring what effect it has.[26] *Refusal of sexual intercourse* can also be cruelty if it is persisted in without excuse and causes injury to health[27]; and the use of *contraceptives*, or the practice of *coitus interruptus* are certainly cruelty if carried on with the knowledge that they are causing injury to the other party's health.

Mr Justice Sachs in *Knott* v. *Knott*[28] called such conduct 'criminal', 'at any rate where the husband adopts a course which preserves to himself a measure of sexual enjoyment'.

19. *Gollins* v. *Gollins* [1964] A.C. 644.
20. *Baker* v. *Baker* [1955] 1 W.L.R. 1011.
21. *Renwick* v. *Renwick* (1960) *The Times*, 9 March.
22. *Higginson* v. *Higginson* (1960) *The Times*, 12 February.
23. *Cooper* v. *Cooper* [1955] P. 99.
24. *Wright* v. *Wright* [1960] 1 All E.R. 678.
25. *Cooper* v. *Cooper* [1955] P. 99; and *Ivens* v. *Ivens* [1955] P. 129.
26. *Walker* v. *Walker* [1961] 2 All E.R. 14.
27. *Sheldon* v. *Sheldon* [1966] P. 62.
28. *Knott* v. *Knott* [1955] P. 249.

The same considerations apply to a refusal to have children, save that here there is a distinction between the sexes: a wife may have a good defence if she can show that her refusal was due to an inordinate fear of childbirth;[29] there has been no reported case of a husband pleading that he refused intercourse because he feared for his wife's sufferings in bearing children.

Sexual perversions whether indulged in within the marriage or outside it, may be cruelty or unreasonable conduct. Sodomy on the part of a husband was a ground for divorce, whether committed on his wife or with another person, and without any evidence of injury to health. But a wife's lesbianism was only cruelty: now it would be unreasonable conduct.[30] Where unnatural conduct is alleged between husband and wife, it is very difficult to prove, since corroboration is usually impossible and the complaining party is usually an accomplice – consent is, of course, a complete defence.[31] The difficulty in these cases is to know what is perversion, since in sexual matters one man's meat is another man's poison. A common charge in cruelty and unreasonable behaviour cases, for instance, is that the husband has made 'excessive sexual demands' on his wife, but who can lay down any rule as to the amount of intercourse which is normal and what is 'excessive'? Again, wives often take part willingly at first, and with enjoyment, in elaborations of the sexual act which later, when passion has died, they describe as revolting and cruel; but the test is, how were these acts received at the time? It can be seen how difficult the Court's task is in such cases, and with what care charges of sexual cruelty must be examined.

Defences

Apart from an outright denial, there are three obvious defences to a charge of cruelty or unreasonable behaviour: pro-

29. *Forbes* v. *Forbes* [1956] P. 16; *Fowler* v. *Fowler* (1952) 2 T.L.R. 143.
30. *Gardner* v. *Gardner* [1947] 1 All E.R. 630.
31. *Statham* v. *Statham* [1929] P. 131; although this is not so if unreasonable behaviour is alleged.

vocation, self-defence and consent. If a man strikes his wife when he finds her committing adultery he cannot be said to be cruel, or to be behaving unreasonably, nor if he injures her in an attempt to ward off an attack, nor if she consents to physical violence in the course of love-making. But the violence used must be in proportion to the provocation or the attack. It would be no defence to a man who had knocked his wife unconscious to prove that she had just slapped his face.[32]

Insanity is no longer a defence to cruelty, nor, therefore, can it be a defence to a charge of unreasonable behaviour. But for many years there was doubt as to the effect of a Respondent's insanity. Whether or not it should be a defence to a charge of cruelty depends on the purpose of a divorce decree: is it intended to protect the injured spouse, or is it a form of punishment for the cruel one? The old judges certainly regarded the law of cruelty as protective, but the difficulty of that view was that it must lead to a finding of cruelty where there could be no possible intent to injure – that is, where the acts complained of were due entirely to disease of the mind. The concept of responsibility for wrongful acts was thought to be a vital principle of modern English law, and in 1953 in *Swan* v. *Swan*[33] the Court of Appeal held that insanity was a complete defence to a charge of cruelty. The definition of insanity for this purpose was the same as in the criminal law: to establish this defence, a man must show that as a result of disease of the mind, *either* he did not know the nature and quality of his acts, *or* he did not know his acts were wrong. This definition is that imposed by a set of answers, given to certain questions from the House of Lords, by all the judges after the acquittal of one Daniel McNaghten on the ground of insanity when he was charged with the murder of Sir Robert Peel's private secretary in mistake for that statesman: these conclusions of the judges are always known as 'the McNaghten Rules', and they have been the binding authority on criminal insanity since 1843. Anyone who came within this definition of insanity – one

32. *Stick* v. *Stick* [1967] 1 All E.R. 323.
33. [1953] P. 258.

which, incidentally, could never be recognized by any medical man, let alone a psychiatrist – could not therefore be guilty of cruelty. Indeed, 'insanity' in the generally accepted sense was not essential to the defence: if the injurious act was committed under a delusion that the act was justified, it could not be cruel, although other acts committed by the same person over the same period of time might be cruel if they were not the result of those delusions.[34] Thus a man might be perfectly sane in general, yet for the purpose of certain acts he could come within the McNaghten Rules and therefore be legally – although not medically – insane. This was only one of the unsatisfactory results of the application of a rule of thumb to the test of responsibility.

But in 1963 the law changed completely. The House of Lords ruled in *Williams* v. *Williams*[35] – but only as in *Gollins* (see page 167) by a majority of three to two – that insanity was no defence to a charge of cruelty: even if the acts complained of were a direct result of severe mental illness, they are still cruelty if they caused injury, or apprehension of injury, to the other spouse. This is the final answer to the question posed on the previous page: a divorce is for the protection of the innocent, and the 'guilt' of the offending party is irrelevant. The results of this decision have been far-reaching, as they struck at the very root of the matrimonial offence as the only acceptable ground for divorce. Why should not physical illness, as well as mental disturbance and failure of character, be a ground for divorce? A wife can suffer as much as the result of her husband's cancer as from the effects of his schizophrenia. It was hard to reconcile this development of the law with the reaction which took place after *Gollins* (see p. 167) and it became clear that the state of the law relating to cruelty made the doctrine of the matrimonial offence as the only ground for dissolution quite untenable. The Divorce Reform Act, 1969, by abolishing the matrimonial offence as the *direct* ground for divorce, removed this anomaly in the divorce court at least. In Magis-

34. *Elphinstone* v. *Elphinstone* (1962) 106 S.J. 392.
35. [1964] A.C. 698.

trates' Courts it still persists.

The effect of resumption or continuance of cohabitation after the conduct complained of has been dealt with on p. 139 with reference to divorce. In the Magistrates' Courts condonation remains a bar (see p. 101).

9 Desertion and Separation

One of the clearest possible indications that a marriage has broken down is that the spouses are living permanently apart. This separation may be by agreement, because they have both found the married state inconvenient or intolerable, or it may be due to a unilateral withdrawal from that state by one spouse from the other. The Divorce Reform Act, 1969, in making breakdown the sole ground for dissolution of marriage, logically made separation one of the facts which may be relied on as proof of breakdown. For the first time, separation without any element of guilt becomes a ground for dissolution. This has made a profound difference to the whole law relating to desertion, but it must be remembered that in Magistrates' Courts innocent or consensual separation is no ground for an order, and both in these courts and in divorce cases where one spouse will not consent to a divorce, the law of desertion will remain of considerable importance. In particular, two years' separation will be sufficient for a divorce even without the other spouse's consent if desertion can be proved against the Respondent; if there is no desertion in law, then five years of separation must pass before the Petitioner can seek a decree[1] unless the Respondent consents to a divorce.

Desertion

Since the basis of the marriage contract is the agreement to live together, it follows that it must be a breach of that contract, and therefore a matrimonial offence, for one spouse to desert the other. So much is clear, but the difficulty arises in defining what amounts to desertion. Obviously there must be some partings in marriage – the husband who

1. Divorce Reform Act, 1969, s.2(1) (c) and (e).

serves abroad in the Forces and the woman who goes away to nurse a sick relative can hardly be said to be in desertion – and equally there must be occasions when one party is entitled to leave because the other's conduct is intolerable. No law would be so harsh as to expect a wife to stay in the house where her husband was living with his mistress, or to go on living with a man whose cruelty threatened her life. Under the Divorce Reform Act, 1969 a spouse is entitled to a divorce if the marriage has broken down because of the other's behaviour (see p. 131). We have already seen (p. 83) that the law recognizes the right of spouses to agree to live apart, so there can be no desertion where the separation is by consent. These are obvious examples, but the complexities of the law lie in those cases where the Courts must decide what amounts to justification for leaving, who in fact brought about the separation, or whether there was consent.

Definition

Desertion has always been a matrimonial offence, which the Ecclesiastical Courts could punish by excommunication or imprisonment, and it could be the ground for a restitution decree (see p. 85) or judicial separation, but it was not a ground for dissolution until 1937 (see p. 62). Although so long regarded as a matrimonial offence, like cruelty it has never been exactly defined. The essence of desertion is the withdrawal by one spouse from a state of things – the whole of the rights and obligations incidental to marriage – without any justification and without the consent of the other. It is not enough that there should be withdrawal from the matrimonial home: a man may stay in the home but make it such a hell for his wife that she is forced to leave, and he will then be in desertion, not she. To constitute the offence itself, as opposed to being proof of breakdown, the separation need not take place for any particular length of time, but there must be an intention on the part of the deserter to bring life together permanently to an end – the most prolonged absence, even if induced by pique or a desire to avoid responsibilites, will not amount to desertion if the intention to return eventually is still there. But the intention to go is not enough in itself: there must in fact be a separation. Thus until these two elements coincide – an actual physical separation and an intention to remain apart for ever – there can be no desertion: there must be both *animus* and *factum deserendi.*

One of these two elements may be present for many years without there being desertion, but if at any time the other requirement is satisfied the offence will start from that date. *Beeken* v. *Beeken*[2] vividly illustrates this. In 1941 a man and his wife were interned by the Japanese in a camp at Amoy, China, where they occupied twin beds in the same room. Early in 1942 the wife became friendly with a Norwegian, began to spend all her free time with him, and refused to have intercourse with her husband. By the end of 1942 the wife was asking her husband to promise to divorce her on her release, but he refused. Throughout this time they were perforce living together, but although they were at arms' length neither seems to have tried to persuade their captors to let them live separately. In June 1943 the Japanese moved them to Shanghai and put them in separate camps. In March 1944 the wife was allowed to visit her husband, and she then asked again about divorce and said that she was determined to marry the Norwegian. After their release in 1945 the wife never rejoined her husband. When the husband petitioned for divorce in 1947 on the ground that his wife had deserted him for three[2a] years or more, the judge held that there had been no desertion either in 1942 or in 1944, because at the earlier date they were living together, albeit without any choice in the matter, and later they were separated by their captors, not of their own motion. Three judges in the Court of Appeal unanimously rejected this decision and gave the husband his divorce: they held that in 1944 the wife already had the intention to desert, and at the time of the actual separation desertion became complete.

2. [1948] P. 302.

2a. Three years desertion was necessary for a decree before 1 January 1971.

Two of the appeal judges agreed with the earlier decision that there could be no desertion in 1942 because the parties were still living together, although against the wife's will; but Lord Justice Bucknill did not agree with this, saying 'If spouses are compelled by their gaolers to live in the same bedroom, the reasoning which prevents a spouse from establishing desertion where they voluntarily share the same bedroom seems to me to disappear.' It is rare in peacetime for married couples to be shut up in one room by force, but probably if a wife were compelled to share her husband's home by some insuperable difficulty, desertion could still arise.

It is not always easy to say whether in fact there has been a physical separation, there must be a complete end to all cohabitation. It is not sufficient that some of the rights and obligations of matrimony have been abandoned; if a wife withdraws to a separate bedroom and refuses to have intercourse of any kind with her husband, yet continues to cook for him or to take her meals at the same table, there is not sufficient separation. But since 'desertion is not a withdrawal from a place, but from a state of things', there can be desertion even if husband and wife continue under the same roof, provided they live as two separate households. When accommodation is difficult it may be impossible for the party who is minded to leave – especially a wife with small children – to find anywhere else to live at short notice, but if the intention is there and all marital relations are broken off, there can still be desertion. By section 2(5) of the Divorce Reform Act, 1969 a husband and wife shall be treated as living apart unless they are living with each other in the same household.

Constructive desertion

It makes no difference which party leaves the matrimonial home: provided one of them has the firm intention to bring married life to an end, and either leaves or behaves in such a way as to force the other out, that one will be in desertion. As the President of the Divorce Division, Sir Henry Duke, said in *Pulford* v. *Pulford*[3] in 1923:

3. [1923] P. 18.

'Desertion is not the withdrawal from a place, but from a state of things. The husband may live in a place and make it impossible for his wife to live there, though it is she and not he that actually withdraws; and that state of things may be desertion of the wife. The law does not deal with the mere matter of place. What it seeks to enforce is the recognition and discharge of the common obligation of the married state.'

Where one drives the other out, it is called 'constructive' desertion. The sort of conduct which is regarded as sufficient in law to drive the other out has never been defined, but it must be something substantial. An obvious case would be where a husband physically put his wife out in the street and barred the doors against her, but such conduct is rare. It is not necessary that any expulsive words should be used, but there must be conduct from which the Court can *infer* that there was an intention to drive out. For instance, where a husband behaves in such a way that he knows his wife's health will be affected if he continues and she will be obliged to leave him – as where a husband persists in familiarity with another woman,[4] or invades his wife's personal freedom by insisting on her submitting to the fanatical rules of the sect of Jehovah's Witnesses,[5] – it will be no defence to him to say that he did not *want* her to leave. A man is intended to presume the natural and probable consequences of his actions.[6] This presumption can be rebutted by evidence to the contrary, but where the conduct is serious it is almost impossible to do so. Certainly it is not enough to say 'I knew she would go if I did not change, but I still hoped she would stay.' But if there is no mental capacity to form an intention, there is no desertion.[7]

How bad must conduct be to amount to 'driving out'? Not every blameworthy act justifies the other partner in leaving: the conduct must be of a grave and weighty character, not just part of what Lord Justice Asquith called 'the reasonable wear and tear of married life', for if that were to be a ground

4. *Morse* v. *Morse* (1959) *The Times*, 2 June.
5. *Patching* v. *Patching* (1958) *The Times*, 25 April.
6. *Lang* v. *Lang* (1955) A.C. 402.
7. *Perry* v. *Perry* [1963] 3 All E.R. 766.

for divorce, 'a heavy toll would be levied on the institution of matrimony'. Mere neglect, refusal of sexual intercourse, drunkenness (without violence), sulking and taciturnity are usually not sufficient of themselves, for everyone who marries must be prepared to accept some defects of temperament and behaviour. Yet during the last ten years the courts have leaned towards a more critical standard of matrimonial behaviour. The change is well illustrated by two cases in the Court of Appeal, one in 1947 and the other in 1962. In the first case[7a] a farmer's wife complained of her husband's rude and inconsiderate behaviour to her, and in particular his neglect of her for the society of his pigman. When she complained that she was humiliated by this unusual association, her husband told her 'if she did not like it, she could clear out and go and live with her mother'. She petitioned for divorce, and succeeded at first instance, but on appeal three judges unanimously held that his conduct was not expulsive, nor did it justify her in leaving, and accordingly he was granted a decree on his cross-petition. This decision effectively checked any tendency to introduce divorce for mere matrimonial unhappiness by a side-wind. Yet judges found a way to grant a decree in many cases less promising than *Buchler* and this inevitably led to inconsistency. For example, in one case[8] a husband was refused a decree although forced to leave by his wife's persistent sluttish behaviour which he found quite intolerable, while in another[9] a wife who persisted in keeping an inordinate number of cats against her husband's will was held to be in constructive desertion.

But in 1962 the Court of Appeal's judgments in *Hall* v. *Hall*[10] brought some clarity into this branch of the law. A wife petitioned on the ground that she had been driven out by her husband's drunkenness; he came home late and noisily, but there was no evidence that he knew that his conduct

7a. *Buchler* v. *Buchler* [1947] P. 25.
8. *Bartholomew* v. *Bartholomew* [1952] 2 All E.R. 1035.
9. *Winnan* v. *Winnan* [1949] P. 174.
10. 12 [1963] P. 375.

distressed her or was likely to drive her out. The Divisional Court held that this was not constructive desertion, since drunkenness, with its ordinary accompaniments of rowdiness and inconvenience to those who had to deal with the drunkard, in the absence of disgusting or violent conduct could not be said to be something that an ordinary wife should not be expected to put up with. In other words, it was conduct such as a wife bargained to endure when she marries 'for better, for worse'. But the Court of Appeal overruled this decision, and granted her a decree, Lord Justice Danckwerts saying that he would not accept that a spouse makes any such bargain in a country which allows divorce when the marriage breaks down, and that in such a country the phrase 'for better, for worse' is 'something of a cynical jest'.

Here we can see at work the process of evolution of judicial thought which laid the foundation for the recent changes in the law. Nevertheless, the test of constructive desertion is still this: was the conduct of such a grave and weighty nature as to make cohabitation virtually impossible?[11] (In spite of the remark of Lord Justice Diplock in *Hall* v. *Hall* that he awaited with some philological excitement an example of conduct which was 'grave' without being 'weighty', the phrase is too honoured by age and usage to be abandoned now.) Grave and weighty misconduct may either establish constructive desertion, or give the other spouse a just cause for leaving and thus be a defence to a charge of desertion (see p. 181).

Desertion, cruelty and 'unreasonable' behaviour

Conduct which could amount to constructive desertion may also be cruelty (see p. 166) provided that it causes injury to health or apprehension of such injury. It will certainly amount to unreasonable behaviour for the purposes of section 2(1)(b) of the Divorce Reform Act, 1969 even without injury to health. But where cruelty is still a ground for relief (that is, in the Magistrates' Court) it is not possible to build

11. *Saunders* v. *Saunders* [1965] P. 499.

up a case of constructive desertion out of what is really a case of unproved cruelty. A weak case of cruelty cannot be dressed up as a constructive desertion,[12] and where a cruelty petition is dismissed because the offence was not proved, the same facts cannot be relied on as establishing constructive desertion,[13] on the principle of estoppel by *res judicata.*

Defences to desertion

Since there can be no desertion unless one party leaves against the will of the other, *an agreement to separate* will be a complete defence to a charge of desertion. The agreement may be by word of mouth, in writing (as by exchange of letters or formal agreement), or in a deed. There is no distinction between these forms of agreement except that oral consent is more difficult to prove, and an ordinary document not drafted by a lawyer may be susceptible to differing interpretations. However the agreement is made, it is wiped out if the parties come back together again, or if they repudiate the agreement in some way or other. For instance, if one party fails to comply with one of the basic terms of a separation deed – such as the payment of maintenance – and the other party makes no attempt to enforce that term, the agreement will usually be at an end, and will then be no defence to desertion.

Sometimes consent to the separation can be inferred from conduct. If it is clear that the wife heaved a sigh of relief when her husband decided to leave, because she was only waiting for an opportunity to go to her lover or to live in the South of France, then he is not in desertion. But if her sigh of relief is induced by the prospect of escape from a marriage made intolerable by her husband's conduct, then he will be in desertion, since she does not want him to go *qua* husband, but only because he has already broken up the marriage. Even if the spouse who is ordered out had long wanted to leave, there will still be desertion in the absence of explicit consent after consultation: in *Phair* v. *Phair*[14] the

12. *Pike* v. *Pike* [1954] P. 81.
13. *Foster* v. *Foster* [1954] P. 67; but see *Thoday* v. *Thoday* [1964] p. 181.
14. [1963] 107 S.J. 554.

Court of Appeal said a finding of desertion in such a case, although the law, would seem to laymen 'a travesty of the real facts'. Once the desertion has begun against the consent of the deserted party, the latter need not continue to want the erring spouse back; even adultery on the part of the injured party will not bring desertion to an end if it has clearly had no effect on the mind of the deserter – in other words, adultery only matters in such a case if it is known to the other party and prevents his or her return to cohabitation.[15]

If the spouse who leaves has a just cause or reasonable excuse for doing so, he will not be guilty of desertion. The sort of conduct which will give the deserting spouse a reasonable excuse is much the same as that which would amount to constructive desertion: it must be grave and weighty, not simply something causing matrimonial unhappiness, but it need not amount to an offence such as adultery or cruelty nor, it seems, need it be quite as serious as that which is required for constructive desertion. Excessive or revolting sexual demands,[16] unjustified refusal of sexual intercourse,[17] insistence on the practice of *coitus interruptus*,[18] inordinate jealousy – all these have been held to be valid excuses for the other party to leave. It is also a defence if the spouse who leaves does so because of a reasonable belief in the other's adultery; where a husband came home late at night on leave from the army and found three men in the house, one in his wife's bedroom, although he had no evidence sufficient to prove adultery, he was justified in leaving her.[19] But the suspicion must be a reasonable one, and it must be induced by conduct; a man is not justified in believing in his wife's adultery because he hears gossip about her, or even if he is told of it by his own mother.[20] And where evidence causing a suspicion (not cer-

15. *Herod* v. *Herod* [1937] P. 11.
16. *Holborn* v. *Holborn* [1947] 1 All E.R. 32.
17. *Glenister* v. *Glenister* [1945] P. 34; *Cann* v. *Cann* (1967) 111 S.J. 810.
18. *G.* v. *G.* [1930] P. 72.
19. *Rice* v. *Raynold-Spring-Rice* [1948] 1 All E.R. 188.
20. *Elliott* v. *Elliott* [1956] P. 160.

tainty) of adultery comes into the possession of a spouse, it is incumbent on that spouse to give the other the opportunity to give an explanation within a reasonable time, otherwise the belief in adultery will not be held to be reasonable.[21]

Quite apart from any excuse, there may be a perfectly good reason for the separation, such as illness, imprisonment, or war, and then there can be no desertion. Since there must be an *intention* to desert, and that intention must continue or the desertion comes to an end, a spouse who leaves the other when insane, or who becomes insane later, cannot logically be in desertion. But a strict application of this rule caused much injustice, and in 1958 the Divorce (Insanity and Desertion) Act made it possible for the High Court (not magistrates) to regard desertion as *continuing* even if the deserter later becomes incapable of forming any intent to desert. Since the 1969 Act repealed section 1 of the Matrimonial Causes Act, 1965, which incorporated the provision, it is no longer available, but presumably most of such cases will fall under intolerable conduct or, failing this, separation for five years. Desertion still cannot *start*, however, unless the guilty party is capable of forming the intent.

Right to choose matrimonial home

Who is entitled to choose the matrimonial home? This is a thorny question. The refusal to live together from the beginning of the marriage can be desertion even though there is strictly no 'state of things' to withdraw from. Since the husband usually has a duty to provide for his wife and family, it might be thought that he would have the right to decide, but there is no absolute rule. The Courts have been exasperatingly vague about this question. The parties must be 'reasonable', they say; the husband's job is important[22] but the wife's may be even more vital and neither party has a casting vote.[23] The husband must provide reasonable accommodation in the place of his choice, but there is no rigid

21. *Marsden* v. *Marsden* [1968] P. 544.
22. *Dunn* v. *Dunn* [1949] P. 98.
23. *McGowan* v. *McGowan* [1948] 2 All E.R. 1032.

test of what is 'reasonable'; it depends on the background and financial circumstances of both parties. However, if they agree before marriage that they will live in a certain place, and then one of them goes back on the agreement, that one will probably be in desertion.

Termination of desertion

Desertion is brought to an end if the parties come back to live together again, or if the deserter makes a genuine offer to return. But the offer must be sincere, and it must be such that the injured party would be unreasonable to refuse it. If an approach is made for purely tactical reasons – such as the avoidance of a maintenance order – then it will not bring the desertion to an end, and where the deserter has behaved very badly in the past, he will have to convince the other of his good intentions for the future. If the deserted party refuses a genuine offer to return, he becomes in desertion himself from the date of the refusal. It is sometimes very difficult to assess the *bona fides* of such an offer.

To bring desertion to an end, the resumption of the marriage state must be complete. It is not enough that there should be an isolated act of sexual intercourse, or even several acts; this may only be part of an attempt at reconciliation, and the courts will not penalize such efforts.[23a] There will be no end to the desertion unless the parties go back to live together as they did before the separation. Desertion will also be terminated by a decree of judicial separation or by a separation order in the Magistrates' Court, but not by an order which is simply for the payment of maintenance.

Remedies for desertion

Once the desertion takes place, a matrimonial offence has been committed and the injured party has a remedy in the Courts. However short the duration of the desertion, it is a ground for an order in the Magistrates' Court. The latter must not be a separation order since it brings desertion to an end and therefore prevents divorce proceedings later; it may

23a. Divorce Reform Act, 1969 s.3(5): and see p. 133.

be, and usually is, merely an order for maintenance. Only if the desertion has continued for two years or more does it become a ground for divorce or judicial separation. Desertion as a ground for divorce was introduced for the first time in the 1937 Act, but from then until 1969 the period of separation had to be three years or more. The provision that it must have continued for at least three years was imposed as a rough test of the permanence of the breakdown of the marriage. Desertion for two years is now considered adequate evidence of permanent breakdown.

Desertion by the applicant spouse may be a defence to an application for an order under section 6 of the Matrimonial Proceedings and Property Act, 1970.

Insanity and desertion

We have seen the relationship between insanity and cruelty, and the way in which the law's attitude changed (see pp. 170–71). Because desertion cannot be initiated nor continue without the necessary *animus*, insanity also has an important bearing on the law relating to desertion. Thus however long the separation, if the respondent spouse was suffering from mental illness which prevented the formation of the intention to desert or to remain away, there could be no offence of desertion. When desertion was first introduced as a ground for dissolution in 1937, incurable insanity was also made a ground for divorce – the first time that a breach was made in the principle of the matrimonial offence and the negation of the view that divorce was not for the protection of the wrong-doer but for the punishment of the wrong-doer (nevertheless this view persisted in some judicial quarters for almost another thirty years).

By the Matrimonial Causes Act, 1965[24] a petition for divorce could be presented on the ground that the Respondent was incurably of unsound mind and had been continuously under care and treatment for a period of at least five years immediately preceding the presentation of the petition. Care and treatment was defined as being liable to be detained

24. s.1(1)(a)(iv).

under the Mental Health Act, 1959, or receiving continuous treatment in certain institutions. This section has now been repealed by the Divorce Reform Act, 1969, and insanity of itself is no longer a ground for dissolution. Where one spouse is mentally ill and is taken away for treatment, there will be three possibilities of dissolution open to the other spouse:

1. If the Respondent is capable of giving consent, a decree could be obtained after two years' separation. But if there is serious mental illness, requiring treatment in an institution, it is unlikely that the Respondent would be capable of such consent. Very strong medical evidence would be required to satisfy the court in relation to consent.

2. Separation for five years will be evidence of breakdown and thus grounds for divorce without proof either of consent or insanity. This will be the most usual ground where one spouse is incurably insane. Evidence that the Respondent had been in a hospital for five years would establish that the marriage had broken down irretrievably.

3. Desertion for two years. Where a spouse does not want to wait for five years to divorce a partner suffering from mental illness, is there any chance of proving desertion? If sane at the inception of the desertion, he could form the intention to desert, but does the supervention of insanity prevent the necessary intention from continuing? By section 1(i)(ii) of the Matrimonial Causes Act, 1965, the Court was given the power to treat a period of desertion as having continued at a time when the deserting party was incapable of continuing the necessary intention if the evidence before the Court was such that, had the Respondent not been so incapable, the Court would have inferred that that intention continued at that time. That saving clause now appears in section 2(4) of the 1969 Act. The reasoning in the judgment of Mr. Justice Cairns in *Kaczmarz* v. *Kaczmarz* relating to the effects of mental disease on both the inception and continuation of desertion, are still applicable in this respect.[25]

25. [1967] 1 All E.R. 416.

But wherever a Respondent is suffering from mental illness, the Official Solicitor as guardian *ad litem* will contest the suit if any allegation of misconduct is made and can be relied on to oppose strongly any finding of desertion. The evidence of irretrievable breakdown would have to be cogent before a court would grant a decree in such a case.

In most cases of insanity or mental ill-health the Petitioner will be able to establish that the Respondent's behaviour was such that the Petitioner cannot reasonably be expected to live with the Respondent.

Part Three **The Children**

Introduction

The first two parts of this book have been concerned entirely with the relationship between the two parties to the marriage and in turn their relationship with the law. This part deals with the children, whether of a marriage or not, and the law controlling them both within the family and within the state. As we shall see, the legal position of children in both cases has changed enormously in the present century. Divorce, once a process concerned only with the rights and wrongs of the spouses, has been made dependent on the satisfaction of the Court with the arrangements for the children – not only those born to the parties but any children accepted by them into the family. The stigma of illegitimacy has almost gone. Adoption is strictly controlled. In disputes between parents, or between parents and foster parents, the child's interest has become paramount. The Poor Law provisions for the abandoned in orphanages and the punishment meted out in the reformatories and later in approved schools, are all swept away and now every homeless, uncontrollable or delinquent child may come under the umbrella of a care order, giving the local authority parental rights.

Wardship – to be dealt with in the Family Division of the High Court from 1 October 1971 – the guardianship jurisdiction in Magistrates' Courts, and the wide legislation controlling the education, the protection and the employment of children all make their contribution to the welfare of the young as outlined in this section.

10 Parent and Child

In the last fifty years there have been several revolutions in the family, but none has been more striking than the change that has taken place in the relationship between parents and their children. Within a few decades the customary rights on which the authority of the Victorian father was founded almost completely withered away. Meanwhile, as parents have lost many of their rights, they have also been relieved of some of the burdens of parenthood by the growth of the welfare state. The law has recognized this change, indeed has contributed to it in many ways, but there are still plenty of anomalies left which are atavistic survivals from historical attitudes towards the family. Where there is confusion in the law relating to children, this is usually due to such survivals and is further complicated, as we find throughout family law, by the attempt to fit an ancient institution into a new world.

The more highly civilized a society becomes, and the longer the period during which the child requires education and support, the fewer rights do parents exert and the more conscious of their liabilities do they become. Among primitive people, living entirely off the land, children are the greatest asset a man can have, since they increase his material prosperity by their labour and thereby add to his status among his fellows. The stories of the Old Testament vividly illustrate the value of children in a nomadic society: sons to care for the flocks and fight off marauders, and daughters to care for the men of the family and to produce new stock, stood first in a man's riches, and a barren marriage was the supreme disaster. First in many of the Old Testament stories comes the catalogue of the character's family.

In a modern industrial society children are the greatest future assets of the state, while to their parents, from the material point of view at any event, they bring mainly burdens. The primitive instinct to have children remains as strong as ever, but the rewards are no longer economic and parental pride is tempered by the weight of responsibility which children bring. In Europe there was a long intermediate phase when children were valued mostly for the continuity they brought to the family: feudalism depended on the inheritance of status and property, and a man could see in his children the defeat of his mortality and the promise that his estates would remain intact in perpetuity. English law reflects all these different attitudes to children, and alongside the care which a modern state must show for its most precious assets we find relics of legal rights and duties which derive from feudal times and from even more primitive concepts of parenthood. The law has always been reluctant to interfere between parent and child – or rather, between father and child, since it was not until late in the nineteenth century that a mother had any legal rights whatsoever – and even today in some respects a child is regarded by the law as a piece of family property. As we shall see in the next chapter, statute law has now given to local authorities powers of such magnitude over children coming into their care, and the classes of such children have been so greatly extended, that this reluctance seems to have been finally overcome, and the child's interest almost universally preferred to parental rights.

Legitimate and illegitimate children

All systems of law, it seems, differentiate between the children born into the family and those outside it, regarding only those born or conceived within marriage as legitimate in the sense that they are subject to the law relating to the family. Certainly our common law, and all the legal systems which are based on Roman law, make a rigid distinction between the two kinds of child. Even Soviet law, which in 1918 abolished all distinction between legitimate and illegitimate children, was forced in 1944 to recognize certain differences between children whose parents had registered their marriage and those whose parents had not. Legitimacy may mean different things and be called by different names in various legal systems, and the law may soften the edges of the distinction between children born in and out of wedlock (as has happened in England in recent years), but it seems impossible to obliterate the concept altogether. The attitude of the Courts to adoption illustrates this: in a recent case[1] the Court of Appeal held that the advantages for an illegitimate child of being adopted, and thereby ceasing to be a bastard, outweighed the loss of his connection with his real father, however devoted the latter might be. This is a good example of the way in which the law and the family are inextricably bound up together. (See also the blood test cases cited on p. 153.)

The English common law rule is that no child can be legitimate unless it is either born or conceived in wedlock. This means that a posthumous child if conceived during marriage or one born of pre-marital intercourse if born during marriage is legitimate, but where a marriage is later declared to be null and void, any children born of the union would, by that rule, be bastards; and this was the position until 1950. But by two Acts of Parliament[2] the legitimacy of such children is now presumed whether their parents' marriage was void from the beginning (provided both or either of the parents reasonably believed the marriage to be valid at the time of conception), or was a voidable marriage which was later annulled. In 1926[3] legislation was passed which tempered the harshness of the common law rule: an illegitimate child could be legitimated by the subsequent marriage of its parents, provided that neither the father nor the mother was married to a third person at the time of the birth. In 1959[4] this proviso was abolished, and now all illegitimate children are automatically legitimated if and when their parents subsequently marry.

1. *Re E. (P) (an Infant)* [1969] 1 All E.R. 323.
2. Matrimonial Causes Act, 1950, s.9, and Legitimacy Act, 1959, s.2.
3. Legitimacy Act, 1926.
4. Legitimacy Act, 1959.

But there still remains a distinction between common law and statutory legitimacy. No child who is legitimated by operation of law can inherit titles or honours, and his legitimacy is not retrospective, but dates only from the time of his parents' marriage. Thus he can only inherit as a legitimate child under a will if the will was made after the date of legitimation, or under an intestacy only if the death occurs after that date.[5] And his seniority among the family for purposes of inheritance is determined by the date of his legitimation, so that he takes his place after all legitimate children born before that date. Apart from these differences, the legitimated child has exactly the same legal status as a legitimate one; as was said by a Chancery judge in *re Lowe, Stewart* v. *Lowe*[6] soon after legitimation by law was first made possible:

'Legitimacy is a question of status. This status of legitimacy can be obtained by being born legitimate or by being legitimated by virtue of the provisions of the Act. The plaintiff had attained that status, and it is an irrelevant consideration whether she attained it in one way or in the other.'

In that case the new statutory legitimation worked most unfairly. The parents of two illegitimate children later married; one child, a son, died in 1919, but a daughter survived to be legitimated by the 1926 Act. When the father died intestate in 1928, the Court held that only the daughter could inherit his estate, and the son's children were excluded because he was never a legitimate child. In such a way do sudden changes in the law lead to injustice.

The definition of legitimacy is not the same in all countries – for instance, in France a child conceived before marriage is not legitimate, although it is legitimated by the subsequent marriage – so that it may be necessary to decide what legal

5. Since primogeniture is now in practice only applicable to the inheritance of titles, this distinction is of little importance today. But under the feudal system – which persisted in estate law in some form until 1925 – it was vital.

6. [1929] 2 Ch. 210.

standards should be applied in testing the legitimacy of any given child. The English Courts in these cases apply the law of the *father's* domicile – they look at the law of this country to decide whether or not the child is legitimate. So that if two Greeks, domiciled in Greece, marry in England before a Greek priest – a marriage which is void here, though valid under Greek law – their children will be legitimate in English law, because the law of the father's domicile will so regard them. In the same way we accept the children of polygamous marriages as legitimate, provided the marriage is valid by the law of the father's domicile.

Sometimes it is important to be able to show that a child is *not* legitimate, as for instance where inheritance of titles or estates depends on who is the eldest son. If the child was born during marriage, the law presumes in favour of its legitimacy. It has been said that the evidence which will rebut this presumption must be 'strong, distinct, satisfactory, and conclusive', but since the Family Law Reform Act, 1969 came into force, the presumption has been more easily retractable. Section 26 is as follows:

> Any presumption of law as to the legitimacy or illegitimacy of any person may in any civil proceedings be rebutted by evidence which shows that it is *more probable than not* that that person is illegitimate or legitimate (...) and it shall not be necessary to prove that fact beyond reasonable doubt in order to rebut that presumption.

If the Court can be satisfied that intercourse was impossible at the time of conception, as for instance where the husband was abroad, then the child will be held to be illegitimate. Similarly if the husband is proved to have been impotent at the time, or even if intercourse was so unlikely that it is more probable than not that it did not occur, illegitimacy can be established. The *Aylesford Peerage Case* in 1885 illustrates how the old presumption operated. The Committee for Privileges of the House of Lords bastardized a child on evidence that intercourse between husband and wife was inherently very unlikely, although technically possible. Lady Aylesford, the wife of the seventh Earl, gave birth to a son in Paris after she had been living as the mistress of the Marquis of Blandford for five years and had been separated from her husband during that period. However, husband and wife had met from time to time, and indeed they were together in London at about the time of the child's conception. When the Earl died and his brother petitioned for a summons to the House of Lords as eighth Earl of Aylesford, Lady Aylesford opposed his petition and set up her own son as the rightful heir. Their Lordships held that the presumption of the son's legitimacy had been rebutted because there was no evidence that Lady Aylesford had had any real opportunity for intercourse with the Earl, and because it was in any case very unlikely that the Earl would have had intercourse with her when he knew of her adultery. These considerations, and the conduct of the Marquis of Blandford in arranging for the birth and maintaining the child later, all made the illegitimacy beyond any reasonable doubt. Now it would be unnecessary for the evidence to go so far.

If intercourse between husband and wife took place at or near the time of conception, then even if the wife had intercourse with another man about that same time it is difficult to prove the child illegitimate. But it can be done. If the white wife of a white husband gave birth to a black baby, the Court would no doubt accept that the child could not be legitimate. More technical applications of the science of eugenics may be applied in some cases. It is known that parents who have combinations of certain blood-groups cannot possibly give birth to a child of certain other blood-groups. If the child can be shown to have a blood-group which could not have been derived from the mating of husband and wife, then the genes producing that group must have been introduced from outside the marriage and the child is conclusively proved to be illegitimate.[7] But this is not quite as useful a test as it appears at first sight. In the first place, the child may well be illegitimate even if its

7. e.g. *Liff* v. *Liff* [1948] W.N. 128; *B.* v. *Attorney-General* (*N.E.B.* intervening) [1965] 1 All E.R. 62.

blood-group is compatible with the husband's and wife's groups; secondly, since the result of testing only rarely proves legitimacy, but only illegitimacy, such a test is against the child's interest and will generally be refused by whoever has custody of the child. But blood tests have been relied on in several reported cases and are likely to become of increasing importance in determining parentage (see the cases referred to on p. 153 and the Family Law Reform Act of 1969, section 20, which is not yet in force).

Only the High Court can hear *legitimacy* suits (under section 39 of the Matrimonial Causes Act, 1969) although a finding of adultery either in the County Court or the Magistrates' Court may entail a finding of fact which makes a child a bastard. But such a finding only operates *inter partes*: only the High Court can make a declaration of legitimacy *in rem*. The County Court, however, has power to make a declaration of legitimation by operation of statute.

Adoption

Children can enter the family either by birth or by adoption. Although the practice of taking children from outside into the family, and bringing them up as if they were members of the family by birth, has existed from time immemorial, English law did not recognize any change of status in the adopted child until 1926.[8] Under the common law, a person who stands *in loco parentis* to a child puts himself in a position of trust, and his relations with the child will be judged by higher standards than if he were a father. But before statutory adoption was introduced, there could be no transfer of the rights and duties of a parent to a stranger, not even to a relative. It is true that adoption deeds were often executed, under which the adopter undertook to accept liability for the child, but it is doubtful how far these were enforceable – certainly they would not have been allowed to operate to the detriment of the child. Even now that adoption is recognized by law, a stranger may still stand *in loco parentis* to a child; in particular, if a father maintains his

8. Adoption of Children Act, 1926.

illegitimate child and takes him into his family, this will be regarded as an adoption for certain purposes, so that the father may make himself liable for the child's future support.

The reasons for the reluctance of the law to recognize true adoption are easily understood. If adoption were easy, it would be open to great abuse: the sale of children, the neglect of those who were adopted by feckless people who soon tired of them, the confusion of family relations – all these undesirable results might follow. But a system of legal adoption, rigidly controlled and giving permanency to the new family, obviously has a useful place in society, giving to childless couples the opportunity to complete their families and to orphans the benefits of a settled home and parental affection. Most European countries made provision for adoption much earlier than we did, and in Ancient Rome it was a recognized way of extending the family. In the East it is often relied on to preserve the rites of ancestor worship. There is great diversity in the style of adoption recognized by different legal systems, and in the effects of adoption, but nearly all countries demand an agreement between the adopters and the parents of the child, while in most cases the courts have a discretion to grant or refuse confirmation. Only in England and Sweden is adoption limited to minors, although all countries follow the Roman rule that adoption imitates nature and therefore the adopter must be considerably older than the child. Again, the lower age-limit for the adopter varies greatly: in England and the Scandinavian countries it is twenty-five; in Switzerland, France, and Austria, forty; in Spain, forty-five; and in Germany no one under fifty may adopt a child.

In England legal adoption can only take place by means of an order of a Court. In the High Court the order is made in the Chancery Division, but most adoption orders are made in County Courts or Magistrates' Courts. In any case, the proceedings are secret and informal, and the inquiry thorough; the Court must be satisfied that all the elaborate conditions prescribed by law have been complied with, and after examining all the circumstances and seeing the applicant the court still has a discretion to refuse the adoption order. Only an unmarried minor (that is, a person under eighteen) may be adopted, and a female infant may not be adopted by a sole male applicant unless there are some very special circumstances to justify such an exceptional order, as there might be where a father had brought up his illegitimate daughter entirely by himself and there was no other person with any interest in the child. The child to be adopted must be living in England or Wales at the time, although foreign birth or domicile is irrelevant.

English adoption law, as codified by the Adoption Acts of 1950 and 1958, attempts to balance the claims (which may well compete with each other) of the three parties involved, that is, the adopters, the natural parents, and the child. Stringent qualifications are laid down for proposed adopters. An order will not be made in favour of more than one adopter, except in the case of a married couple, where both may adopt jointly. Either the mother or the father of an illegitimate child may adopt it, either alone or together with his or her spouse. In rare cases grandparents have been allowed to adopt their grandchildren, but the courts are reluctant to make such orders, and will probably only do so where the applicants are relatively young and are exceptionally well suited to stand in the position of parents. The courts cannot make an order in favour of a married applicant unless the other spouse consents to the adoption. Age is important: no sole adopter may be under twenty-five, unless a relative of the child, when the limit is reduced to twenty-one; where there are two applicants both must be over twenty-one and one must be over twenty-five, unless one is a relative of the child. The applicant must live in England at the time of the hearing, and until 1958 also had to be domiciled in England; but it is now possible for persons of foreign domicile to obtain a provisional adoption order in this country, which enables the child to be taken abroad by the applicant in order that full adoption can take place in the country of the applicant's domicile. This relaxation has been very useful in helping adoption societies in placing homeless children who are coloured or have some special religion; it has also made it possible for wealthy Americans to fill their quivers here.

The most important condition for adoption is the consent of the parents and guardians of the child. For this purpose, the father of an illegitimate child is not regarded as a parent, although he must be notified of the proceedings if he is liable to maintain the child, either under an affiliation order or an agreement, and he may be heard on the application. It is not possible for him to prevent the adoption if the Court is satisfied with the arrangements, but he can have considerable nuisance value. The father of an illegitimate child is now allowed to claim the custody of that child; if he makes such an application this will tie the hands of the Court hearing the adoption proceedings, since no adoption order can be made until the claim to custody has been settled.[9] By this means an awkward father can hold up the adoption indefinitely, in spite of the fact that his consent is not necessary. Many adoptions concern illegitimate babies whose mothers arrange to dispose of them during the desperate months before the birth, but may well change their minds when motherhood is complete and they hold the cause of their misfortunes in their arms. Obviously no mother should be allowed to abandon her rights to her child without a full understanding of the implications; accordingly the law provides that a mother shall not be capable of giving effective consent until her child is at least six weeks old. The parent or guardian may consent by appearing at court and giving evidence, but usually a document is completed which must be signed by the person consenting and attested by a justice of the peace, justice's clerk, or officer of a County Court. Once the consent has been given, the parent or guardian may not take the child from the proposed adopters while the application is pending, without the leave of the Court, but as we shall see the consent is not irrevocable.

The condition of consent is imposed to protect all parties from adoption orders being made against the will of the

9. Re Adoption Application no. 41/61 [1963] Ch. 315.

natural parents or other persons charged with responsibility for the child; it must not be abused by vindictive people who have not the child's interest at heart. Therefore if consent is unreasonably withheld, or if the parent has abandoned or neglected or ill-treated the child, then the Court may dispense with the consent. It is not easy to say what the Courts will regard as 'unreasonable': the fact that the child would be better off if adopted is certainly no ground for saying that the parent is unreasonable in withholding consent – and only in very exceptional cases will the Courts hold that a parent is unreasonable in withholding consent. In *re D. (an Infant)*,[10] when the consent of the father of an illegitimate child, who was liable to maintain the child, was still necessary, the father refused to consent to the child's adoption, giving no reasons save that he loved his son. Since he was at the time of the application serving a life sentence as the reprieved murderer of the unfortunate child's mother, it is perhaps not surprising the court held that his refusal to consent was unreasonable.

Until very recently the attitude of the Courts to dispensing with consent has been governed by the principle that in adoption, unlike custody proceedings, the interests of the child are not paramount; the rights of the natural parent are also to be given due consideration and the withholding of consent has been respected in all but the clearest cases of unreasonableness. But recently there has been a division of judicial attitude as shown by two cases in the Court of Appeal[11] one of which has now been to the House of Lords. In the first case, *re W. (an Infant)*,[11a] the test imposed was whether or not the mother's conduct in withholding consent was culpable against the infant. In the second case the test was 'would a reasonable parent regard a refusal to the adoption as involving a serious risk of affecting the whole future happiness of the child?'. Since 'a reasonable

10. [1958] 1 All E.R. 427.

11. *Re W. (an infant)* [1970] 3 All E.R. 970, and *Re B. (an infant)* [1970] 3 All E.R. 1008.

11a. [1971] 2 All E.R. 49. H.L.

parent' would put the welfare of the child before her own wishes, this latter test seems undistinguishable from the test of the paramount interest of the child.

Even if the necessary consents are given, they can be withdrawn at any time up to the making of the order, even at the Court hearing itself. Since the Court may not make an adoption order unless the child has been continuously in the care and possession[12] of the proposed adopters for three months immediately preceding the hearing (not including any period when the child was under six weeks), there is ample time for the parent to reconsider the decision to part with the child. During this three months' probationary period there are other safeguards: the would-be adopters, unless one of them is a parent of the child, must give at least three months' notice to the local authority of their intention, so that the children's officer may have an opportunity to supervise the circumstances of the child's new home.

When all these conditions have been fulfilled, the case may come on for hearing. It is necessary for the child's interests to be safeguarded, and to this end a 'guardian *ad litem*' is appointed by the Court. Usually this will be the children's officer in the County Court or Magistrates' Court, but in the Chancery Division of the High Court the Official Solicitor is appointed. Whoever the guardian may be, he or she must, among other things, investigate fully all the circumstances of the proposed adoption, in particular the home conditions, means, and health of the applicants and, if the child is old enough to understand, find out whether he or she wishes to be adopted. The report made by the guardian *ad litem* is confidential, and is not available to the parties, but is read by the judge or magistrates at the hearing of the application and is of decisive importance.

Once the adoption order is made, and the time for appeal has passed, it is final, and the child becomes a member of his adopter's family as if he were a natural child: he takes his

12. A County Court judge has held that a child at boarding school cannot be in 'care and possession' of the adopters, but this seems to be going too far and would probably not be followed.

adoptive father's nationality and domicile, he will benefit from the father's estate if he should die intestate, even if there are other children born within the family, and he is entitled by law to support from his adopters. His own parents' rights and liabilities are completely wiped out. But in one respect an adopted child can never be the equal of his brothers and sisters by adoption: he cannot inherit any title or honour, since these depend on blood alone.

At a time like the present, when the demand for children to adopt far outruns the supply, the introduction of unwanted children to couples anxious to adopt might well develop into a racket little better than the baby-farming of Dickens's time. To prevent any such scandal the law forbids the publication of advertisements relating to adoption, or any payment or reward for allowing or arranging an adoption. It is also forbidden to take a British child out of the United Kingdom for the purposes of adoption unless under a provisional adoption order. Furthermore, it is an offence for any body of persons other than a registered adoption society to make any arrangements for the adoption of any child. The penalties are heavy – six months' imprisonment or a fine of £100 – but it is easy to imagine ways round these laws and no doubt breaches do occur without detection. But on the whole, adoption works very well in this country, and it has certainly added a good deal to the sum of human happiness.

However, there is pressure for reform of the law in several aspects. As we have seen, the interest of the child is not paramount in adoption proceedings, as it is in custodial cases and sometimes the law acts against the child's interest in paying regard to parental rights. Where a child has been fostered with a good and loving couple from birth and they want to adopt the child, under the present law their application would be almost hopeless if either parent withheld consent; a mother may demand her child from foster-parents after many years of absence, thus breaking up the only home the child has ever known and perhaps causing untold injury. It may be that these *de facto* adoptions should be given legal effect after a certain period, whatever the natural parents' wishes may be.

Both the Law Commission and a Home Office Committee under the Chairmanship of Sir William Houghton are considering these and other problems connected with adoption. But with the increase in child care services it is generally felt that the need for adoption is not so great today; it is a kind of legal deceit upon the child, and threatens that sense of identity which psychiatrists and child workers regard as of such importance. It seems likely that fostering and guardianship will increase at the expense of adoption: these two methods of dealing with a homeless child leave him with the opportunity, at a later stage, to seek out and renew his ties with his natural parent or parents.

Registration of children

However a child enters the family – by birth in wedlock, by legitimation, or by adoption – he must be duly enrolled in the records of the state. When first born, whether legitimate or not, his arrival in the world must be registered, by either his mother or his father, or by someone present at the birth, or by the occupier of the house where he was born, or by someone who has charge of him. One of these people must give particulars of the birth to the registrar of births and deaths of the district within forty-two days, and if this is not done, the parents are each liable on conviction to a fine of £2.00. In return for the information, the parent is handed a birth certificate, which shows the facts entered in the register – date and place of birth, names and sex of child, and names of father and mother. This certificate, which is required for so many purposes during life, may reveal the fact of illegitimacy: if the column for the father's name is left blank, or his name is other than that of the mother, the wretched child carries with him for ever the evidence of his own bastardy. Some slight remedy for this unfortunate situation is now available in the form of a 'short certificate of birth', which is available on payment of fifteen pence and which mercifully omits all particulars of parentage. Where an illegitimate child is later made legitimate by his parents' marriage, they may re-register the child's birth and he will then have an impeccable certificate.

Adopted illegitimate children are not quite so fortunate. Their adoption must be registered in the Adopted Children Register, and the Register of Births is amended by the addition of the word 'adopted'. To avoid the evidence of illegitimacy the child must avail himself of the doubtful smoke-screen of the short birth certificate.

Parental rights and liabilities

One of the principles of the old legal concept of the family was a father's rights to the services of his infant children. Both his wife and his children were regarded as his property, as were his servants, and anyone who damaged this property by physical injury, or enticed or seduced them away, or harboured them, was liable in damages.

All these torts derived from the medieval action *per quod servitium amisit*, and they are now only of historic interest. Actions for seduction, enticement and harbouring were abolished by the Law Reform (Miscellaneous Provisions) Act, 1970, but had for many years been obsolete. There remains the claim for loss of services of a child due to personal injury, but this must be a rare cause for action, since very few children under eighteen years now give services of pecuniary value to their fathers.

Although as we have said the law is reluctant to interfere between parent and child, it has always recognized certain rights on both sides. Under the common law, the father has the right to the custody of his legitimate child, and although a mother now has equal rights to apply to a court for custody, until there is some court order the position remains the same as it has always been: the father has the right to determine his child's religion, the way he is educated, where he shall live, and all that pertains to his upbringing.[13] This natural jurisdiction of the father gives him the right to chas-

13. Subject, of course, to the restrictions imposed by statutes relating to education and child welfare.

tise his child, but the punishment must be reasonable; if it amounts to cruelty or neglect, the father can be convicted of a criminal offence in exactly the same way as any other person maltreating a child. This right to punish can be delegated by the father to a schoolmaster or any other person (an elder brother has no right to punish his younger brother or sisters, unless he is *in loco parentis* in the absence of the father). If the father dies, the mother assumes the right to custody of the child.

The liabilities of parents are more important than their rights. It has always been a father's moral duty to support his children. In the past this duty, although recognized by the law, was only imposed in an indirect way. As late as 1827 a Lord Chancellor said:[14] 'The courts of law can enforce the rights of the father, but they are not equal to the office of enforcing the duties of the father.' For example, where a child is entitled to an inheritance, the court will not order maintenance for the child to be paid out of that inheritance unless 'from the poverty of his parent he is in danger of perishing for want'.[15] The courts have shown themselves loathe to allow a father to make inroads into his child's estate, even for the necessities of life; but the Honourable John Verney, Master of the Rolls, said in *Fawkner* v. *Watts*, in 1741:

> 'I shall not dispute but every father and mother, by the law of nature, is under an obligation *to maintain* their own children, but yet this may be varied by circumstances; for suppose the father or mother should be in a low or mean condition in the world, thc Court will order, especially in the case of the mother, that the child should be maintained out of a provision left to it by a collateral relation.'[16]

In fact, this question could hardly arise to day, since it is the practice in drafting wills to leave money on trust for the beneficiaries during their infancy, with the right to the

14. *Wellesley* v. *The Duke of Beaufort* (1827) 2 Russ. 1.
15. *Butler* v. *Freeman and Butler* (1743) 3 Atk. 60.
16. *Fawkner* v. *Watts* (1742) 1 Atk. 406.

trustees to advance money for education and general maintenance.

By successive Acts of Parliament the law has gradually imposed more and more strictly upon parents the legal obligation to perform the undoubted moral duty of maintaining their offspring. Since the state took some responsibility for the care of the needy the Poor Law Acts have always made the father legally liable to prevent his family from becoming a charge on the rates (see p. 37). In the next chapter these and other legal duties which the state now imposes on parents are described.

In general, parents are not liable on their children's contracts or for their debts. If a minor enters into any contract, whether for goods or services or for money lent, it is unenforceable[17] unless it is for necessaries – these are tested as they were in the case of a wife (see p. 38) – and the other party cannot look to the father or mother to fulfil the contract. Sometimes a parent is asked to sign the contract as a guarantor, and then, of course, he will be liable. Yet a father will be liable for certain items of maintenance provided by others for his children as, for example, where a schoolmaster sues the father for a child's education and board, even though there is no direct contract between the father and the schoolmaster, the action will succeed. This applies even if the 'father' is only a person *in loco parentis*, as where he has taken on his wife's children by a former marriage.[18]

Nor is a parent as a general rule liable for his child's torts; that is to say the wrongful, but not criminal, acts for which the law supplies a remedy. The child himself is liable, provided he is old enough to distinguish right from wrong, but he is not usually worth suing and his parents cannot be made to pay any damages ordered. But there are cases where a parent may become liable for his child's wrongdoing: for example, if a father incites or even permits his son to shoot birds in the neighbour's garden, and the neighbour is injured,

17. Infants Relief Act, 1874.
18. *Stone* v. *Carr* (1799) 3 Esp. 1.

the father, will be liable in damages. Similarly, if a parent fails to supervise a child in his charge, or is in control of some dangerous thing and is negligent in allowing the child to use it, then the parent will be liable for any injury caused to others. But this responsibility is limited, and a parent is not expected to watch his children every moment of the day, or indeed to do anything more than what the reasonable and prudent parent would be expected to do. Where, in *Donaldson* v. *McNiven*,[19] a father allowed his thirteen-year-old son to have an air-gun on condition that it was never used outside the house – it was intended that it should only be fired in the cellar – and the boy broke his promise and fired it in a near-by alley-way, injuring another child, the court held that the father was not liable in damages as he had done all that could be reasonably expected of him by extracting a promise that the gun would not be used in the street. In that case both the late Lord Goddard (then Lord Chief Justice) and the late Lord Justice Birkett made it clear that they did not see anything wrong in a father allowing his thirteen-year-old son to have an air-gun, but the result might have been different if the weapon had been more dangerous. Where a father knew his fifteen-year-old son was of such a disposition as not to be trusted with an air-gun, and the boy shot the plaintiff, the father was held liable.[20]

A parent has no direct responsibility for his child's crimes, although he will be liable for punishment if he incites the child or is an accessory to the offence. But the Courts have in recent years been given the power to order parents to pay fines imposed on their children who have been convicted of crimes. The parent may also be ordered to pay any compensation to the victim of the crime which the child has been ordered to pay, or any order for costs. Such an order will not be made against a parent unless the court is satisfied that the parent has been neglectful of his duties or has in some way conduced to the offence. Furthermore, a parent may be ordered by the Court to give security for the good behaviour

19. [1952] 1 All E.R. 1213.
20. *Court* v. *Wyatt* (*The Times*), 25 June 1960.

of a child of his who has been charged with any offence.[21] The age of criminal responsibility of children is ten years old (it was eight until 1963).[22]

For the duty to maintain children in matrimonial proceedings, see pp. 252–7.

Custody and care and control

The father's authority in the family has been completely undermined by a series of laws which have been passed since 1886[23] and which limit his absolute natural right to custody and control to such an extent that it has become little more than an archaic survival. The mother now has equal rights with the father before the Courts: if she is dissatisfied with the way in which the child is being brought up, she can apply – as can the father – to the High Court or to the Magistrates' Court for an order for the custody of the child. At the hearing the Court

> 'shall regard the welfare of the infant as the first and paramount consideration, and shall not take into consideration whether from any other point of view the claim of the father, or any right at common law possessed by the father . . . is superior to that of the mother, or the claim of the mother is superior to that of the father.'[24]

Although since 1886 the mother had had the right to apply to the Court for custody, it was not until 1925 that her equality was so clearly stressed – and more important still, the welfare of the child made paramount *by statute*.

With the increase in divorce, custody proceedings have become common and they are given the greatest importance by the Courts. Custody orders may now be made in relation to any child under eighteen. It is through this jurisdiction that some control can be exercised over the children of broken marriages, and much has been done in recent years to widen the Court's powers in this respect. Court welfare

21. Children and Young Persons Act, 1933, s.55.
22. Children and Young Persons Act, 1963, s.16(1).
23. Guardianship of Infants Act, 1886.
24. Guardianship of Infants Act, 1925. See now Guardianship of Minor's Act, 1971.

officers are available in the High Court and the County Court to report to the judge on the conditions under which the children are living, or under which it is proposed that they shall live, and in the Magistrates' Court the probation officers fulfil this function. No divorce decree may be made absolute where there are children of the family[25] unless the judge has expressed himself satisfied with the arrangements made for the children. By section 17 of the Matrimonial Proceedings and Property Act, 1970. It is laid down that a court shall not make a decree of divorce or nullity absolute, nor make a decree of judicial separation, unless satisfied that satisfactory arrangements have been made for the welfare of every minor of the family who is under sixteen or is receiving educational instruction or training or that it is impracticable for the parties to make such arrangements. The judge must therefore hear evidence and make inquiry as to the children's present care and future prospects, and if he is not satisfied he can order a Court Welfare Officer to investigate or require the parents to provide evidence of more satisfactory arrangements. This sanction is a most useful weapon in making parents shoulder their responsibility for their children before they can get their 'freedom' – usually to remarry and perhaps have other children. The judge also has power under section 36 of the 1965 Act to commit the care of the child to a local authority 'where there are exceptional circumstances making it impracticable or undesirable for the child to be entrusted to either of the parties to the marriage or to any other individual'. This is a serious invasion of parental rights which is only exercised sparingly, but it can be useful in cases where both parents are either unable to make a home for the child or totally unfitted to do so.

In deciding which parent is to have custody of a child, the Courts have changed their attitude considerably in the last

25. This class is very wide: see the Matrimonial Causes Act, 1965, s.46 and Matrimonial Proceedings and Property Act, s.26(1). It includes *any* child who has been treated by both parties as a child of the family and who is under the age of sixteen or receiving education or training.

twenty years. Although judges had frequently stressed that the most important factor was the welfare of the child, and the Act of 1925 had given statutory force to the principle that the child's interests are 'paramount', until quite recently this admirable rule was by no means absolute. This is a good example of the way in which words change their meaning with the alteration of the moral climate. Until the 1950s the word 'paramount' in this context was modified by the prejudice of society against the adultress: however desirable she might be as a mother, and however much the children might suffer by being separated from her, to allow her to care for them was more than a highly principled judge could stomach. At that time, an adultress had not the slightest hope of keeping her children, or indeed of ever seeing them again (a father who had committed adultery was not, however, deprived of his children's custody for that reason). A hundred years ago Sir Cresswell Cresswell, one of the early divorce judges, said in *Seddon* v. *Seddon and Doyle*:

> It will probably have a salutary effect on the interests of public morality, that it should be known that a woman, if found guilty of adultery, will forfeit, as far as this Court is concerned, all right to custody of or access to her children.[26]

Until 1910 this remained the rule, which was universally applied, however trivial the mother's offence or however unsuitable the father. It is impossible to estimate the weight of human misery behind those carefully calculated words of Sir Cresswell, but undoubtedly, at the time, they did no more than express the moral attitude of all right-minded people. There could be no more vivid instance of the inequality of the sexes: a woman had to choose between her lover and her children, while a man could keep his mistress and yet remain head of his family and enjoy the love and respect of his children.

Just before the First World War some cracks began to show in this monstrous edifice. In *Stark* v. *Stark and Hit-*

26. (1862) 2 Sw. and Tr. 640.

chins,[27] where a mother had been divorced on the ground of adultery and had then married the co-respondent, the sixteen-year-old daughter, who was in the custody of her father, ran away to her mother. The father attempted to have the mother committed to prison for contempt of Court, and she was in fact committed for one week by the trial judge; but when she appealed against this decision, the Court of Appeal behaved in a most enlightened way, and discharged both the committal and the custody orders. The *real* effect of discharging the custody order was to leave the custody with the father, under the operation of the common law, but as he could scarcely enforce this right against a daughter of sixteen, the *practical* result was to free the child to live with her mother. The Court said that the mother's adultery

'ought not to be regarded for all time and under all circumstances as sufficient to disentitle the mother to access to her daughter, or even to the custody of her daughter.'

The Court went on to lay down the principle which applies today:

'It is always to be borne in mind that the benefit and interest of the infant is the paramount consideration[28] and not the punishment of the guilty spouse.'

Even after this case, the Courts were reluctant to let a 'guilty' mother have access to her child, and it was almost unknown for her to be given custody. As late as 1951 a judge refused to allow a mother who had married the co-respondent in the divorce the care and control of her child, a girl of two years of age, although the mother was clearly the best person to bring up the child in the circumstances. The reason the judge gave was that it could never be in the interests of the child to be entrusted to the care of a woman who had committed adultery once and who therefore might commit it again! The Court of Appeal said that this was quite a wrong conclusion, and allowed the mother to have

27. [1910] P. 190.
28. This was before such a test was imposed by statute in 1925.

the care and control, although leaving the custody with the father.[29]

Today, the word 'paramount' is given its full meaning in the Courts, and the child's interest ousts all other considerations, whether legal, moral, or ethical. Generally speaking a mother will not be deprived of the care and control of her children while they are very young, even if she is the 'guilty party', unless she is utterly unfitted for motherhood. A prostitute, or a woman who has been proved to be cruel or neglectful towards her children, would certainly not be allowed to have them with her; but even a good mother cannot expect to have her children *as of right* if she is the cause of the disruption of the family, especially if she did so for another man. Lord Denning said in an unreported case in 1962: 'When a mother breaks up her home she must realize she does not have the right to take the children away with her.' The Court of Appeal has recently said[30] that although the best place for a child of three and three-quarters is with his mother, other things being equal, where a mother goes off and leaves the child for a long period to live with another man, the child should stay in the care of his father. (In that case the Court also stressed the importance of the judge seeing the contesting parties: although custody applications are supported by affidavit evidence, the judge has power to call the deponents before him either for cross-examination or to be questioned by the court.) In fact, no rules can be laid down: every case will be decided on its own facts, and often the judges have an almost impossible task in deciding which of two parents should bring up a child. Where children are used as weapons in their parents' matrimonial fights a judge need only decide where lies the best hope for a stable future for the children; but sometimes,

29. This is a not uncommon course. It means that the parent with custody has the ultimate authority over the child's upbringing, while the physical control remains for the time being at least with the other parent, who is better able to give day-to-day care. Magistrates have no jurisdiction to make such an order.

30. *H.* v. *H. and C.* [1969] 1 All E.R. 262.

where both parents are equally devoted, the decision is heart-breaking.

Custody applications can be made even if the parents are living together, and irrespective of whether or not divorce or separation proceedings have been started. If a divorce petition has been filed, the Divorce Court will deal with the application; if not, it must be brought in the Magistrates' Court or in the Chancery Division. In any case the hearing will be in private, and the Court will be able to order maintenance at the same time as it settles questions of custody, care and control, and access. There is a right of appeal against any such decision, but as the question of custody is one for the discretion of the Court, an appeal can only succeed if this discretion can be shown to have been exercised quite wrongly. In divorce cases parties other than the parents can, with leave of the Court, intervene in the suit on questions relating to the children, but in the Magistrates' Court only the spouses can be heard (except for the local authority or the probation officer in certain circumstances, and then only at the request of the court). But whoever applies, the Court has a completely free hand in disposing of the child's future, and either custody or care and control may be given to third parties, even to a local authority. In these days it is very rare for a parent deprived of custody to be refused all contact with the child – access has been described by the Court of Appeal as 'the basic right of every parent' – but in rare cases, where the parent is utterly without merit and likely to cause moral or physical danger to the child, access may be refused. Under section 18(3) of the Matrimonial Proceedings and Property Act, 1970,[31] the Court has power on granting a decree of divorce or judicial separation to make an order that the parent by reason of whose misconduct the decree is made is unfit to have the custody of the children of the marriage. Such a declaration of unfitness debars the parent concerned from being entitled as of right to custody or guardianship on the death of the other parent.

No order relating to children is final: either parent may

31. Formerly s.34(2) of the Matrimonial Causes Act, 1965.

come back to the Court at any time for a variation. Custody and maintenance orders may be made relating to children up to twenty-one years, or in certain cases – as where education is incomplete – beyond that age. But no court will order a child over sixteen to live with either parent against its will. It does not matter where the child is living; provided it is a British subject, the English courts can make an order even if the child is abroad and even though it may be impossible to enforce the order. An order made by a foreign court will be taken into account by the English courts, but it is in no way binding and the child's interests are the prime consideration. At one time only children of both the parties to the marriage could be made the subject of a custody order, but now the Court has jurisdiction over all 'children of the family' – this includes any child, whether legitimate or not, born to or adopted by either of the spouses, provided it has been treated by both parties as a child of their family. Thus a child of one party by a previous marriage is a 'child of the family' if it has lived with them after the remarriage, or has even been supported by the step-father or step-mother.

As we have seen (p. 99), magistrates can make an order relating to the children of the family whenever matrimonial proceedings have been *started* before them. The County Court has the jurisdiction to deal with the children, on the application of one of the parties or some other interested person, as soon as a divorce petition is filed. When the case is transferred to the High Court, on becoming defended, application must be made to a judge of the Divorce Division. But even when the divorce suit is to be brought in the County Court, the High Court has power to grant an injunction for the protection of the children of the family.[32] No divorce decree can be made absolute until the Court is satisfied as to the welfare of the children. These provisions of the law, combined with the present wide definition of 'children of the family', are probably the best that the law can be expected to do to ensure that the children of broken homes do not suffer more than is inevitable. In the last resort their fate

32. *L.* v. *L.* (1969) 113 S.J. 88.

depends on their parents: civilized people should not project their sexual jealousy and frustration on to their helpless children, and undoubtedly many couples come to sensible arrangements about the family with the minimum of disturbance, but all too often the children are forced into divided loyalties and emotional insecurity. No Act of Parliament can prevent this, but at least the material environment can be controlled, and since 1958[33] the law has made it more difficult for parents who break up their marriages to neglect their children physically.

33. Matrimonial Proceedings (Children) Act, 1958, now Matrimonial Proceedings and Property Act, 1970.

11 State and Child

As the basis of society moves, in the words of Maine, 'from status to contract', so does the child progress from being first and foremost his father's chattel to a position regulated by law and largely independent of his family. A modern state, living by technology, must see that its children are educated and physically cared for to properly survive in a modern society, and parents can no longer be left to bring up their children as they please, but must conform to the requirements of the state. So the law has come to govern the upbringing of children more and more, in spite of the English distaste for interference in the family, and the area of the parents' discretion is now very much narrowed down. This is perhaps one of the most potent influences in the new relationship between parents and children. When authority is so circumscribed by the law, it cannot receive the same respect as when it is absolute, or at least freely exercised.

Although until recently the state as such interfered very little with children and left them almost completely to the mercy of their parents, the sovereign has always had a special interest in the helpless subjects of the Crown, including minors and mental defectives. This is a relic of the feudal bond whereby the king, as liege-lord, was obliged to maintain and defend his people in return for service and obedience. Part of this feudal concept is the sovereign's prerogative right to protect the persons and estates of infants, idiots, and persons of unsound mind. The king as *parens patriae* at one time received petitions directly and made orders for the care and protection of his infant subjects. Later he exercised these powers through his Lord Chancellor, the Keeper of the Royal Conscience, but with the end of feudalism – which came slowly and late in the law as might be expected – the Chancellor's Court of Wards and Liveries was abolished[1] and the prerogative was transferred to the Court of Chancery.

Wards of court

The way in which this royal prerogative was, and is, called into play is by making the infant a *ward of Court*. The Court can then appoint a guardian and give such directions as to the infant's upbringing or welfare as may be necessary, and the ward may not marry or leave the jurisdiction without leave of the Court. It is evident that this parental interest of the sovereign in his infant subjects was mainly directed towards those who had property; until 1949 a child became a ward of Court automatically on the commencement of an action in his or her name, or on payment into Court of any money or securities in which the infant was interested, and it was chiefly in these two ways that the jurisdiction came to be exercised. Although in theory the king was father to all his liege children, whether born to lord or serf, in practice only those with landed or other property interests ever came within the exercise of the royal prerogative. Wardship procedure was particularly useful, in the days when a woman's property vested in her husband on marriage,[2] in preventing fortune-seekers from marrying heiresses and thus laying hands on their property.

For centuries the judges of the Chancery Division have exercised this jurisdiction over children, standing so to speak in the shoes of the sovereign as universal parent to the State. But in recent years wardship proceedings have become increasingly inappropriate to the Chancery Division: with legal aid to help them, more and more parents have used the procedure to resolve their difficulties, whether they arise from defiance of parental authority or from their own squabbles over custody. The property element has gone out of wardship, and it has become an important part of the law

1. Tenures Abolition Act, 1660.
2. That is, before the Married Women's Property Act, 1882.

of domestic relations. For this reason all wardship jurisdiction is to be transferred to the new Family Division of the High Court.

Since 1949[3] a child can only be made a ward of Court only by order of the Court, not merely by starting some action relating to property, or by payment of money into Court on his behalf. In fact, the infant becomes a ward immediately an originating summons is issued in the Chancery Division, which is useful, because wardship procedure is often an urgent measure taken to prevent some irrevocable act, such as marriage or taking a child out of the country. But this system is open to abuse, and there have been cases where infants have been made wards for spurious reasons. It is now necessary for a supporting affidavit to be produced on application for the summons except in cases where the Court official issuing the summons is satisfied that there is extreme urgency. But unless the summons is followed up by making an appointment for a hearing by the Court, the wardship lapses after twenty-one days. The effect of wardship is far-reaching: a ward may not leave the country without the Court's consent, and to marry a ward or assist in such a marriage is contempt of court punishable by imprisonment. A parent or other interested party has only to publicize the wardship sufficiently to put all registrars and ministers of religion on their guard against performing any such marriage. No passport will be issued to a ward, and the Home Office notifies ports where necessary to prevent the infant from leaving the country. But these are not the only reasons why children are made wards of court: sometimes a parent who wishes to arrange the education or upbringing of a child against the will of the other parent seeks the guidance of the Court and the security of a wardship order. The child then becomes the ultimate responsibility of the Court: although one of the parents, or some third party, may be appointed guardian, all major decisions relating to education, upbringing, religion, and marriage must be taken by the Court, and the guardian can at any time apply to the Court for guidance. Anyone who intereferes with the Court's authority,

3. Law Reform (Miscellaneous Provisions) Act, 1949.

even the ward himself, may be punished by committal to prison for contempt of Court. This is a very powerful weapon, and many undesirable suitors have been frightened away, and many parents checked in their plans to whisk their children out of the reach of the other parent, by the knowledge that the tipstaff was waiting to support the authority of the Court by carrying them off to Brixton or Holloway. Wardship is a particularly interesting example of how an ancient prerogative procedure can be adapted to modern needs – and evidence of the flexibility of the law to set against those examples we have seen of its rigidity.

The principles on which the judges of the Family Division will act will no doubt follow those which applied in the Chancery Division. These are not easy to define, since the judge has a wide discretion to make any order for the benefit of the infant. The case is generally heard *in camera* to avoid harmful publicity, but sometimes, as where a ward has disappeared, publicity may be helpful and the judge opens the Court to enable his orders to be as widely published as possible by press reports. If the judge does not consider that the Court should retain control over the infant he will make an order dewarding him, otherwise he will confirm the wardship, which will then continue until the age of majority[4] or until further order.[4a]

There are today three main classes of applicant in wardship cases:

1. United parents make their child, usually a daughter, a ward either in order to prevent her from marrying or associating with an undesirable partner, or to bring her back into the bosom of the family when she has left home and is thought to be in moral danger. Here the Court will intervene to prevent a hasty, disastrous marriage, but may give consent to the marriage against the parents' wishes after a full investigation. The judge is unlikely to order an infant over school age to return home against his or her will unless there is strong evidence of moral danger.

4. Now 18: see Family Law Reform Act, 1969, s.1(1).

4a. Under s.6 of the Family Law Reform Act, maintenance can now be ordered in wardship cases.

2. One parent seeks to wrest a child from the custody of the other, estranged, parent. In this case the Court has the difficult task of deciding between the rival claims of parents, and applies the same principles as operate in the Divorce Courts (see p. 208 *et seq.*). But in this jurisdiction there is very often a foreign element: where one parent lives abroad and the other in England there is inevitably some bias in favour of the parent resident here, since once the child is removed from its jurisdiction the Court loses all control, and cannot put matters right if things turn out badly. Where there is an order of a foreign Court in relation to the custody of the infant, the English Court will take account of this but will not necessarily follow the order, since that would be to abdicate the duty imposed on the Court as *parens patriae*.[5] The paramount interest of the child prevails over questions of parental guilt or innocence in matrimonial matters, foreign orders, and the comity of nations; even kidnapping by one parent, although frowned on by the Courts, is not met with the automatic response of an order to return the child.[6]

3. Foster-parents or would-be adopters seek to hold the custody of a child in their care against the wishes of the child's own parent or parents. These are difficult and often tragic cases. A parent's right to bring up, and to love and to receive love from, his own offspring is not easily displaced, even by the overriding interest of the child's welfare. While there is nothing in tradition or law in this country which approaches the Roman idea of *patri potestas* – still part of the code of some Latin countries – nevertheless the ties of blood are strong and a Court will require very cogent evidence indeed that the child's interest demands that he be separated from his own parent before denying him the obvious advantages of growing up with his own father or mother or both. In *Re Thain*,[7] decided a year after the Guardianship of Infants Act, 1925 first gave statutory force to the paramount interest of the child, the Court held that a

5. *Re E.* (*an infant*) C.A. [1967] Ch. 761.
6. *Re E.* (*an infant*) supra and *Re. T.* (*infants*) [1968] 1 Ch. 704.
7. [1926] Ch. 676.

young girl, brought up by loving relatives for six years after her mother's death, should nevertheless be returned to the custody of her father since it was in her paramount interest to be brought up by him, although there was undoubted evidence that she was secure and happy with her foster-parents and there was no certainty that the change would be for her good. This case was thought for many years to be authority for the proposition that it must be in the best interests of a child to be in the custody of his own parent, and that unimpeachable parents would never be deprived by the Courts of their child if they could provide a good home for him. This was reinforced by the decision in *Re C. (M.A.)*[8] which received much publicity as the 'blood-tie case'. There a child of eighteen months was taken away from an excellent home with foster-parents, would-be adopters, and given into the care of her putative father and his wife. But in *J.* v. *C.*[9] the House of Lords refused to take a ten-year-old boy from foster-parents with whom he had lived for most of his life and return him to his unimpeachable Spanish parents, who ardently desired his return.

Child welfare

No law can create good parents, but much can be done to limit the effect of bad ones. Even in a highly developed welfare state, parents are obliged by law to maintain their children, as we shall see in the next chapter; but the provision of money and the necessities of life is by no means the end of parenthood, and the law now goes considerably further in the physical and moral protection of children. Under the common law every parent (and everyone standing *in loco parentis*) has a duty to protect his children. If the child dies as the result of neglect, abandonment, or excessive chastisement, the parent will be guilty of manslaughter at least; if he intended the child's death, he will be guilty of murder. The general law as to assault applies within the family, and a father who injures his child can be convicted

8. [1966] 1 W.L.R. 646.
9. [1970] A.C. 668.

of common assault, aggravated assault, or grievous bodily harm in the same way as a stranger. But these common law sanctions were not enough to prevent parents from neglecting their children, since actual injury to health had to be proved in cases where there was no actual assault, and until 1889 the law could not intervene where there was nothing more than a threat to the child's life or health. In that year the Prevention of Cruelty to, and Better Protection of, Children Act was passed, making it an offence for any person over sixteen having the custody, control, or charge of a child to ill-treat, neglect, abandon, or expose that child, or to cause or procure such ill-treatment, in a manner likely to cause the child unnecessary suffering. This Act also imposed certain very limited restrictions on the employment of children, for example, as beggars or in the licensed trade, and further – a much more revolutionary step – gave the Courts power to take children out of the custody of their parents in certain circumstances.

This Act established for the first time the principle that the state would interfere in the family in order to prevent hardship or danger to the children. It opened a breach in the wall of the Englishman's castle, through which in later years there has poured an army of children's officers, probation officers, education officers, and welfare workers of all kinds. A series of Children and Young Persons Acts has extended the principle, and the present law[10] contains specific provisions against almost any conceivable sort of injury or neglect. Failure to provide proper medical treatment for a child was made an offence by an Act of 1908:[11] in the case of *Oakey* v. *Jackson*[12] it was held that if a parent refuses to allow his child to undergo a necessary operation, he is guilty of such failure. In that case, the magistrates held that the statute did not mean that the father was under a legal liability to allow the operation to be performed, but they were overruled by the Divisional Court, who found that 'in the particular cir-

10. Children and Young Persons Acts, 1933 to 1956.
11. Children Act, 1908, s. 12.
12. [1914] 1 K.B. 216.

cumstances' the father was liable. The Court qualified this by saying that not every refusal to permit an operation would amount to 'failure to provide adequate medical aid' – every case must be judged on its particular facts. The test is whether the parent behaved reasonably, therefore the cogency of the medical advice and the likelihood of injury to health must be taken into account.

It will be seen that under the present law, which is as follows, almost any ill-treatment of children can be an offence:

If any person who has attained the age of sixteen years and has the custody, charge, or care of any child or young person under that age, wilfully assaults, ill-treats, neglects, abandons, or exposes him, or causes him to be assaulted, ill-treated, neglected, abandoned, or exposed, in a manner likely to cause him unnecessary suffering or injury to health (including injury to or loss of sight, or hearing, or limb, or organ of the body, and any mental derangement), that person shall be guilty of a misdemeanour.[13]

This covers almost everything from starving a child to death to shutting it up in a chicken-run. More specifically, it is an offence for an adult to go to bed under the influence of drink with an infant under three years of age, if the infant should suffocate (section 1(2)(b)) ('overlaying' was at one time a serious problem); or to be drunk in a public place while in charge of a child under seven;[14] or for an adult who has charge of a child over four and under sixteen years to allow him to live in a brothel;[15] or to allow a child under twelve to be in a room containing an open fire or other heating appliance not sufficiently protected to guard against the risk of the child being burnt or scalded, if the child is killed or seriously injured and the adult in charge has not taken reasonable precautions, (section 11). Then there is a mass of statute law forbidding the sale of drink,[16] tobacco,[17] and

13. Children and Young Persons Act, 1933, s. 1.
14. Licensing Act, 1953, s. 2(1).
15. Children and Young Persons Act, 1933, s. 3(1).
16. Licensing Act, 1953, s. 128(1).
17. Children and Young Persons Act, 1933, s. 7.

firearms[18] to children and ensuring their safety at entertainments[19] and cinemas.[20]

Under the old Poor Law provisions, children who were without effective parents or guardians became the responsibility of the parish, with results for the children which depended largely on the individual characters of the officials under whose care they came. Since the servants of Bumbledom were ill-paid, lowly regarded, and generally quite untrained, the plight of orphans and neglected children was always sad and often wretched. Dickens's picture in *Oliver Twist* of the Poor Laws in action was probably not much of an exaggeration. But since 1945 there has grown up a body of social legislation which has swept away the last traces of care by the parish, replacing it with an elaborate scheme to cover all ordinary need. Under the modern law[21] all orphaned or abandoned children become the responsibility of the County Councils – or the equivalent London County authority – and this includes all children whose parents are for some reason (sickness, imprisonment, or any other circumstances) prevented from looking after them. The local authority has power to take any child into care, provided a parent or guardian does not desire to take over the care of the child. These children are looked after by trained and devoted people in good accommodation, but however excellent the care it cannot take the place of home life, and the statute (section 1(3)) imposes on the local authority the duty to secure that the child shall be handed over to a parent or relative wherever that course is consistent with the welfare of the child. But where the parents are dead or incapacitated or quite unfit to resume the care of the child, the local authority may assume entire parental rights by passing a resolution to that effect. The resolution must be served on any parent or guardian whose whereabouts are known, and

18. Firearms Act, 1937, ss. 16 and 19, and the Air Guns and Shot Guns etc., Act, 1962.

19. Children and Young Persons Act, 1933, s. 12.

20. Cinematograph Act, 1952, ss. 2, 3, and 4.

21. Children Act, 1948, s. 1(1).

if no objection is received within one month, the local authority becomes the legal parent of the child, with all the rights of custody which can be enforced against the whole world, even the parents:[21a]

This is a very big invasion of the family by the state, but it is nothing to compare with the powers given to the Juvenile Courts and the local authority under the Children and Young Persons Act, 1969. This Act,[22] which revolutionizes the law relating to the young, aims 'to prevent the deprived and delinquent child of today from becoming the deprived, inadequate, unstable or criminal citizen of tomorrow'. To this end criminal prosecutions of children are to be abolished and local authorities are charged with the duty to inquire into any case in their area where there is a suggestion that a child may require to be brought before a Juvenile Court and if it then appears that there are grounds for making a care order, to bring the child before the Court. Furthermore, no care proceedings may be brought without notice to the local authority.

The child is brought before the Juvenile Court by a local authority, constable, or authorized person (that is authorized by the Home Office). His parent cannot bring him to Court as under the former law. When the child appears before the Court the Magistrates must investigate the case to find out if he is in need of care and control and if at the same time any of the following conditions exist:

1. His proper development is being avoidably prevented or neglected, his health is being avoidably impaired or neglected or he is being ill-treated.

2. It is probable that the condition set out in the preceding paragraph will be satisfied in his case, having regard to the fact that the Court or another court has found that that con-

21a. Children Act, 1948, s.2.

22. Its provisions are to be brought in gradually over a period of years, but the sections referred to in this chapter (relating to care and supervision orders) are expected to be in force by the end of 1970.

dition is or was satisfied in the case of another child or young person who is or was a member of the household to which he belongs.

3. He is exposed to moral danger.

4. He is beyond the control of his parent or guardian.

5. He is of compulsory school age within the meaning of the Education Act, 1944 and is not receiving efficient full-time education suitable to his age, ability and aptitude.

6. He is guilty of an offence, excluding homicide.[23]

If satisfied that one or more of these conditions is established, the magistrates can make one of the following orders:

1. An order requiring his parent or guardian to enter into a recognizance to take proper care of him and exercise proper control over him.

2. A supervision order.

3. A care order (other than an interim order).

4. A hospital order within the meaning of part 5 of the Mental Health Act 1959.

5. A guardianship order within the meaning of that Act.

A *supervision order* places the child under the local authority, who may require the child to live in a specified place, receive treatment or participate in activities as directed by the authority. The child may be put under a probation officer, who will be part of the local authority organization.

A *care order* gives the local authority complete authority over the child to the exclusion of parental rights: the authority shall receive the child into and keep him in their care 'notwithstanding any claim by his parent or guardian' while the order is in force (section 24). The discretion of the authority in dealing with the child is much wider than it was under earlier Acts, such as the Children and Young Persons Act, 1933 ('fit person' orders). The Children Act, 1948

23. Children and Young Persons Act, 1969, s. 1.

imposed a duty on the authority to exercise their already wide power 'to further [the child's] best interests and afford him opportunity for proper development', but section 27(2) of the new Act relieves them of this check on their powers.

The result is that the Children's Department of the Town Hall can on its own initiative, subject to the magistrates' decision and the right of appeal to Quarter Sessions, take over the whole control and disposition of any child who is neglected, out of hand, in trouble with the law, or not being educated 'efficiently'. It is true that the parents can oppose the making of a care order, or apply for it to be set aside, but the very title of the order must make it difficult to oppose if there is any evidence that the child is out of control.

These orders replace the former fit person and approved school orders. Approved schools are to be replaced altogether in time by 'community homes' which will house all children in care, whether neglected or guilty of criminal offences. But it should be noted that the rights and duties of the local authority to take abandoned children into care and to assume parental powers under sections 1 and 2 of the Children Act, 1948 (see p. 224) are unaffected by the new code.

Many will be anxious about the sweeping powers now given to the local Children's Departments, but on the other side it is arguable that the former power of the law to intervene in the family was not wide enough. There are undoubtedly many hidden cases of neglect and ill-treatment. For instance, recent work on the 'battered baby syndrome',[24] which has revealed that really serious ill-treatment is often passed off as accidental injury, underlines the need for wider powers to discover, and remedy, problem families. It is often worse than useless to send either or both parents to prison: what may be needed is treatment while avoiding the break-up of the home, which may do the child

24. A condition in which a child is found to have multiple injuries, often fractures, received at different times. One or both parents may be sadistic, or suffering from a psychological disturbance. Many of these children are illegitimate or conceived out of wedlock.

more harm than the physical violence he has already suffered. It is very difficult to find any way to effect this solution within the present law relating to children.

Education

The law controls the upbringing of children to a remarkable extent today through compulsory education and restriction on employment. Before the late nineteenth century, a parent could please himself whether or not he sent his child to school – that is, if he had the means to do so, or was lucky enough to find education provided by charity. Since 1833 there had been a certain amount of Treasury assistance for education, but there was no general system of elementary education until 1870.[25] In 1893[26] school attendance was made compulsory: the father's moral duty to educate his children was converted into a legal duty, and at the same time the state took the obligation to provide schooling off his shoulders. Under the present law,[27] it is 'the duty of the parent of every child of compulsory school age' – that is, between five and fifteen – 'to cause him to receive efficient full-time education suitable to his age, ability, and aptitude, either by regular attendance at school or otherwise.' If the local authority believe that this duty is not being fulfilled, it can serve a 'school attendance order' on the parent specifying a school at which the child must attend; if this order is disobeyed, the parent is guilty of an offence, punishable by a fine of one pound in the first instance, five pounds for a second offence, and ten pounds or one month's imprisonment for subsequent offences.

The statutory obligation to educate children is not only an invasion of parental authority; it is also a restriction on the prerogative right of the sovereign, as exercised by the courts, to give orders for the care and upbringing of infants. This was illustrated by *Re Baker* (*Infants*)[28] decided in 1961. A

25. Elementary Education Act, 1870.
26. Elementary Education (School Attendance) Act, 1893.
27. Education Act, 1944.
28. [1962] Ch. 201.

mother of seven children, living apart from her husband and holding strong views against organized education, steadfastly refused to send her children to school. She believed that she could give them a better education at home than they would get at any school, and in particular that she could bring them up to have more original and independent minds than if they were pressed into any educational mould. (She later defended her principles most ably in the correspondence columns of *The Times*.) The Norfolk County Council did not agree that the mother was providing the 'efficient full-time education' required by the Act, and served her with school attendance orders which she disregarded. She was convicted, appealed, and lost her appeal; she was convicted again, and again lost her appeal; having lost all along the line, she still refused to comply with the orders. The Council could continue to prosecute her, and no doubt she would eventually have been sent to prison, but this would not of itself get the children to school: it was pointless to punish the mother, since clearly nothing would deflect her from her views. Finally, the Council went to the Chancery Division and made the children wards of Court, asking for direction as to their education. But this manoeuvre failed, not because the judge had any sympathy with the mother's views, but because the jurisdiction of the Court had been ousted by the Education Acts in this particular matter. The royal prerogative does not extend to interference with Acts of Parliament: the Court could not prevent the making of a school attendance order, nor could it enforce such an order; the statute provided the means of enforcement, and these must be followed.

A determined parent could thus keep his child away from school and if the child was well controlled and kept out of trouble the authorities could do little about it. But under section 1(e) of the Children and Young Persons Act, 1969 the local authority can bring a child before the Juvenile Court in care proceedings (see p. 226) solely on the ground that he is not receiving 'efficient full-time education'. Then, unless the parent enters into a recognizance to take proper care of him, a care order or supervision order will be made, which will give the local authority effective powers to see that he does attend school – even to the point of removing him entirely from parental control.

Employment of children

A further restriction on parental rights is the law against employment of children. In the working-class family a hundred years ago a child was regarded as an investment – a mouth to feed until he was grown sufficiently to bring home a wage each week, but then an asset, that wage being the property of the head of the family to be used as he thought fit, either for the general welfare of the family or for the indulgence of the father. It took the devotion of a Shaftesbury to break down this custom, and the resistance from the workers was as bitter as that of the industrialists who saw the end of a cheap source of labour. The law grew slowly, clamping down on one form of slavery after another. The position now is that no child may be employed until he is two years short of the upper age limit for compulsory education – at present, that means not under thirteen – and in any event not during school hours, or before 6 a.m. or after 8 p.m., or for more than two hours on a schoolday or a Sunday; nor may he be required to lift, carry, or move anything so heavy as to be likely to cause injury to him.[29]

We have seen that the Juvenile Courts and the criminal law of course assists in protection from moral danger by punishing rape and indecent assaults on children, sexual intercourse with girls under sixteen, and incest. It throws an interesting light on the growth of moral standards within the family that incest was not made a criminal offence until 1908, no doubt partly because it was endemic both in isolated rural areas and in overcrowded slums, and partly because of the reluctance of the law to invade the privacy of the family – perhaps also there was reluctance to recognize that squalor and poverty could reduce men to the level of

29. Children and Young Persons Act, 1933, s. 18.

beasts, and that society was responsible for such degradation.

There are many incidental ways in which the state has taken over the duties of parents – school meals, the school medical and dental services, the provision of nurseries for the children of mothers who work, subsidized housing, grants for further education – all these relieve the parents and give all children, from good and bad, rich and poor homes alike, a measure of opportunity at the beginning of their lives. Whether this lessening of parental responsibility and authority is desirable is still a matter on which opinions vary: some see in it the decay of the family as a social unit, while others believe that the 'democratic' family of today is an infinitely better thing for all its members than the rigid structure it has replaced. One thing is certain: the old type of family was utterly unsuited to modern conditions, and could not have survived unchanged. The law has played a big part in moulding the new style of family although, as we shall see in the next chapter, some of the changes in the law put great strains on family life.

Part Four Maintenance and Property

Introduction

'But then one is always excited by descriptions of money changing hands. It's much more fundamental than sex.'[1] Whether more fundamental or not, the excitement is certainly very easily transferred from love to property: the progress from passionate love through sexual jealousy to quarrelling over the Crown Derby is too common to be ignored. When marriages break down the real question for the lawyers today is not who can win a hollow personal victory by proving that the other was guilty of a matrimonial offence, but who shall support whom and to what extent; who shall take what share of the matrimonial property; and how shall financial justice be done throughout the family. These questions test the skills of bench, bar and solicitors perhaps more than anything else in matrimonial law.

There have been great changes in matrimonial property law in recent years and in this section we see the effects of the Act of 1970 on the law relating to maintenance of wives, husbands and children. The rights of both parties to occupy the matrimonial home and the resolution of their claims to its ownership have also been radically changed.

Community of property in marriage, while it failed to win sufficient support in Parliament to become part of our matrimonial law, can now be effected by the judges in the exercise of the wide discretion given to them under the new Acts. The principles on which this discretion will be exercised are examined in this part of the book, together with the law on financial provision after the death of the party.

1. Nigel Dennis, *Cards of Identity*.

12 The Right to Support

It is a principle of English social law that no one shall be allowed to become a charge on the state while there is some member of his immediate family capable of maintaining him. In this respect the law intervenes decisively in the family: welfare state or no welfare state, a man or woman attracts on marriage the liability for the basic necessaries of life of husband, wife, and children, and he or she cannot contract out of this liability. No mutual agreement not to ask for maintenance can oust the right of the state to look to one spouse for the maintenance of the other.

There is nothing new in this principle. Under the old Poor Law, if a wife or children became a charge on the parish, the cost of their maintenance could, in theory at any rate, be recovered from the husband. But it was at that time also a principle of law that a husband could not be obliged to maintain his wife if he were not legally bound to do so – in other words, if she had committed adultery or deserted him, the expense of her maintenance could not be recovered from him. The modern law is contained in the National Assistance Act, 1948, which set up a National Assistance Board to supersede the old Poor Law machinery, and gave the Board[1] the right to apply to a Court to recover any sums paid out, from anyone liable to maintain the assisted person. In cases brought under this Act, it has been held that a husband cannot shift his liability on to the community simply because he is no longer bound to maintain his wife at common law (for example, where she has entered into an agreement not to ask for maintenance as in *National*

1. Replaced by the Supplementary Benefits Commission.

Assistance Board v. *Parkes*[2]), but there is no *absolute liability* to maintain a wife imposed on a husband by the National Assistance Act; in *National Assistance Board* v. *Wilkinson*[3] the Divisional Court held that where a husband had been deserted by his wife, he could not be ordered to repay to the National Assistance Board the sums they had paid out to the wife.

Wife maintenance

This duty to support the other members of the family – which, incidentally, does not go so far as to impose any duty on children to maintain their parents or siblings – is a matter entirely between the state and the individual. The law was much slower to enforce the moral duties within the family itself. Since, prior to 1882, married women could not own the bare necessities of life, a husband was inevitably liable to provide his wife with some sort of maintenance. Indeed, this can be regarded simply as an application of the legal fiction of unity between husband and wife, and we have already seen how it worked out in practice and how, until very recently, a husband could be sued for necessaries supplied to his wife (pp. 37–8). But the right to pledge a husband's credit was a dubious advantage, since it depended on finding a tradesman willing to give credit, and it was a practice which is clearly subject to the law of diminishing returns. What wives needed was a *legal* right to maintenance, and for a long time they had no such thing. The Ecclesiastical Courts had the power to order maintenance when making a decree of divorce *a mensa et thoro*, and we have seen that even the guilty wife had the protection of 'The Ladies' Friend' in parliamentary divorces (see p. 59), but for those wives who were unwilling or unable to take divorce proceedings there was no possible machinery for obtaining maintenance however guilty the husband. Unless something could be negotiated, or the husband's family could be prevailed on to help – and polite social blackmail usually procured such

2. [1955] 2 Q.B. 506.
3. [1952] 2 Q.B. 648.

support among the wealthy classes – the deserted wife was thrown back on her own relations or the parish.

But in 1878 for the first time a wife was given the legal right to maintenance from a husband who ill-treated her. An Act[4] of that year gave any court (including a Magistrates' Court) which convicted a husband of an aggravated assault on his wife the power to award maintenance to the wife. This Act was soon repealed, but it was replaced by a much more far-reaching statute[5] which gave wives the right to apply to magistrates for maintenance where their husbands had treated them with persistent cruelty, had deserted them, assaulted them, or wilfully neglected to maintain them. The maximum weekly sum that could be ordered at that time was two pounds. Other grounds have been added from time to time, and the maximum weekly order increased, until today the grounds are as set out in chapter 4, and the magistrates can make an order for any amount.[6]

Meanwhile, the new Divorce Court set up in 1857 had the power to order maintenance up to any sum in all cases of divorce, so that the working-class wife could obtain an order suitable to her needs from the magistrates and the wealthier woman could seek more appropriate maintenance in the Divorce Court. But for many years there remained a gap: a woman who was not willing or able to divorce her husband could not go to the High Court, but was limited to the maximum sum which the magistrates could award. She could have two pounds a week or nothing. This position continued until 1949, when the High Court was given power to order a husband who has been guilty of wilful neglect to provide reasonable maintenance for his wife or infant children to make her periodical payments without any limit on the amount.[7]

The position today, then, is that a wife who has been neglected, deserted, or ill-treated has a choice: she may go to

4. Matrimonial Causes Act, 1878, s. 4.
5. Summary Jurisdiction (Married Women) Act, 1895.
6. Maintenance Orders Act, 1968.
7. Now s. 22 of Matrimonial Causes Act, 1965.

the Magistrates' Court; she can start proceedings for divorce or judicial separation, when she will be able to apply for maintenance pending the hearing of the case, and full financial relief afterwards; or she can apply to the Divorce County Court, without starting any other proceedings, for an order for maintenance under section 6 of the Matrimonial Proceedings and Property Act, 1970. A husband is liable for maintenance even if the marriage is polygamous.[8]

Whichever procedure the wife chooses, the principles on which the sum is computed are much the same. As a very rough rule, and subject to many qualifications, the Courts have followed the practice of the old Ecclesiastical Courts, and awarded the wife a sum which would bring her income up to one-third of the total joint incomes of husband and wife. Thus, if she earned nothing, and her husband earned £1500 a year, he would probably be ordered to pay her £500; if she earned, or had a private income of £500 herself, she would get about £150; if she had £800 of her own, she would get nothing. But this was by no means a rule of law, and in recent years it has been generally regarded as discredited (although in fact followed to a great extent). The Divisional Court has suggested a different approach.[9] The principle is that a wife should not suffer financially as a result of the breakdown of the marriage, or at least no more than is inevitable when one source of income has to maintain two homes. The wife should not be relegated to a lower standard of life than the husband, although both may have to suffer some reduction in available income. Where the joint income is small, the principle to be applied is this: the husband must be left with sufficient to keep him at subsistence level, having regard to all essential expenses such as travelling to work; out of the surplus the wife should be allotted a sum, sufficient for her subsistence, then the children should each receive enough to keep them; thereafter, if there is any surplus, it should be allotted in such a way as to do justice to all the parties concerned. But it must be stressed

8. *Din* v. *National Assistance Board* [1967] 2 Q.B. 213.
9. *Kershaw* v. *Kershaw* [1966] P. 13, *Ashley* v. *Ashley* [1968] P. 582.

that this approach is only suitable for the modest income. Where incomes are larger, the husband is likely to keep a larger proportion of his income. When dealing with very large incomes the Courts try to assess what sum is necessary to keep the wife in the same manner as when she lived with her husband. Whatever sum is awarded to the wife is quite separate from any award made for the children, and in assessing the sum to be ordered for wife or children, any assistance received by them by way of social security payments must not be taken into account (see *Ashley* v. *Ashley* above).

In general, it has been a defence to a husband on any application for maintenance to show that his wife had committed a matrimonial offence. Even when the suit is pending, where the wife is proved to have committed adultery she will not necessarily obtain an order. But although a woman who has been the cause of breaking up the marriage cannot expect to be paid maintenance thereafter, the Court has discretion to make an award.

In the past a small compassionate allowance was sometimes awarded to a 'guilty' wife. But the courts have recently recognized that the party who was found guilty by decree was not necessarily the cause of the breakdown of the marriage, and would award proper maintenance to a wife even if she had, for example, committed adultery, if the length of the marriage and the position of the children warranted it.[10] Now that breakdown is to be the only ground for a decree, it will be necessary to consider who caused the breakdown as well as the matters laid down by statute when ordering financial relief. In spite of the abolition of the matrimonial offence as a ground for dissolution it seems that a full investigation of guilt and innocence will still be necessary to decide the parties' financial obligations. By section 5(1) of the Matrimonial Proceedings and Property Act, 1970:

it shall be the duty of the Court in deciding whether to exercise its powers [to order financial relief] in relation to a party to the

10. See *Porter* v. *Porter* [1969] 3 All E.R. 640.

marriage and, if so, in what manner, to have regard to all the circumstances of the case, including the following matters; that is to say:

(*a*) the income, earning capacity, property and other financial resources which each of the parties to the marriage has or is likely to have in the foreseeable future;

(*b*) the financial needs, obligations and responsibilities which each of the parties to the marriage has or is likely to have in the foreseeable future;

(*c*) the standard of living enjoyed by the family before the breakdown of the marriage;

(*d*) the age of each party to the marriage and the duration of the marriage;

(*e*) the contributions made by each of the parties to the welfare of the family, including any contribution made by looking after the home or caring for the family;

(*f*) in the case of proceedings for divorce or nullity of marriage, the value to either of the parties to the marriage of any benefit (for example, a pension) which by reason of the dissolution or annulment of the marriage, that party will lose the chances of acquiring;

and so to exercise those powers as to place the parties, so far as it is practicable and, having regard to their conduct, just to do so, in the financial position in which they would have been if the marriage had not broken down and each had properly discharged his or her financial obligations and responsibilities towards the other.[11]

It will be seen that the 'conduct of the parties' is still to be taken into account. Such conduct can be canvassed in maintenance proceedings even if not alleged in the divorce.[12] It is therefore not necessary to fight a defended divorce suit in order to bring out bad conduct by the other spouse which might affect the award of maintenance.

It is interesting to note that the matters now laid down by statute as those on which the court should exercise discretion

11. The principles to be applied on awarding child maintenance are set out on pp. 254–9.

12. *Tumath* v. *Tumath* [1970] But as to the question of estoppel, see *Porter* v. *Porter* [1971] 2 All E.R. 1037.

in deciding what is reasonable have not greatly changed since 1891 when Lord Justice Lindley set them out in *Wood* v. *Wood*.[13]

The circumstances which have to be taken into account are: (1) the conduct of the parties; (2) their positions in life, and their ages and their respective means; (3) the amount of the provision actually made; (4) the existence . . . of children . . . (5) any other circumstances which may be important in any particular case.

What has changed since 1891 is the *application* of these principles. The law is 'alive and moving with the times and is not a creature of dead or moribund thought' said Lord Justice Sachs in *Porter* v. *Porter*,[14] thus changing social standards – particularly the attitude to a wife's adultery – mean that today the courts will pay more attention to the length of cohabitation and the true cause of the breakdown of the marriage than to the bare facts on which a decree is granted. There is usually a good deal more in the breakdown of a marriage than is revealed at the hearing of an undefended suit, and it is on the whole picture of the marriage that the Court must decide what is reasonable. We have come a long way from the time when a single act of adultery would inevitably deprive a wife of all rights to support (or even the right to see her children; see p. 211). Today, a wife who has lived many years with her husband, and after the divorce is without any means, will be awarded maintenance even if she has committed a matrimonial offence, except in very rare cases. It seems likely that the Courts will continue to apply the same principles under the 1970 act as they have done in recent years, subject to the developments to be expected from a law that is 'alive and moving with the times'.

All questions of ancillary relief initially come before a County Court registrar on evidence given on affidavit.[15]

13. [1891] P. 272.
14. [1969] 3 All E.R. 640.
15. There is a right of appeal from the registrar to a judge in Chambers, and thence to the Court of Appeal, and from a High Court Judge or a County Court Judge to the Court of Appeal.

But where conduct of the parties is an important issue the application will be heard by a High Court judge. Under the Divorce Rules provision is made for the Court – either registrar or judge – to transfer the case to the High Court where the court 'considers that the application gives rise to a contested issue of conduct of a nature which is likely materially to affect the question whether any, or what, order should be made'. If the application is transferred, it is heard by a High Court Judge.

As may be imagined, it is not always easy to discover the true financial position of the parties: both husbands and wives who do not receive fixed incomes can cloud the issue by 'arranging' their affairs, and it is not unknown for well-dressed businessmen with large motor-cars to produce accounts showing a distressing situation in which, on the face of it, they should be on Supplementary Benefit rather than ordered to maintain wives and children. But the Courts have a way of dealing with this sort of thing. In *F.* v. *F.*[16] the husband had no capital, his income for tax purposes was only about sixty pounds a year and he was in debt for many thousands of pounds, but the Court took into consideration his ability to raise money and the manner in which he was living, and gave the wife – who had, incidentally, committed adultery and had some earning power herself – an order for seven pounds weekly. It is no way out for a husband to demonstrate that he has no income whatsoever; a man who invested all his money in a mink farm, from which he received no payment but had his living expenses, was ordered, in *Donaldson* v. *Donaldson*[17], to pay his wife a sum appropriate to the manner in which he lived. And, if a man decides that he is not going to work in order to support his family, the fact that he has no income will not save him from paying maintenance, for it is partly on the *ability* to pay that the Court bases the order, and that ability is judged by his qualifications and past performance as much as by his present earnings. It is not unknown, however, for men to refuse

16. [1955] P. 236.
17. [1958] 2 All E.R. 660.

promotion to more responsible positions if that would involve them in paying more maintenance, and that is something about which the Court can do nothing – nobody can be compelled to work harder than before in order to inflate a maintenance order.

The wife's ability to earn also affects the amount awarded to her. But in the case of a wife who has never worked, or never worked during marriage, the Court will usually not expect her to go out to work simply to keep down her husband's liability for maintenance, certainly not if she has young children to look after.[18] Where, however, a wife is young and has no small children, even if she has not worked during the marriage, allowance may be made for her earning capacity and the order reduced accordingly. There are no hard and fast rules, and each case will be decided on its own facts, but the general principle is that a wife (at all events an innocent one[19]) – should be restored as closely as possible to the economic situation in which she would have been if the marriage had not broken down.

An unfortunate result of the application of these principles in allotting maintenance is that many injured wives are encouraged to remain idle, when they would be much happier and lead fuller lives if they took employment instead of sitting at home and brooding over their wrongs. There is something rather demoralizing about being kept by a man, who is probably hated and who certainly receives nothing in return for the provision he makes, and many women are too proud to live as *rentiers* of their ex-husbands. Of course, where there are small children it is different, but it is regrettable that able-bodied women should be encouraged to contract out of life because if they take a job their maintenance will be reduced.

18. *Rose* v. *Rose* [1951] P. 29; *Le Roy Lewis* v. *Le Roy Lewis* [1955] P. 1.

19. But see *Porter* v. *Porter* (p. 239).

Maintenance in the Magistrates' Court

In any proceedings brought under the Matrimonial Proceedings (Magistrates Courts) Act, 1960 the magistrates may make any of the following orders:

1. The husband shall pay to the wife such weekly sum as the Court considers reasonable in all the circumstances of the case;

2. Where the husband's earning capacity is impaired through age, illness or disability, that the wife shall pay to the husband such weekly sum as the Court considers reasonable in all the circumstances of the case;

3. Either the husband or the wife or both maintain any child of the family by weekly payments until the child reaches sixteen (or the order may be extended up to twenty-one years if the child remains dependant).

There is no financial limit to the amount of these orders. The principles applied in assessing the amount of any order are the same as in the High Court and County Court (see pp. 239–40). But there are some important differences. No order will be made in favour of a complainant who has committed adultery during the marriage, unless the adultery was condoned or connived at, or conduced to by the wilful neglect or misconduct of the defendant. If the parties are cohabiting at the time of the order, it is not enforceable until they cease to live together, and lapses altogether if they stay together for three months from the date of the order. The order also ceases to have effect if they resume cohabitation. Divorce has no effect on the order. Proceedings for revocation or variation of the order may be taken at any time if there is a change of circumstances. Remarriage brings both types of order to an end.

Financial relief in High Court and County Court

All the provisions relating to financial relief in matrimonial cases are now to be found in the Matrimonial Proceedings and Property Act 1970.

20. See also chapter 4.

Maintenance pending suit[21]

This replaces the old alimony pending suit which was based on the wife's common law right to necessaries (see p. 38).

On the filing of any petition for divorce, nullity or judicial separation, the Court may order either husband or wife to maintain the other spouse. This maintenance can, and normally will, continue until the determination of the suit – that is, the date of decree absolute.

The sum to be awarded is governed by what 'the court thinks reasonable'. Orders for alimony pending suit were assessed on what was needed to keep the wife's head above water until the suit had been heard, and were usually substantially less than the final maintenance order. As a rule of thumb, but not a rule of law of practice, she was often given a sum which would bring her income up to one-fifth of their joint incomes, but where the husband had a very small or very large income all questions of proportion were disregarded (see p. 238 for the 'level' of subsistence test). It seems likely that the same principles will continue to be applied. The considerations to be taken into account when other ancillary relief under section 5 (see p. 240) do not apply to orders pending suit.

Supplementary Benefit payments to the wife and children may be taken into account in ordering maintenance pending suit. However, the benefit will usually be reduced once the order has been made. Accordingly a practice has been worked out whereby any order pending suit where the wife is receiving benefit is post-dated by fourteen days and the registrar immediately notifies the Supplementary Benefits Commission in order that payments can be adjusted. In these circumstances the benefit received need not be taken into account when making the order. Application may be made any time up to decree absolute and the order may be backdated to the date of the petition, credit being given for all sums already paid.

21. S. 1.

Financial provision on or after decree[22]

On making any decree of divorce, nullity or judicial separation, or at any time after the decree, the Court may make one or more of the following orders:

1. Either party will make periodical payments to the other in such amounts, at such intervals and for such term as may be specified;
2. Either party will secure such periodical payments as may be ordered;
3. Either party will pay to the other such lump sum or sums as may be specified.

The principles which are to govern the Court in making any of these orders have already been discussed (p. 240).

An order for *periodical payments* (maintenance) or secured provision may be made for any term, beginning not earlier than the date of the application (or in the case of decrees of divorce or nullity, from decree absolute), and continuing not longer than the joint lives of the parties, or until remarriage of the party in whose favour the order is made, whichever is shorter.[23] The order may be varied or discharged if there is a change of circumstances. Proceedings for enforcement of arrears may not now be taken in respect of arrears due more than twelve months before starting the proceedings without leave of the Court, and arrears may be remitted as the Court thinks fit.[24] Furthermore, where there has been overpayment in view of a change of circumstances, the court can order repayment of the excess.[25]

An order for a *lump sum payment* may be made to enable the applicant 'to meet any liabilities or expenses reasonably incurred by him or her in maintaining himself or herself or any child of the family' before making an application for financial provision.[26] This is a new power, which should be useful in remedying the injustice suffered by wives who have to spend their own savings or borrow money in order to set

22. s. 2(1).
23. s. 7(1) and (2).
24. s. 9(1) and (7).
25. ss. 10 and 4.
26. s. 2(2)(a).

up a separate home on leaving their husbands. The Court may also provide for the payment of the lump sum by instalments.[27]

It was the intention of Parliament to increase the scope of lump sum payments wherever capital is available. A once-for-all settlement on the breakdown of a marriage is very desirable, since it brings an end to financial wrangling between the parties and gives the wife an independence which must help her in starting a new life with the minimum of bitterness. So often money disputes prolong the arid emotional struggles in which the marriage foundered. But there are obvious risks. A woman may fritter away her lump sum and she cannot then seek any further relief, since a lump sum order cannot be varied as can a maintenance order.[28] But there is a question whether a further lump sum can be advanced in such circumstances.

If she is awarded both a lump sum and a maintenance order, what happens to the latter if she gets rid of her capital? In theory the order could be varied under section 9, but this is unlikely. As the Lord Chancellor said in the debate on the Bill, 'I do not think any provision could be inserted in the Bill making it impossible for anybody to spend the lump sum, but I think such a person would get little sympathy if he or she tried to obtain an increase in the periodical payments simply because the lump sum had been squandered.'[29]

No doubts the Courts will take into consideration the financial responsibility of the applicant, and where there is a risk that the money may be frittered away, an instalment order, with provision for the instalments to be secured, could be made.[30]

When either periodical payments of maintenance or a lump sum payment, or both, are ordered, the Court may order the husband to secure the whole or part of any sums ordered. An order for security ties up the husband's capital, and no such order will be made on his business assets, nor will a general charge be ordered on all his assets: specific

27. s. 2(2)(b).
28. s. 9(2).
29. Hansard, H.L. Vol. 305 no. 10, vol. 855.
30. s. 2(2)(b) and see p. 245.

property may be charged (for example, a house or stocks and shares) and, if necessary the Court will refer the matter to conveyancing counsel to the Court to draw up a suitable deed. An order for security is not operative until decree absolute, and the Court may refuse to make the decree absolute until the necessary steps have been taken to secure the specified property. It used to be thought that no more than one third of the husband's total assets should be charged, but this idea has gone the way of the other 'rules of thumb' in financial relief: the court's discretion is completely unfettered, but in general the fact that a large sum is secured will be reflected in a lower order for maintenance.[31] Orders for secured provision may be varied or discharged as may any other order to support. A wife could be ordered to secure a sum for her husband's maintenance when she divorced him on the grounds of insanity,[32] and this is now extended to cases where a decree is granted under section 2(1) of the Divorce Reform Act, 1969 and the Court is satisfied that the husband is insane.[33]

All orders for periodical payments and secured provision come to an end on remarriage of the person in whose favour such an order was made.[33a]

Orders for transfer of property and variation of settlements[34]
The Courts are now given wide powers to redistribute, and to settle or resettle, the property of either spouse on granting a decree. These provisions are dealt with in chapter 13.

Wilful neglect to maintain[35]
Quite apart from any proceedings for dissolution or separation, either party to a marriage may apply to the Divorce Court for maintenance on the sole ground that the other

31. *Chichester* v. *Chichester* (1936) P. 129.
32. Matrimonial Causes Act, 1965, s. 16(3).
33. Divorce Reform Act, 1965, Schedule 1(5).
33a. Matrimonial Proceedings and Property Act, 1970, s. 7.
34. Matrimonial Proceedings and Property Act, 1970, s. 4.
35. Matrimonial Proceedings and Property Act, 1970, s. 6.

spouse has wilfully neglected to maintain him or (more usually) her, or the children of the family. (This is an alternative procedure to an application to Magistrates, see pp. 87–104). 'Wilful' implies a failure to maintain adequately in view of one's means. If the person is already paying maintenance in accordance with an order of a Court, and there has been no change in circumstances since the date of the order, he cannot be held guilty of wilful neglect.[36] The principles on which the order is made are those operating in all maintenance applications (see p. 99). A matrimonial offence on the part of the wife may or may not prevent her from obtaining an order; certainly if she refuses to return to cohabitation without just cause she will not obtain an order,[37] nor will she if the couple parted by mutual agreement.[38]

The application is made to a County Court judge in the first instance by originating application, verified by an affidavit, but if the respondent contests the case (that is, denies wilful neglect) it will be transferred to the High Court. In either case the judge may, if he finds wilful neglect proved, make an order forthwith or refer the matter to a registrar to investigate the means of the parties. There is now power to make an interim order where 'the applicant or child is in immediate need of financial assistance'.[39] Periodical payments may be ordered for the joint lives of the parties, or payment of a lump sum may be ordered, or both.[40] This is a considerable enlargement of the powers given to the court under section 22 of the Matrimonial Causes Act, 1965. The final order for periodical payments may be altered when secured.

Effects of taxation on maintenance orders

It would seem, on the face of it, that men must inevitably be deterred from breaking up too many marriages by the econ-

36. *Smith* v. *Smith* (1962) 106 S.J. 611 C.A.
37. *Dyson* v. *Dyson* [1954] P. 198.
38. *Stringer* v. *Stringer* (1952) P. 171.
39. Matrimonial Proceedings and Property Act, 1970, s. 6 (5).
40. ibid., s. 6 (6).

omic burden of maintenance. But by a combination of our curious fiscal system and the operation of the welfare state, for quite a large section of the community, the very rich and the rather poor, maintenance is much less of a problem than might be expected. To take the effect of taxation first of all: a man earning £10,000 a year, who is ordered to pay his wife £3000 deducts tax at the standard rate and in fact only pays her £1763, and she reclaims tax overpaid having regard to her allowances; furthermore instead of being taxed on £10,000 he is taxed on £7000 and avoids surtax on the top £3000 – a saving to him of several hundred pounds. If he remarries and is divorced again, his second wife will only receive a similar proportion of his uncharged income, but even her smaller allotment will further reduce his liability for tax. The wives recover some of the tax deducted, since by reason of allowances they are not liable to pay tax on the whole amount, so that in effect the taxpayers as a whole are paying quite a considerable slice of the rich man's maintenance orders.

At the other end of the scale the community also helps to keep wives whose husbands have left them. A man who is earning fifteen pounds a week may be ordered to pay his first wife and family five pounds, but he cannot pay much more – blood cannot be got out of a stone – and if the wife cannot live she must draw Supplementary Benefit.[41] If he remarries and again breaks up his marriage, there just is not enough money available for anything more than a nominal order in favour of the second wife, and she and any successive wives there may be must be supported by the state.[41a] Any children will of course increase the payments made by the Supplementary Benefits Commission, or the children may have to be brought up by the local authority. Provided he only has one at a time, the feckless man can have as many wives as the richest sheik. This subsidized polygamy for the richest and the poorest in the land cannot have been the intention of Parliament, but the more complex the economic

41. *Roberts* v. *Roberts* [1970] P. 118.
41a. But not the current wife, if he is unemployed.

structure of a society, the more likely is it that such anomalies will occur. Certainly maintenance is a great burden on the middle-income husband, especially if all his income is fixed and therefore immediately apparent; the man with an expense account or other benefits in kind will often find himself better off, in spite of the principle that ability to pay may be assessed by examination of a man's way of life, because of the difficulty of pinning down the value of these extra benefits.

Avoidance of orders for support

It is only human to want to avoid paying out money for something which brings no return, and husbands have shown considerable ingenuity in avoiding or reducing orders for maintenance of their estranged wives. It is not very difficult to devise some scheme to divest oneself of capital and income without losing all the benefits – advising on this sort of thing has become a profession of itself in the field of income tax and estate duty – and many men have handed over substantial property to their mistresses, subsequent wives, business interests, and families in order to present a more modest picture to the court. But this practice has now been made more difficult (although still not entirely stopped) by a provision[42] which gives the court the power to set aside, or to prevent, any disposition of property made with the intention of defeating the wife's claim for financial provision – and 'defeating' includes 'reducing'. Once the wife can show that the effect of the disposition has been, or will be, to reduce or defeat her claim, the husband is presumed to have done it for this purpose and it is then for him to prove that he had no such intention. If a disposition was made less than three years before the date of the application, there is a presumption that the intention was to defeat the claim for relief. But a disposition for valuable consideration, other than marriage, to a *bona fide* purchaser for value will not be set aside. Thus, if a man sells his house to a friend, even for a very low sum, in order to reduce his capital, unless the

42. Matrimonial Proceedings and Property Act, 1970, s. 16.

friend knew of the strategem, the sale will not be set aside. What this law does prevent is the wholesale transfer of a man's estate into the hands of a woman with whom he is living, or the creation of family trusts, for the avoidance of maintenance obligations.

Maintenance out of deceased spouse's estate

Even death is now no release from the liability to maintain a wife. We have seen that a wife who is cut out of her husband's will is able to apply to the court for provision out of his estate but until 1 January 1959[43] no such rights existed against the estate of a former husband. Now, any former wife (or husband) who has not remarried can apply to the court within six months of the date when representation of the estate of the former husband (or wife) was taken out, or at any time before the distribution of the estate is complete with the permission of the court, for an order for payments to be made out of the estate until death or remarriage. The order will only be made if the court considers that it would have been reasonable for the deceased to have made some provision, and all the circumstances will be considered – the conduct of the parties, the income of the survivor, any capital sums paid in the past, the size and nature of the estate and the interests of other dependants and beneficiaries under the will or on the intestacy, as the case may be.

Child maintenance

Curiously, the law was much slower to act in respect of maintenance of children than that of wives. The criminal law would punish a man who neglected his child sufficiently to cause severe suffering, but apart from the liability under the Poor Law to relieve the parish of the burden of maintaining his children, a father had at common law, as we have seen, no more than a moral obligation to support them. Children have no right to pledge their father's credit, and a trader

43. Matrimonial Causes (Property and Maintenance) Act, 1958, s. 3, now Matrimonial Causes Act, 1965, s. 26 as amended by Family Provision Act, 1966.

who supplies an infant with necessaries will be unable to recover the price from the father – he must content himself with suing the child, if that is worth doing. In the same way a father is liable for any necessary expenses incurred on behalf of his children by a servant who has charge of them,[44] and presumably a schoolmaster or anyone else who takes charge of children must also have an implied authority to pledge the father's credit. This remained the position until 1857;[45] although a wife could be given maintenance by the Ecclesiastical Courts, no provision could be made for her children, and it was only when divorce jurisdiction was transferred to the High Court that there was any power to order a husband to maintain his children. This of course was only of any use in the rare cases where a woman was able to bring divorce proceedings, and the deserted wife was still without any remedy unless she could prove that her husband had committed adultery coupled with some other offence. And for the working-class wife there was no remedy whatsoever, however much she might suffer at her husband's hands: if he would not provide for the children voluntarily, they were thrown on the parish with all the degradation that entailed.

Even when wives were given some limited rights in the Magistrates' Courts by the Acts of 1878 and 1895 (see p. 237) there was still no power to order maintenance for the children except in divorce cases. It was not until 1920[46] that magistrates were enabled to include in a separation order some provision for the children, and then the maximum sum that they could award for each child was ten shillings. This sum was increased to thirty shillings in 1949 and later to fifty shillings. Now, there is no financial limit[47] and the mother as well as the father can be ordered to contribute.[48]

44. *Cooper* v. *Phillips* (1831) 4 C. & P. 581.
45. Matrimonial Causes Act, 1857.
46. Married Women (Maintenance) Act, 1920, s. 1.
47. Maintenance Orders Act, 1968.
48. Matrimonial Proceedings (Magistrates' Courts) Act, 1960, s. 2(h).

Again, there was a gap. A mother who was separated from her husband and was not in a position to take proceedings against him because he had committed no matrimonial offence, or a wife who was forced by economic circumstances to remain with her husband, had no legal sanction to compel her husband to maintain the children. But in 1925[49] both the High Court and Magistrates' Courts were given the power to make orders for the maintenance as well as the custody of any child on the application of either the father or the mother. The amount of the order was then limited in the Magistrates' Court, but the High Court could make any suitable order under this provision.

The High Court or County Court may now make an order for either parent to make periodical payments for a child of the family, or to make a lump sum payment or payments, either on or after decree, or where there has been wilful neglect to maintain.[50]

The principles to be applied in making financial provision for a child of the family are set out in section 5(2) of the Act of 1970 as follows:

It shall be the duty of the court [. . .] to have regard to all the circumstances of the case, including [. . .]

(a) the financial needs of the child;
(b) the income, earning capacity (if any), property and other financial resources of the child;
(c) any physical or mental disability of the child;
(d) the standard of living enjoyed by the family before the breakdown of the marriage;
(e) the manner in which he was being and in which the parties to the marriage expected him to be educated or trained;
and so to exercise those powers as to place the child, so far as is practicable and, having regard to the [income, earning capacity, financial needs, obligations, and responsibilities of the parties to the marriage,] just to do so, in the financial position in which the child would have been if the marriage had not broken down and each of those parties had properly discharged his or her financial obligations and responsibilities towards him.

49. Guardianship of Infants Act, 1925, s. 3.
50. Matrimonial Proceedings and Property Act, 1970, ss. 3 and 6.

Similar considerations apply in the Magistrates' Court.

No order under sections 3 or 6 above can be made in favour of a child over eighteen years of age unless the child is receiving instruction or training over that age, and in the first instance the order will not generally extend beyond the statutory school-leaving age.

A considerable tax advantage can be gained by having the order made payable direct to the child. The father deducts tax at the standard rate, but as the child usually has not other income, he is entitled to reclaim a large part of the tax deducted. But by section 15 of the Finance Act, 1968, it was provided that the unearned income of infants should henceforth[51] be aggregated with the income of the father if both parents are living together or, where they are living apart, with the income of the mother for any period during which she has actual custody of the infant.[52] That provision made many thousands of child maintenance orders inappropriate but from 5 April 1971 the aggregation provision is abolished.[53] One again, a divorced or separated father could educate and maintain his children entirely out of untaxed income; he still pays the maintenance less tax, and therefore, if his income is high enough, he will pay only a few shillings in the pound for his son's fees at public school and his allowance at university. This reversal of the law will no doubt be a great encouragement to fee-paying schools of all kinds. But it seems unjust that a divorced man may be so much better off than the man whose marriage survives.

To summarize, then, there are seven different ways in which husbands and wives can today be made to support each other or their children:

1. A wife or a husband can apply for an order on various grounds in the Magistrates' Court, and the justices may then order either spouse to maintain the other (see p. 99).
2. A wife or a husband can start matrimonial proceedings of

51. From 5 April, 1969.
52. Finance Act, 1968, s. 8.
53. Finance Act, 1971.

any sort in the Magistrates' Court, and the justices may then – even if they are not asked to do so – order either husband or wife to pay maintenance for any child of the family (see p. 100).

3. A wife may apply to the County Court for maintenance for herself and the children on the ground that the other spouse has wilfully neglected to maintain them without having to prove any other matrimonial offence (see p. 237).

4. A father may be ordered to pay maintenance for his children if they are given into the custody of his wife in an application by either parent to the High Court or the magistrates under the Guardianship of Infants Act, 1925 (see p. 209) or in wardship proceedings.

5. On any decree of divorce, judicial separation, nullity, or restitution of conjugal rights, the County Court may make any order for the payment of maintenance to any child of the family.

6. The Supplementary Benefits Commission may recover in the Magistrates' Court, from either husband or wife, the cost of assistance given in respect of the other spouse or any child under sixteen.

7. Either parent may be ordered by the Magistrates' Court to contribute to the maintenance of any child who has been placed in the custody of a guardian, or is in an approved school, or is in the care of a local authority, or has been committed to the care of a fit person (see p. 100).

The power of the courts to make orders for support within the family cannot be ousted by any private arrangement between the parties. The state has an interest in seeing that the family is self-supporting, and it would be against public policy to allow husbands and wives to agree together not to apply to the courts for maintenance (see p. 84). But sometimes it is in the interests of both parties to agree to a lump-sum settlement of their mutual rights and liabilities: for example, a woman may want to make a new life overseas, where she expects to be able to support herself, and her former husband may be in a position to pay her a substantial sum in exchange for her agreement not to make any further demands on him. She gains by having something to start her off in her new life, he gains by knowing the limit of his liabilities. There is nothing inherently wrong in such an arrangement, except that it will not be binding on the wife if she later finds that she needs maintenance, so that no husband can safely enter into it. Happily there is a way out of this impasse: if the agreement is incorporated in an order of the Divorce Court, then it will be binding on both parties, and it will be impossible for the wife to make any application in future.[54]

Enforcement of maintenance orders

It is one thing to get an order for maintenance, and quite another to enforce it. We have already seen how such orders are enforced in the Magistrates' Courts (see p. 103). The position in the High Court is more complicated, because all the means available for enforcing judgments may also be used in respect of maintenance orders. A full description of these methods would entail a review of a large part of the law and would occupy a separate volume: the ancient writs of *fieri facias*, sequestration, and *distringas* can be employed, the debtor can be committed to prison for contempt, a judgment summons may be issued, or a receiver may be appointed. Alternatively, a judgment summons may be issued in the County Court, which is a much simpler and more effective procedure than in the High Court. Better still, a High Court order can be registered in the Magistrates' Court, and it is then much more easily collected. The end result is the same in any case: if the money is not paid, and the means of the debtor are adequate, he will go to prison. This does not happen except as a last resort, after the debtor has been given every chance to pay, and if his means are small he may be given the opportunity to pay off the arrears by instalments.

Sometimes a reluctant husband spends all his earnings so

54. *L.* v. *L.* [1962] P. at p. 108 and *M.* v. *M.* [1967] P. 313.

that there is nothing left with which to pay maintenance. The only remedy then is to send him to prison, which does not help his wife and children. It is now possible[55] for any Court to make an order by which his earnings can be attached as soon as he is in arrears by as much as a month. The order specifies two figures: the *normal deduction rate,* which is the amount which the Court thinks should be paid each week out of his earnings, and the *protected earnings rate,* which is the amount below which his earnings must not be reduced by any deduction made under the order. The employer is served with this order, and is then bound to pay over the appropriate amount each week to the officer of the Court specified in the order. It was hoped that this sensible arrangement, for many years in use in Scotland, would reduce substantially the number of men sent to swell the prison population for what is a civil, not a criminal, offence, and to which in any event the remedy of detention is particularly ill-suited. But it has not worked well in practice since it is only too easy for the man to change his job so frequently that he shakes off the effects of the attachment order. The only way to ensure payment would be to have the order stamped on his insurance card, and make it obligatory on the employer to fulfil the provisions of the order.

Another way in which men evade payment of maintenance orders is to leave the country to settle somewhere where the order cannot be enforced. But within the Commonwealth there are now so many countries with which we have reciprocal arrangements for the enforcement of maintenance orders that the escaping husband will be forced to go to some entirely foreign country. The Republic of Ireland remains the handiest haven for men who want to shrug off their family responsibilities.

55. Maintenance Orders Act, 1958, Part II.

13 Property in the Family

This chapter deals with a subject which has seen more change than any other aspect of family law in recent years, in particular under the Matrimonial Proceedings and Property Act, 1970, which came into force on 1 January 1971. It is too early to say how this Act will be applied by the Courts, but it may well bring about more fundamental changes in the patterns of marriage, divorce and separation than any previous statute. The provisions of the Act only come into operation on breakdown of marriage, but they will inevitably affect the attitudes of men and women to each other in questions of property, both before and during marriage. To appreciate the changes about to take place, the historical development of this branch of the law must be understood. As a quick-change social transformation it is a fascinating study. Much of our law is concerned with property rights, but until quite recently this branch of the law did not invade the privacy of marriage. There, no dispute could arise: all was simple, since under the common law everything belonged to the husband. On marriage, a woman forfeited all her proprietary rights, and henceforward she could neither acquire, nor enjoy, nor dispose of any property, whether in the form of land or chattels, independently of her husband. This meant that she could enter into no contracts, nor could she sue or be sued. 'What's yours is mine, what's mine's my own' could be said with truth by any English husband before the eighties of the last century.

If a woman owned a house, from the moment of her marriage her husband became entitled to all the rents and profits from that house and could mortgage or sell it without her consent. (But if she survived him, the house would revert to her on his death, and he could not prevent this from happening by disposing of it elsewhere by his will.) Even a wife's most personal possessions belonged to the husband for all practical purposes: her clothes, her jewels, her books, and her furniture, whether they had been acquired before or after marriage, whether gifts from her family or bought out of her own fortune or earnings – all were his, and he could dispose of them at any time during his life or leave them to someone else in his will. There was a modest exception to this rule in that such personal things as came under the definition of 'paraphernalia' reverted to the wife on the husband's death and he could not dispose of these things in his will. The word paraphernalia covered such articles of apparel and personal ornaments as were suitable to the wife's rank or degree – diamonds and sables for the duchess, a good serge coat and skirt and pinchbeck brooch for the wife of the artisan.

This application of the legal fiction of the unity of husband and wife was softened a little by the Courts of Equity, which protected property given to a woman for her separate use during the period of her marriage, so that it could not be appropriated by the husband during her life, although it became his on her death. This meant that fathers could provide some sort of security for their daughters on marriage, and husbands could, if they wished, renounce their common law rights and declare that the wife's property should continue to belong to her for her sole and separate use. The usual way of doing this was to convey the property to trustees, who held it on the terms of the trust for the benefit of the wife (who was usually restrained from dealing with the capital during her marriage). The drafting and construction of the documents by which such arrangements were made was a profitable field for the lawyers.

Then, on 18 August 1882, the Married Women's Property Act was given the royal assent, and by a stroke of the pen the emancipation of women was made inevitable. It is doubtful if the conventional Queen knew what she had started on that August day at Balmoral, when she gave her assent to this

Act of Parliament. What would she have thought if she had foreseen the direct and indirect results of this legislation – women in every trade and profession, even invading the House of Lords itself, doing as they wished with their lives and their possessions, their husbands powerless to stop them after the sanction of financial control had been torn from their hands! The words of the first section of the Act sound innocent enough, but they brought about the most profound revolution in the whole structure of the family:

A married woman shall, in accordance with the provisions of this Act, be capable of acquiring, holding, and disposing by will or otherwise, of any real or personal property as her separate property, in the same manner as if she were a feme sole, without the intervention of a trustee.

At last women were to have a status of their own, and not be classified together with lunatics and children as creatures unfitted to deal with property directly. Every woman, the Act continues,

shall be entitled to have and to hold and to dispose of . . . as her separate property all real and personal property, her title to which . . . shall accrue after the commencement of this Act, including any wages, earnings, money, and property so gained or acquired. . . .

It is difficult to believe, when reading those words, that little more than eighty years ago a woman's earnings became her husband's property, over which she had no control whatsoever. In the working-class family the husband could, and often did, send his wife out to work and take all her wages for his own indulgence – and the law could not interfere. (It will be remembered that it was not until 1895 that a husband could be ordered by the justices even to maintain his wife. See p. 237.)

Although this change in the law gave women a new status and a new opportunity for freedom, it had another less desirable effect. Before 1882 disputes over property within the family were limited to the construction of wills and settlements among the well-to-do: in the vast majority of marriages there could be no argument, as everything belonged to the husband. But now that married women could own property, and could protect it by all the means provided by the law, it was inevitable that there should be disputes between husband and wife as to ownership. Parliament foresaw this, and to prevent expensive and public legal battles between spouses in the courts, provided them with a cheap, expeditious, and private way of settling their differences:

> In any question between husband and wife as to the title to or possession of property, either party, or any . . . bank, corporation, company, public body, or society . . . in whose books any stocks, funds, or shares of either party are standing, may apply *by summons or otherwise in a summary way* to any Judge of the High Court of Justice . . . or to the Judge of the County Court of the district . . . and the Judge . . . may make such order with respect to the property in dispute . . as he thinks fit, or may direct such application to stand over from time to time, and any inquiry touching the matters in question to be made in such manner as he shall think fit.[1]

The words in italics mean, in practice, that the judge (or master or registrar) hears the dispute in his chambers (in the High Court – in the County Court the judge sits in open Court), and the whole case is conducted with considerably less formality than generally attends the hearing of an action.[2] But although the section provides for a relatively informal way of settling disputes, it is purely procedural and does not give the Court any discretion to go behind the legal rights of the parties, once these have been determined. As we shall see, because in so many cases the task of discovering the legal rights of the parties is well-nigh impossible, the Courts tended to exercise a kind of 'palm-tree justice' under this section, taking the words 'may make such order . . . as he thinks fit' as conferring a wide discretion. This tendency has

1. Married Women's Property Act, 1882, s. 17.

2. Loans between husband and wife cannot be dealt with under this procedure; *Crystall* v. *Crystall* [1963] 1 W.L.R. 574.

now been finally halted (see p. 269). The 'revolution' brought about by this statute was slow and halting. Wives did not become the equals of their husbands in property matters overnight. This is an area into which the law steps delicately; as late as 1952 Lord Denning said in *Bendall* v. *McWhirter*:[3] 'A wife is no longer her husband's chattel. She is *beginning* to be regarded by the law as a partner in all affairs which are their common concern.' The fiction of legal unity between the spouses still throws a long shadow over the married state. The task is made more difficult by the parties themselves; even if the law no longer regards a woman's personality as being swallowed up in her husband's on marriage, men and women persist to a remarkable degree in holding, at least at the start of marriage, the romantic view – which may be the teaching of the Churches but is certainly not supported by the law – that they have joined in a sacramental union of estates as well as bodies. In consequence they enter into no formal agreements, they make no settled plans, and they keep no record of the distribution of ownership within the home, and it is only when they fall out that they begin to question what exactly belongs to whom. It really is quite extraordinary how even the most businesslike people, with responsible public lives, enter into marriage in a kind of rosy haze, without any idea as to their mutual proprietary rights. Indeed, in some respects the law encourages this attitude. They muddle along well enough while they agree, acting very much in the spirit of the old legal fiction of unity – one pays the mortgage one month, the other the next, while one keeps up the hire-purchase payments on the washing-machine and the other puts money into the post office for a rainy day. But if they should fall out and separate, who then should have the washing-machine? What claim can they each make to the house and the savings?

Over the years, the decided cases have built up a body of principle on which these disputes are decided. In the first place, although the Court under the Act of 1882 had to exercise some discretion in dividing up matrimonial property

3. [1952] 2 Q.B. 475.

in certain cases, this discretion can only be exercised where there is doubt as to the intention of the parties. The ordinary law applies between husband and wife just as it does between other people: if there is evidence of any agreement, whether oral or in writing, as to the ownership of any property in dispute, the Court will give effect to that agreement. For instance, if a man and woman agree together at the beginning of their marriage that they will share the ownership of the home and its contents, whatever each contributes thereafter the Court will award them equal shares when the home is broken up and sold. Or if property was clearly bought by one party with the intention of retaining its ownership – as for instance where a wife buys a sewing-machine out of her own earnings – then the Court will give effect to that intention.

Sometimes it is very difficult to unravel the facts in retrospect, especially when the minds and memories of the spouses are clouded with the bitterness of intervening quarrels. But there are some guidelines which may be followed, and all sorts of shreds of evidence may assist in deciding ownership. For example, who used the property? Who provided the money for its purchase? If it was a gift, who was the giver? Sometimes, as in the case of a house, there is a document which on the face of it shows who is entitled to the property; or there may be a document which, while not proving title, gives a strong indication of intention, as with the registration book of a motor-car. Where it is quite impossible to spell out any intention, then the Court falls back on the old legal doctrine 'Equity leans towards equality' – in other words, share and share alike.

Special rules apply to gifts. Where a present is made specifically to one spouse, or is later treated by the parties as being the property of one, or is clearly only of use to one – for example, a mink coat will be assumed to have been intended for the wife alone – that one will be held to have been the donee and will have an absolute right to the gift. But where the present was made without any indication as to who was intended to be the recipient, then it will be deemed to belong to the spouse who is the friend or relation of the giver. Thus, wedding presents are divided up according to which side they came from, unless there is some indication that a present was intended to be personal. (If a girl is given a pearl necklace on her wedding-day by her father-in-law, she will keep that for herself, just as her husband will keep the gold cigarette case given to him by her father.)

Possessions of this type are relatively easy to sort out, but the situation is much more difficult where gifts between husband and wife are in dispute. Until very recently different considerations have applied depending on whether the husband or the wife was the donor. If a husband puts property or buys shares in his wife's name, the law has presumed that he intended to make a gift of the property, and it was for him to rebut the presumption by proving that no gift was intended.[4] There was no such presumption where the wife made a gift to the husband. This presumption of advancement is no longer of much assistance to a wife: in *Pettit* v. *Pettit*[5] the House of Lords said that the strength of the presumption had been much diminished and in *Falconer* v. *Falconer*[6] the Court of Appeal said that the presumption has no place, or at any rate very little place, in our law today. It arose, said Lord Denning, M.R., in Victorian days 'when a wife was utterly subordinate to her husband'.

Gifts and contributions to matrimonial property are now treated in the same way, whoever makes them: if the surrounding circumstances show that a gift was intended, the law will so hold; if on the other hand it can be inferred from the parties' conduct that they did not intend a gift in whole or in part, then the donee will hold the whole or the part in trust for the donor. We shall refer to this principle later when dealing with the matrimonial home. Here the sexes are still unequal before the law: if a husband puts property into his wife's name – a good example is shares in a

4. *Silver* v. *Silver* [1958] 1 W.L.R.259.

5. [1970] A.C. 777; per Lord Reid at P. 793; per Lord Diplock at P. 823.

6. [1970] 3 All E.R. 449; per Lord Denning at p. 452.

company – or hands it into her possession, or lets her use it, the law presumes that he intended to make her a gift of it, and it will be for him to prove that no gift was intended; but where a wife puts property into her husband's name or otherwise passes it over to him, there is no such presumption – indeed if the property is valuable the law assumes that she intended her husband to hold it in trust for her, and the burden is on him to prove that there was in fact a gift to him.

Clearly, husbands should be careful what they hand over to their wives. Men have been known to transfer property into their wives' names in order to defeat their creditors, but a husband who does this cannot later turn round and say that the property does not belong to his wife.[7] It is a common practice for a husband, when buying a house, to have it conveyed into the names of his wife and himself jointly, so that if he dies his wife becomes the sole owner without any further ado, and no duty is payable on the value of her share of the house, at any rate if he does not die within five years of the conveyance. If the marriage breaks up, the husband, who has paid for the house and probably regards it as his property, will find that he cannot go behind the deed: he cannot claim the whole house, for he has shown by the deed that he intended his wife to have a half-share, even if that intention was only formed in order to save death duties. Any other interpretation would mean that he 'intended the transaction to be a mere sham to deceive the estate duty office when the time came', as Lord Justice Donovan as he then was said in *Hine* v. *Hine*[8] where an attempt was made to evade the effects of joint ownership, and the court will not impute any such intention.

The matrimonial home

The purchase of the matrimonial home is often a haphazard matter, and it may be difficult to decide how it should be divided up. The general rule of law, which applies between

7. *Gascoigne* v. *Gascoigne* [1918] K.B. 223.
8. [1962] 3 All E.R. 345.

parties who are not married, is that whoever provided any part of the purchase price is entitled to a similar proportion of the proceeds of sale. This is true whoever has the legal title to the property. The legal owner holds the property on a resulting trust for the beneficial interest of any contributor to the purchase price, to the extent of the contribution. As we have seen (p. 264) the same rule is applied between husband and wife where possible: if the house is conveyed into the husband's name, but the wife puts down half the deposit and pays half the mortgage repayments out of her own earnings, she will be entitled to half the proceeds of sale. But usually matters are much more complicated than this. If a house is in the husband's name, and he pays a large part of the deposit while the wife contributes only a small sum, and he thereafter pays most of the mortgage repayments but she assists by contributing to the housekeeping out of her own earnings, the court will be unable to calculate exactly what each contributed and will pronounce a judgment of Solomon: each shall take half of the proceeds of sale. As Lord Denning said in *Rimmer* v. *Rimmer*,[9] where the facts were similar:

'It is rather like the case when the husband only goes out to work and the wife looks after the house. If she manages to save money out of the housekeeping allowance, sufficient to buy furniture for the home, which is intended to be a continuing provision for them both, then that furniture does not belong to her absolutely, even though it is bought in her name; nor does it belong absolutely to the husband, even though he provided the housekeeping allowance. It is the result of their joint efforts and is presumed to belong to them jointly.'

This case was one of the earliest attempts to spell out some sort of community of property, and the line of reasoning was certainly not followed by all courts. In *Allen* v. *Allen*[10] for example the Court of Appeal did not consider the fact that the wife earned money towards expenses other than the house gave her any claim to a share in the house. But where there

9. [1953] 1 Q.B. 63.
10. [1961] 3 All E.R. 385.

has been a genuine 'pooling' of earnings, to which the wife has made a substantial contribution, even if the husband has made all the payments towards the house purchase under the mortgage deed, the wife will probably be entitled to a share, usually equal in the absence of any evidence of a contrary intention.[11]

The qualifications in the preceding paragraph are necessary, although they must be aggravating to the student. So much depends on the precise facts of each case. But one thing is quite certain since the recent House of Lords decision in *Gissing* v. *Gissing*:[12] no inference of an intention to give a wife an interest in the matrimonial house will be made merely from the fact that she made contributions to general living expenses which may have relieved her husband of financial burdens, thus enabling him to pay the mortgage instalments, or to pay them more easily. In that case the house was in the husband's name, and he made all payments towards it; but the wife had used her savings to pay for laying out a lawn and the purchase of furniture. This must be compared with *Nixon* v. *Nixon*[13] where a wife had worked in her husband's business without reward, and was held to be entitled to share in the property purchased in the husband's name with the profits of the business. Where a business partnership can be spelt out, the wife will be in the same position as any other partner under the law, whether the proceedings are brought under section 17 of the Married Women's Property Act or by way of a partnership action in the Chancery Division.

Problems abound in this sort of case, and always there is the difficulty of deciding what were the intentions of the parties at the time. Since they often had no intentions frequently the court has to fall back on 'equality'. But the easy solution of sharing the property equally will not be taken if there are indications of any contrary intention, even if this is only a matter of inference. Where a house which cost £2950

11. *Fribance* v. *Fribance* [1956] 1 P. 99.
12. [1970] 2 All E.R. 780.
13. [1969] 3 All E.R. 1133.

was conveyed into the names of husband and wife jointly, £2000 being paid by the wife and the rest being raised by mortgage which the husband repaid entirely by himself, a County Court judge held that they were entitled to the proceeds of sale in equal shares. But the Court of Appeal in this case[14] said that this was wrong: the wife must just have her £2000 out of the proceeds of sale, and only on the balance could the principle of 'equality is equity' begin to operate, since it was clear that the parties had always intended that the £2000 should remain the wife's in any event. The wife was entitled to a half-share of the balance, because she had helped her husband to repay the mortgage indirectly by taking in paying guests from time to time and by running the house. But it is doubtful whether the same decision would be reached today. In *Hine* Lord Denning went a very long way in holding that the provisions of section 17 of the 1882 Act gave the judge an 'overriding discretion' to make 'such order as appeared fair and just in all the circumstances'. This interpretation was doubted in *National Provincial Bank Ltd* v. *Ainsworth*[15] and may be regarded as a dead letter since the decisions in *Pettit* (see p. 265) and *Gissing* (see p. 268).

The attempts by one section of judicial opinion to set up a kind of community of matrimonial property by regarding the home and its contents as 'family assets' were given their *quietus* in those two cases: the principle is now finally established that the determination of disputes between spouses as to the beneficial interest of one in property legally vested in the other must follow the general law. But as we shall see this principle, which may, indeed must, work harshly in some cases, has been greatly mitigated by the reforms of 1970 (see p. 277).

What if one spouse improves property belonging to the other spouse, by decorations, repairs or extensions? Surely the contributor should be entitled to a share in the increased value? *Appleton* v. *Appleton*[16] was an attempt to do justice

14. *Hine* v. *Hine* [1962] 1 W.L.R. 1124.
15. [1965] A.C. 1175.
16. [1965] 1 All E.R. 44.

in such a situation: the husband, a skilful carpenter, had greatly increased the value of the wife's house during the marriage, and when the marriage broke down he claimed a share in the equity. The Court of Appeal held that even in the absence of any agreement he was entitled to so much of the enhanced value of the property as was due to his work. But this decision was criticized in the House of Lords in *National Provincial Bank Ltd* v. *Ainsworth* and was disapproved in *Pettit* v. *Pettit* (see p. 265). In the latter case a husband expended considerable sums of money and personal effort in redecorating and improving his wife's house, enhancing its value by about £1000. The House of Lords held that in the absence of express agreement, he had no claim to any of that enhanced value although the Court of Appeal, following *Appleton*, had said he was entitled to £300. Lord Reid said (at p. 795) that the law should not be changed by lawyers in such an important matter, but by Parliament. That has been done by the 1970 Act, as we shall see (p. 277) the statute has restored the effect of *Appleton*, and a spouse is now entitled to a share in any property belonging to the other to which he or she has made a 'contribution of a substantial nature'. The share will be such as may have been agreed by the parties, or in default of such agreement, such share as seems just to the court.

Right to remain in matrimonial home

In many cases the most important consideration on the breakdown of the marriage is who shall be entitled to stay on in the matrimonial home. It is no use protecting a wife by way of a maintenance order if she is unable to find accommodation for herself and the children. If she has no proprietary or contractual right to occupy the house, she is now protected by the Matrimonial Homes Act, 1967. Section 1 of this Act gives either a husband or a wife who has no 'estate or interest' in the home the right if in occupation not to be evicted or excluded from the house or any part of it by the other spouse except with the leave of the Court. If not in occupation, he or she has a right to enter and occupy the house with the leave of the Court. These rights of occupation only last so long as the marriage is in being, and so long as the other spouse has a legal right to occupy the house.[17]

If a wife has a share in the matrimonial home – if for instance it is in joint names, but not if she only has a *claim* to a share[18] – the 1970 Act gives her no protection, and she is thrown back on the common law rights which were developed over the years to protect a wife in these circumstances.[19] The 'equity of the deserted wife', as it used wrongfully to be described, gives a deserted wife the right to stay on in the former matrimonial home, but as this only operates against the husband and not mortgagees or purchasers, it is of limited value.

Either husband or wife, if having no legal right to occupy the home, may apply under section 1 of the Matrimonial Homes Act either in the High Court or County Court, for an order that the other spouse do not evict or exclude him or her, or if not in occupation, for an order that he or she enter into occupation. On such application the Court (a Registrar sitting in chambers) may:

make such order as it thinks just and reasonable having regard to the conduct of the spouses in relation to each other and otherwise, to their respective needs and financial resources, to the needs of any children and to all the circumstances of the case, and, without prejudice to the generality of the foregoing provision,

(a) may except part of the dwelling house from a spouse's rights of occupation (and in particular a part used wholly or mainly for or in connection with the trade, business or profession of the other spouse);

(b) may order a spouse occupying the dwelling house or any part thereof by virtue of this section to make periodical payments to the other in respect of the occupation;

(c) may impose on either spouse obligations as to the repair and maintenance of the dwelling house or the discharge of any liabilities in respect of the dwelling house.

17. Matrimonial Homes Act, 1967, s. 1(8).
18. See Matrimonial Proceedings and Property Act, 1970, s. 38(9).
19. *Gurasz* v. *Gurasz* [1970] P. 11.

Orders under this section may, in so far as they have a continuing effect, be limited so as to have effect for a period specified in the order or until further order.[20]

The Act gives added protection in the case of a matrimonial home to which the Rent Acts apply.[20a] Where a marriage is terminated by a decree of divorce or nullity, and one spouse is entitled to occupy the house by virtue of a tenancy to which the Rent Acts apply, or of a statutory tenancy, the Court may order that as from decree absolute the tenancy be transferred to the other spouse. This means that a wife, left by her husband in a house of which he is the tenant, may by order of the Court who grants her a decree step into his shoes, and have all the benefits of a Rent Act tenant: that is, the landlord will only be able to evict her if she is in breach of the tenancy agreement (for instance if she fails to pay the rent), or if he can show that he needs the house for his own occupation and can show greater hardship.

The great value of the Matrimonial Homes Act is preventive. With the wide discretionary powers given to the courts under the 1970 reforms, a spouse has a choice of procedures for ensuring that the matrimonial home goes to the party with the greater need and greater merit (see p. 277) but these procedures are of little use if the house has already been disposed of or the family turned out on the street and this can now be prevented until the Court has considered the merits.

But the wife's licence to remain in the house, whether statutory or at common law, ceases on decree absolute unless the Court has made an order to the contrary.

Quite apart from the Matrimonial Homes Act, the Divorce Court has the power to protect either husband or wife, pending the hearing of the suit, in occupation of the matrimonial home by granting an injunction.

All this makes it impossible for a wife to be driven out of the house, or kept out, by her husband, but it gives her no protection against anyone else. If, for example, the husband

20. Matrimonial Homes Act, s. 1(3) and (4).
20a. Matrimonial Homes Act, s.7.

has mortgaged the house, the mortgagee can gain possession if he is in breach of the covenants of the mortgage deed (*National Provincial Bank Ltd* v. *Ainsworth,* see p. 269) or if he has sold the house she may be turned out by the purchaser if he bought without notice of her occupancy. However, under section 2 of the Matrimonial Homes Act a spouse can register his or her rights of occupation created by the Act under the Land Charges Act, 1925, as a 'Class F' charge. This gives the statutory rights of occupation a priority to any charges registered thereafter. Thus the spouse who owns the house will be effectively prevented from selling or mortgaging the house with the concurrence of the other spouse or without an order of the Court under section 1.[20b]

A 'Class F' land charge will be cancelled by the Chief Land Registrar if he is satisfied

1. that either spouse is dead,
2. that the marriage has been terminated by a decree of the court,
3. that the spouse's rights of occupation which gave rise to the charge have been terminated by an order of the court (that is under section 1).

The Court will, in proper cases, grant an injunction ordering one spouse to leave the house, even if he or she has proprietary rights to the house,[21] or restraining the spouse from entering if not in occupation. Even after the determination of the suit, an injunction can be granted for the protection of spouse or children, but after the marriage has come to an end the Court will not generally interfere with the proprietary rights of a spouse.[22]

20b. But see *Rutherford* v. *Rutherford* [1970] 3 All E.R. 422.

21. *Silverstone* v. *Silverstone* [1953] P. 174 and *Jones* v. *Jones and Another* [1971] 2 All E.R. 737 C.A. where a husband and his mistress were ordered out of a council flat of which the husband was the tenant. But this is a drastic remedy which will only be granted if it is 'completely impossible for the spouses to live together in peace in the same house': *H.* v. *H.* (1971) *The Times*, 20 January.

22. *Montgomery* v. *Montgomery* [1965] P. 46.

This inherent jurisdiction of the Divorce Court to interfere with proprietary rights is an exception to the general rule that the Court will not, in dealing with matrimonial matters, override the established law of property and contract. The basis of the jurisdiction to grant such injunction is set out in Lord Denning's judgment in *Gurasz* v. *Gurasz* (see p. 271):

'Some features of family life are elemental in our society. One is that it is the husband's duty to provide his wife with a roof over her head; and the children, too. So long as the wife behaves herself, she is entitled to remain in the matrimonial home. . . . If he should seek to get rid of her, the Court will restrain him. If he should succeed in making her go, the Court will restore her. In an extreme case, if his conduct is so outrageous as to make it impossible for them to live together the Court will order him to go out and leave her there.'

Joint bank accounts

In deciding who is entitled to the balance in a joint account, the courts will apply the same principles as in determining the ownership of other matrimonial assets. If the parties showed some intention at the time the account was set up of dividing the money in any particular manner, the court will follow that intention. But if there was no agreement, then even if the parties put in unequal amounts the court will divide the money equally between them.[23] The prevalence of hire-purchase often complicates the picture. Sometimes the wife makes the payments as they fall due out of the housekeeping, sometimes out of her own earnings; but usually the purchase was intended to benefit both parties, and both made some contribution, even if the wife's contribution only consisted in running the house and therefore saving her husband's pocket. As we have seen, in those circumstances the court will declare that they have an equal interest, because it is quite impossible to find any other fair way of dealing with the question.

23. *Jones* v. *Maynard* [1951] Ch. 572.

Housekeeping money

This is often a bone of contention. Until 1964, considerable injustice could be done to the careful housewife by the operation of the law, which held that, where the husband was the sole provider, any money saved from the housekeeping belonged to him. So that where a wife bought furniture out of the money she saved[24] or put money on the pools with stake-money from the housekeeping[25] she was unable to claim any share in the property or winnings. This was changed by the Married Women's Property Act, 1964, which gave husband and wife equal shares, in the absence of any agreement to the contrary, in any money saved from housekeeping, or any property purchased with such money.

Nuptial settlements

Until well on into this century, no family of any means would allow a marriage to take place without some sort of a settlement. One reason was, as we have seen, that daughters could thereby have preserved to them some measure of financial independence, but among the landed classes there was a much stronger motive: the land which had been acquired by inheritance or industry must at all costs be kept in the family. Thus, elaborate documents were drawn up which provided for every sort of contingency, and every device of conveyancing was used to keep estates intact and limit the effects of human extravagance and fecklessness. Settlements of land, which were intended to preserve large landed estates from generation to generation, have almost died out because heavy death duties have made this impossible, and even the so-called 'trader's settlement', tying up money and stocks and shares, is rare because of the impact of taxation on the wealthy classes. In fact, a completely new type of settlement has been developed in recent years, chiefly for the avoidance of taxation and death duties, and only incidentally for the

24. *Blackwell* v. *Blackwell* [1943] 2 All E.R. 579.
25. *Hoddinott* v. *Hoddinott* [1949] 2 K.B. 406.

purpose of giving financial support to a marriage. A good example of this is the discretionary settlement: trustees hold a fund for the benefit of a number of different people, with a discretion to distribute the income among the beneficiaries as they think fit. This can be very helpful from the tax point of view, but, more important, no death duties are payable until all the beneficiaries are dead.

But although the old sort of marriage settlement is of little importance today, the word 'settlement' has taken on a new meaning in matrimonial affairs. This has happened because in 1859 the Divorce Court was given the power, after making a decree of divorce or nullity, to vary any ante-nuptial or post-nuptial settlements made on the parties. The power now persists as part of the wide discretion to deal with property on breakdown of marriage under the 1970 Act (see p. 277). The Court can do anything with the settlement in its discretion, but aims at putting the parties as far as possible into the position they would have enjoyed if the marriage had not broken down. The injured party and the children must be protected, and the wrongdoer will not be allowed to benefit from his wrongful acts, but the respective contributions of the parties will be taken into account. In certain cases the Court will extinguish the rights of one party completely, or perhaps re-settle everything on the children. In order to do justice in the greatest possible number of cases, the Courts have construed these words very widely, so that any transfer of property which has a 'nuptial' element about it is held to be a settlement which can be varied under this provision. Out-and-out gifts are excluded, but any property which can be regarded as 'settled' – that is, if it makes some continuing provision, as for example a trust fund or a mortgage deed – can be the subject of an order of the Court, always provided that the transfer of the property related in some way to the marriage. It does not matter who makes the settlement, provided that it is made on the husband or the wife, or both, *in the character* of husband or wife, or to put it in another way, gives benefits to one or other of the parties with reference to their married state. So that where a mother settled £20,000 on the occasion of her son's marriage, the income to go to the son for his life and thereafter to his wife for her life, with other benefits to any children of the marriage and, eight years later, settled a further sum of £86,000 on similar terms, these were held, in *Prinsep* v. *Prinsep*,[26] to be ante-nuptial and post-nuptial settlements which the Court could vary.

Of wider relevance is the decision in *Cook* v. *Cook* that a house conveyed into the name of the husband, to the purchase of which the wife made some contribution, is the subject of a settlement which the Court can vary. This takes us back to the question of the deserted wife's right to remain in the matrimonial home. Even if she loses her rights under the Matrimonial Homes Act, 1967 by divorcing her husband, provided she made some contribution to its purchase, however small, she can ask the court to vary the legal position at any time *after* the divorce. If she is the injured party it may well be that the husband's rights in the house will be limited in some way or even entirely extinguished, depending on the relative positions of the parties and all the surrounding circumstances – foremost among which would be the interests of any children of the family. This she may be able to go on living in the matrimonial home indefinitely, irrespective of the termination of the marriage contract.

The 1970 Act

Since 1 January 1971 the Divorce Court has had wide powers to deal with any sort of matrimonial property.

Section 4 of the Matrimonial Proceedings and Property Act, 1970, reads as follows:

> On granting a decree of divorce, a decree of nullity of marriage or a decree of judicial separation, or at any time thereafter (whether, in the case of a decree of divorce or of nullity of marriage, before or after the decree is made absolute), the Court may, subject to the provisions of sections 8 and 24 (1) of this Act, make any one or more of the following orders, that is to say:

26. [1929] P. 225.

(a) an order that a party to the marriage shall transfer to the other party, to any child of the family or to such person as may be specified in the order for the benefit of such a child such property as may be so specified, being property to which the first-mentioned party is entitled, either in possession or reversion;

(b) an order that a settlement of such property as may be so specified, being property to which a party to the marriage is so entitled, be made to the satisfaction of the Court for the benefit of the other party to the marriage and of the children of the family or either or any of them;

(c) an order varying for the benefit of the parties to the marriage and of the children of the family or either or any of them any ante-nuptial or post-nuptial settlement (including such a settlement made by will or codicil) made on the parties to the marriage;

(d) an order extinguishing or reducing the interest of either of the parties to the marriage under any such settlement; and the Court may make an order under paragraph (c) above notwithstanding that there are no children of the family.

The matters which are to be taken into account in making an order under this section are set out in section 5 (see p. 240) and include the conduct of the parties.

The powers to transfer or to settle any property to which a spouse is entitled, under (a) and (b) are so wide that in effect they produce a modified community of matrimonial property at the discretion of the Court. Once breakdown occurs, no property rights are sacred: whatever deeds were entered into, however clearly the parties spelled out their rights, the Court can overrule all such agreements and make any order which will 'place the parties, so far as it is practicable and, having regard to their conduct, just to do so, in the financial position in which they would have been if the marriage had not broken down and each had properly discharged his or her financial obligations and responsibilities towards the other.'

Although no doubt the Courts will continue to follow the practice that orders for financial relief are not made to punish the wrong-doer, the penalty for matrimonial misconduct may now be very high.

When the Court makes a declaration that property belongs to one or other of the spouses, how does this take effect? It is not much use to be told that you are entitled to half the television set and your wife to half the washing-machine, when both are in the matrimonial home which the court has said belongs equally to both parties and which is at present occupied by your wife. In the case of a house, the court will usually make an order for sale, the proceeds to be divided between the parties in certain proportions – it can be imagined how easy it is to sell a house over the head of the present occupier, especially an embittered wife! – but with items of furniture and other possessions this would be inconvenient and uneconomic. If the parties cannot agree to divide the spoils in some way, the court usually awards some things to one and some to the other, giving overall effect to the value put on their respective contributions to the home.

Insurance

This is a field in which the law favours the family. It was decided a very long time ago, in *Reed* v. *Royal Exchange Assurance Co.*[27] that husbands and wives could insure each other's lives up to any amount, and recover the sum assured without proving any financial loss. In the ordinary way, no one may insure the life of another person unless he has 'an insurable interest' – that is, a financial interest – in that person's life, and may not recover more under the policy than the value of that interest.[28] The Married Women's Property Act, 1882, gave the family further substantial advantages. If either spouse takes out a policy on his or her own life, and expresses it to be for the benefit of the other spouse or the children, this creates a trust in favour of that spouse or children. This means that the person for whose benefit the policy was taken out can sue on the policy, which

27. (1795) Peake, Add Case. 70.
28. Life Assurance Act, 1774, ss. 1 and 3.

would otherwise be impossible because there would be no contract with the insurers. Also, being a beneficiary under a trust the survivor takes the whole of the sum assured, even if the assured is bankrupt or his estate insolvent. A further advantage is that money paid out under such policies, although dutiable, is not aggregated with the deceased's estate for revenue purposes, and therefore does not push the estate up into a higher scale of duty.

Property and children

The general law relating to parents and children in respect of property is sparse. Apart from protecting infants from parental greed by putting parents in the position of trustees when handling their children's property, the law in the main keeps out of this side of family life. Whenever there is a conflict over property between parent and child, the scales are heavily weighed in favour of the child and the Court will scrutinize the parents' conduct carefully. Apart from this, the usual law of contract applies to transactions between parents and their children. In one particular case, however, the law presumes in favour of a child: if a father puts property of any kind into the name of his child (however old) or allows him to have it in his possession, there is a presumption that the father intended a gift to the child. This is similar to the presumption in favour of a wife, and can be rebutted in the same way. Curiously enough, no such presumption arises in the case of a mother and her child, but it takes very little evidence to satisfy the court that in fact a gift was intended.

However, on breakdown of a marriage the Divorce Court now has wide powers to transfer property to, and make settlements on children of the family (see p. 278).

There is a great deal of law protecting infants from predatory adults, and from themselves, but none of this is specific to the family. Children under eighteen can own all sorts of personal property, including stocks and shares, but they cannot hold land: it must be held by adult trustees on their behalf and for their benefit. A parent has no rights over his children's property, and cannot strictly even enter on his infant child's land to receive the rents and profits; if he does do so, he will be regarded as a trustee of those rents and profits. A father cannot give a valid receipt for any property owned by his child. But one right a father has: while the child lives with and is maintained by him, he has a right to the child's earnings. Apparently this right is still honoured in the observance in some parts in the north of Britain, but in most places the young have their own ideas on this branch of the law.

Property after death

The disposition of property after death is an important part of family law, but wills and inheritance form such a large subject that they cannot be dealt with here. Only a few points of general interest will be touched on.

Most people regard the rights to dispose of their property by will as they wish as one of the freedoms to which they are absolutely entitled, but as we have seen (see p. 51) this right is subject to certain obligations to other members of the family. Apart from this, however, all men of full age have always been able to do what they wish with their worldly possessions after their death, provided they complete a written document which complies with the formalities required by law.[29] (Soldiers on active service and mariners at sea can even dispose of their property without a written will.) But a married woman before 1882 could only bequeath property held to her separate use in equity (see p. 260): the rest went to her husband on her death, whatever might have been her wishes. It is only since 1935[30] that a married woman has had an unfettered right to dispose of all her property by will. Any will made by either a man or a woman is revoked on marriage, unless the will was made expressly in contemplation of that particular marriage.[31] Therefore if a

29. Wills Act, 1837.

30. Law Reform (Married Women and Tortfeasors) Act, 1935.

31. No special words need be used, but to avoid revocation the will must make it quite clear that the marriage contemplated was the one which in fact took place.

bachelor wishes to leave all his property to his mother and makes a will to that effect, he must take care to make another will immediately upon his marriage, otherwise he may die intestate – when his widow will get the money instead.

Before the Family Reform Act, 1969, if a testator had both legitimate and illegitimate children a bequest 'to my children' was construed as meaning only the *legitimate* children. But if there are no legitimate children, then he was taken to have meant to benefit the illegitimate ones. Now, 'children' in a will includes both legitimate and illegitimate children. Until 1950 adopted children were in the same position as illegitimate ones: they did not share in any gift to 'children' unless the testator quite clearly intended them to. But since the Adoption Act, 1949, came into operation they have been in exactly the same position as legitimate children in respect of any will or codicil made *after* the adoption order.

The passion of the law for equality in the family extends to the interpretation of wills. There is a presumption of law that a father intends to deal equally with his children and not to favour one at the expense of the others. So if a father during his lifetime gives one son £2000 and the others nothing, and later in his will he leaves '£3000 to each of my children', the one who received the gift during life will only get £1000 while the others will take the full amount. This application of a principle of law – that children must bring into account what they have received during the testator's lifetime – is known as 'the rule against double portions'. Like other presumptions of law, it can be rebutted: in this case by producing evidence that the father intended one child to benefit more than the others.

Where one member of the family dies intestate, there is a set of rules which lay down how the estate is to be divided.[32] On the death of either husband or wife, the survivor takes all the deceased's personal chattels, which include furniture,

32. Administration of Estates Act, 1925, and Intestates' Estates Act, 1952.

clothes, motor-cars, jewellery, wines, and stores, but not anything used for business purposes, nor any money or securities. What happens to the rest of the estate depends on whether or not there are any children of the marriage or any other close relatives living at the death. If there are children, the surviving spouse takes up to £8750 free of death duties and a life interest in half the rest of the estate. Half is held on trust for the children in equal shares, and the other half is held similarly, but subject to the survivor's life interest. If there are no children, but the deceased leaves a parent or brother or sister (not half-brother or half-sister), or issue of such brother or sister, then the surviving spouse takes up to £20,000 and half the residue outright – the other half passing to the parents of the deceased or, if both parents are dead, then to the brothers and sisters in equal shares. If there are no children, and no immediate relatives, the surviving spouse takes all.

A particularly valuable provision of the law,[33] and quite a recent innovation, is that the surviving spouse on an intestacy has the right, subject to certain limitations, to retain the matrimonial home if it is part of the estate. This enables the family to continue under the same roof and avoids the necessity for a forced sale at what is usually a most inconvenient time. The value of the house is set off against any other interest the survivor may receive out of the estate, and if the house is worth more than that interest, he or she may pay the balance to the representatives of the estate. This option must be exercised within a year of the grant of representation, and during that time the personal representatives may not sell the house without the written consent of the surviving spouse. Of course, if the sale of the house is necessary for paying off the deceased's debts or the expenses of administering the estate, then it can be sold for that purpose. This provision applies to all freehold houses and any lease which has two years or more to run at the date of the death. Weekly or monthly tenancies are therefore excluded,

33. Intestates' Estates Act, 1952, and Schedule.

but where the property is controlled under the Rent Acts,[34] the survivor's tenancy is protected: he or she cannot be evicted except by the order of the Court, which will only be made in certain limited circumstances. Because of this provision a surviving spouse may well be better off on an intestacy than where there is a will. If the will leaves the whole estate elsewhere, the survivor can take proceedings under the Inheritance (Family Provision) Act (see p. 52), but under that Act there is no power to preserve the matrimonial home for the survivor. This is a curious anomaly of the law which sometimes causes injustice to an unfortunate wife cut out of her husband's will through no fault of her own.

Under the common law illegitimate children took nothing on a parent's intestacy, and even now they have no claim on a *father's* estate. But under the Family Law Reform Act, 1969, section 14, the rights of illegitimate children to take on the intestacy of a parent are identical to those of legitimate children. Similarly the parent of an illegitimate child takes on his death intestate precisely as if he had been legitimate.

Death due to negligence

Death of the bread-winner can be a terrible blow to the family, even in the welfare state. If a man is injured by the negligence of another, he can claim substantial damages for loss of earnings and pain and suffering, often running into thousands of pounds. But if he dies as a result of negligence the only claim that survives *under common law* for the benefit of his estate is for the loss of expectation of life – a loss on which the courts now place a very low figure, varying between £300 and £600 depending on the age at death and the prospects of 'a predominantly happy life'. This anomalous situation meant that *under the common law* it was cheaper to kill a man than to maim him. During the early nineteenth century this problem became very serious owing

34. That is, where the annual rateable values is £400 or less in London, £200 pounds or less elsewhere, and the tenancy commenced before July 1957.
35. Legitimacy Act, 1926, s. 9.

to the invention of the railway and the prevalence of dangerous machinery, and in 1846[36] Lord Campbell introduced a completely new cause of action. This gave to certain dependants the right to claim for the financial loss which they had suffered as the result of death caused by the negligence of another. Under this Act negligence must be proved, and any contributory negligence on the part of the deceased is taken into account. The only people who can make such a claim are the wife, husband, parent, child (including illegitimate and adopted), grandparent, grandchild, sister, brother, uncle, aunt, niece, nephew or cousin (that is, children of brother, sister, uncle, or aunt) of the deceased. Any of these people can make a claim but will only succeed to the extent that they can show pecuniary loss as a result of the death. This loss must be directly due to the relationship: for example, a wife who has lost the support of her husband can recover the value of that support, but a man who was in partnership with his brother will receive nothing for the business loss he has sustained as a result of the brother's death.

In *Burgess* v. *Florence Nightingale Hospital for Gentlewomen*[37] a man and his wife were professional dancers who appeared as a team and shared their earnings and expenses: the wife died as the result of the negligence of a hospital, but the husband could recover nothing for his loss of income, although he could recover for the increase in his expenses which resulted from her death.

It can be imagined that the assessment of damages is not easy in these cases, and it has become a highly specialized branch of the law. The general principle is to discover how much the 'dependency' was worth annually, and then to multiply this by the numbers of years the deceased might have been expected to continue to support the dependant. For instance, if a widow had been receiving fifteen pounds weekly from the deceased for housekeeping and her own use, and the expense of keeping her husband was about five

36. Fatal Accidents Act, 1846.
37. [1955] All E.R. 511.

pounds a week, the annual dependency figure will be about £520. If the husband was thirty when he died, having therefore a calculated expectation of life of 40·27 years,[38] and he had little prospect of improved earnings, the Court will probably multiply this figure by 15 or 16 to find the value of the widow's loss – that is, she will receive around £6000. If he had good prospects of improving his earning power, she will get more; if he was in bad health, or there is a likelihood of her early remarriage, she will get less. The reason that the multiplier is so much lower than the number of years of the actual expectancy of life is that the value of a lump sum must be taken into consideration. Quite apart from the income on the money, this sort of bird in the hand is worth vastly more than the bird in the bush. In any case the figure can never be more than an inspired guess, and it must be emphasized that only *monetary* loss is taken into account: there is no award for grief and loss of companionship. Whatever sum is calculated as damages, any benefit which results to the claimant as the result of the death, whether under an intestacy or from the deceased's will, must be deducted. For example, if the man quoted above left £2000 to his wife in his will, her claim will be reduced to around £4000. Insurances, pensions, and gratuities payable on death are ignored for this purpose, and are not deducted from the damages. Finally, where there is more than one claimant, the Court apportions the total damages among the dependants, generally giving the largest share to the widow.

It is quite appropriate that this book should end with a rather lengthy and complex chapter on property in the family. As we have seen, the law is reluctant to trespass on those delicate relationships which rely for their maintenance on love and respect. But, before the law, property rights are sacred: the principle that ownership must be protected is so fundamental that the law will even intervene in the privacy of the family to support it. The rules that the law applies today to property disputes within the family are necessarily

38. From life tables given in the Registrar-General's Decennial Supplement, 1951.

complex, because considerations other than those which apply between strangers must be taken into account, and also because as we have seen, there have, since the days of the nineteenth century, been vast changes in the balance of power between men and women, and parents and children. But knowledge of these rules can prevent much confusion and unhappiness. Some of the more obvious traps can be avoided if the legal principles are understood, and their common-sense applications can at least minimize the risk of that most destructive of family evils – the dispute over property.

Table of Cases

Re Adoption Application no. 41/61 [1963] Ch. 315; [1962] 3 All E.R. 553; [1962] 3 W.L.R. 997; 126 J.P. 511; 106 S.J. 649; 60 L.G.R. 478, C.A.; Digest Cont. Vol. A929, 1346a 200

Ali v. *Ali* [1968] P. 564; [1966] 1 All E.R. 664; [1966] 2 W.L.R. 620; Digest Cont. Vol. B128, 924d 115

Allen v. *Allen* [1961] 3 All E.R. 385; [1961] 1 W.L.R. 1186; 105 S.J. 630, C.A. Digest Cont. Vol. A694, 2130ad 267

Alway v. *Alway* (1961) 105 S.J. 725 165–6

Re Andrews [1955] 3 All E.R. 249 53

Angelo v. *Angelo* [1967] 3 All E.R. 314; [1968] 1 W.L.R. 401; 111 S.J. 457 78

Appleton v. *Appleton* [1965] 1 All E.R. 44; [1965] 1 W.L.R. 25; 108 S.J. 919. C.A.; Digest Cont. Vol. B344, 621r 269–70

Argyll (*Margaret, Duchess*) v. *Argyll* (*Duke*) [1967] Ch. 302; [1965] 1 All E.R. 611; [1965] 2 W.L.R. 790; Digest Cont. Vol. B449, 875c 45–6

Armitage v. *Att.-Gen.* [1906] P. 135; 75 L.J. 42; 94 L.T. 614; 22 T.L.R. 306; 11 Digest (Repl.) 483, 1094 76

Ashley v. *Ashley* [1968] P. 582; [1965] 3 All E.R. 554; [1965] 3 W.L.R. 1194; 130 J.P. 1; 110 S.J. 13; Digest Cont. Vol. B382, 6739b 99, 238, 239

Atkins v. *Atkins* [1952] 3 All E.R. 248 168

Att.-Gen. for Alberta v. *Cook* [1926] A.C. 444; [1926] All E.R. Rep. 252; 95 L.J. (P.C.) 102; 134 L.T. 717; 42 T.L.R. 317; 11 Digest (Repl.) 472, 1030 71

Att.-Gen. v. *Yule and Mercantile Bank of India* (1931), 145 L.T. 9; [1931] All E.R. Rep. 400, C.A.; 11 Digest (Repl.) 350, 1818 70

Aylesford Peerage Case (1885) 195–6

Re B. (*an infant*) [1970] 3 All E.R. 1008 199

B. v. *Att.-Gen.* (*N.E.B. intervening*) [1965] P. 278; [1965] 1 All

Table of Statutes

Index